Jacques Pépin

HEART & SOUL IN THE KITCHEN

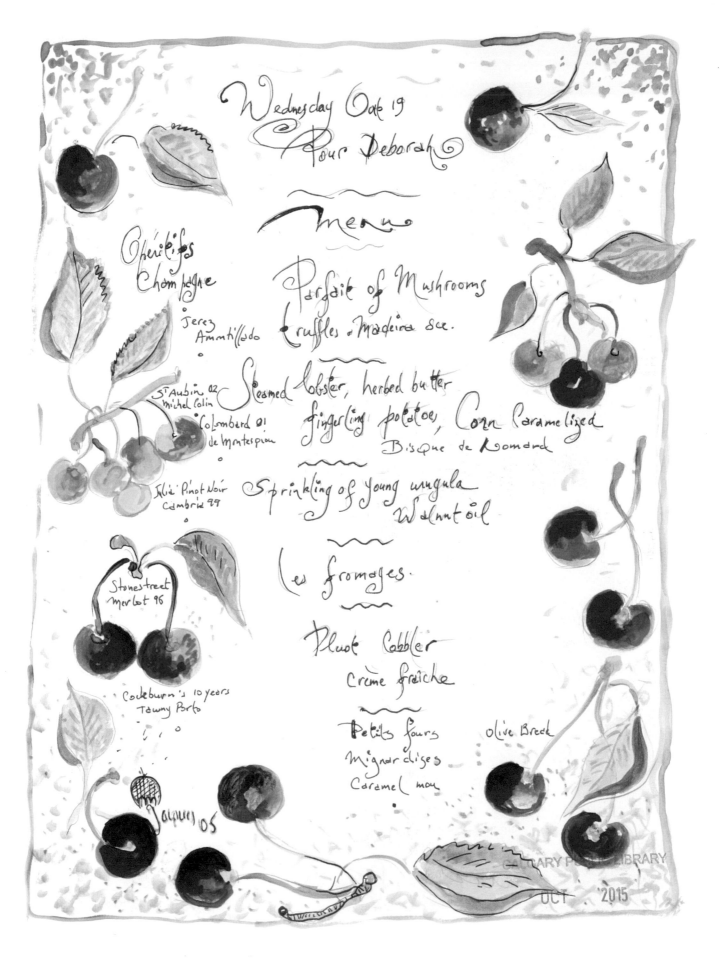

Wednesday Oct 19

Pour Deborah

Menu

Cherities
Champagne

Jerez
Ammtillado

Parfait of Mushrooms
Truffles · Madeira sce.

St Aubin 02
Michel Colin

Colombard 01
de Montespieu

Steamed Lobster, herbed butter
fingerling potatoes, Corn Caramelized
Bisque de Homard

Julie Pinot Noir
Cambria 99

Sprinkling of young arugula
Walnut oil

Les Fromages

Stonestreet
merlot 96

Pluot Cobbler
Crème fraîche

Cockburn's 10 years
Tawny Porto

Petits fours   Olive Bread
Mignardises
Caramel mou

Jacques 05

Jacques Pépin

HEART & SOUL IN THE KITCHEN

Photography by Tom Hopkins Studio

A Rux Martin Book

HOUGHTON MIFFLIN HARCOURT BOSTON NEW YORK 2015

For information about permission to reproduce selections from this book, write to
Permissions, Houghton Mifflin Harcourt Publishing Company, 215 Park Avenue South,
New York, New York 10003.

www.hmhco.com

Library of Congress Cataloging-in-Publication Data available upon request.
ISBN 978-0-544-30198-6 (paper over board); 978-0-544-30226-6 (ebook)

Book design by Endpaper Studio

Printed in China

C&C 10 9 8 7 6 5 4 3 2 1

To my mother, Jeannette,
who taught me how to live and how to cook,
and to my beautiful granddaughter, Shorey,
who loves to cook, eat, and share
and will carry on the family traditions.

Acknowledgments

|||||||||||||||||||||||||||||||||||||||||||||||||||||||||||||||||||||||||||||||||||||||||||||||||||||||

THE MAKING OF *HEART & SOUL*, THE BOOK AND THE companion PBS TV series, was a complicated process that required the combined efforts of many, many good people and took several years. I always count on my wife, Gloria, for advice and ideas and, of course, Norma Galehouse, my longtime assistant. She has worked on two dozen books with me, and I continue to rely on her to make something readable out of the notes I give her. Thanks, also, to Doe Coover, my agent, who was very involved in the production of the book; to Rux Martin, my editor, for her confidence, enthusiasm, and guidance; and to Barry Estabrook, for looking at many of my notes and editing and polishing my writing. I am most grateful, too, for the very thorough copyediting of Judith Sutton, who improved the book greatly. I am indebted to Tom Hopkins for his friendship and the great photographs he took—not only of the food in the book, but also of the artwork I have included. Thanks, too, to Rich Kosenski, who worked with Tom on this project.

I want to thank Jean-Claude Szurdak, my best friend, who spent a great amount of time helping me—going to the market, helping me prepare the food, and then organizing it for the photography sessions. I want also to thank Claudine, my daughter, as well as Rollie Wesen, her husband and my son-in-law, for assisting me with the preparation of some of the dishes.

The television series based on this book is the thirteenth of my series filmed at KQED, the PBS station in San Francisco, over the last twenty-eight years. I want to thank my friends at the station, especially John Boland, the president of KQED and a great supporter, and Michael Isip, the station's Chief Content Officer and series executive producer, whose guidance, confidence, and friendship I rely on. I also want to thank Laureen Chang, who raised money for the series; DeLinda Mrowka, for her work on series promotion and advertisements; and Janet Lim Young, our capable liaison in marketing and client services. And thanks to Wendy Goodfriend, the very talented person in charge of KQED's website, for all her hard work.

In the back kitchen during the filming were, as always, my friends Jean-Claude, David Shalleck, and Michael Pleiss. In addition, I'm grateful to the incredible kitchen staff, Richard Ju and Kelly Gladstone and assistants Kim Kaechele, Carrie Dove, and Hubert Garcia. They not only were competent, but were always happy and smiling.

More than anyone else, I want to thank Tina Salter, my producer of many, many years, for her dedication, professionalism, passion, humor, and kindness, and Christine Swett, her assistant, for her talent and commitment. Thanks, too, to June Ouellette, who did a great job as associate producer. A heartfelt thank-you to Paul Swensen, our director, who replaced our dear departed friend Bruce Franchini. Paul did a great job and was very patient with me, and I thank him for his technical knowledge and endurance.

Thanks again to my friend Jean-Claude, for appearing on several of the shows with me, and thanks to Claudine; to Shorey, my granddaughter; and to Rollie, for being with me on the series too. I also want to give a big thank-you to the technical crew and cameramen for their efficient and skilled work.

Finally, to everyone involved in the book and the series, your cooperation, dedication, and hard work made me look good and I am grateful for that.

Contents

||||||||||||||||||||||||||||||||||||||||||||

Introduction

||||||||||||||||||||||||||||||||||||||||||||||||||||||||||||||||||||||||||||||||||||||||||||||||||||||||||||||||||||||||||||||

THINK OF THIS BOOK AS AN INVITATION TO COME OVER to my house for a meal. Like most gatherings here, it will be accompanied by plenty of interesting conversation about food (French people like to talk about food almost as much as they enjoy eating it), spiced with reminiscences, stories, perhaps a little gossip, and, of course, generous pourings of wine.

Most of the two dozen cookbooks I have written over the past four decades have had specific themes: fast cooking, French cooking, economical cooking, healthy cooking. . . . For this book, mindful that as I approach the age of eighty I have a limited number of cookbooks in my future, I decided to gather a collection of the recipes that I cook at home today.

You'll find the dishes I prepare for quiet evenings when my wife, Gloria, and I are alone. Many of these recipes are also ideal when we have small gatherings of family or friends. I've included some true standbys that I rely on when guests drop by on the spur of the moment. And then there are the festive dishes that I set out when we have large gatherings, particularly in the summer, when dozens of hungry and thirsty folks descend upon our place for afternoons and evenings of spirited *boules* matches on our backyard court. Although the recipes in this book typically serve four or six, almost all of them can be expanded to accommodate bigger groups. In all cases, the recipes are for the food I love to eat and enjoy with those dearest to me. They represent my culinary heart and soul.

The first requirement for anything I serve at my house is that it taste good. No compromises! I don't want people to come away from my table feeling that they have had some sort of "culinary experience." I just want them to say to themselves, "This was really good." I also prepare food with as little fuss as possible, not the least because I want to be able to enjoy the wine, food, and companionship myself.

Creation in the kitchen, for me, means constantly improving the familiar, tweaking and whittling my recipes over the years in a never-ending process of making them better and reducing complication until I arrive at their essential qualities. The result is really tasty food that I (and you) can make as quickly and easily as possible.

Pleasant dining also requires interesting conversation. I have included snippets of text throughout the book drawn from conversations that have taken place in my kitchen. More than one guest has looked shocked when I've pulled a fistful of wilted lettuce or a plastic bag of dry, cracked hunks of miscellaneous cheeses out of the fridge, until I assure her that—trust me—they will become the base of a terrific dish. Someone's comment about the vast array of knives in the block on my counter might inspire a discussion about what to look for in a good knife or a philosophical pronouncement about the value of a sharp knife. Knowing that I favor straightforward fare, where you can recognize exactly what you are eating, friends sometimes nonchalantly solicit my opinion on molecular cuisine and probably get more of an earful than they anticipated. And the gallery of photographs on our hallway

wall provokes questions about what it was like to cook with James Beard, Julia Child, and other "greats."

If you came to lunch here at the height of summer, I might serve you stuffed tomatoes, a dish in the repertoire of every French cook. My zesty take (page 340) calls for hollowed-out large, just-ripe tomatoes filled with a mixture of mushrooms, zucchini, onion, garlic, parsley,

jalapeño peppers, and hot Italian sausage. The tomatoes can be stuffed well ahead of time and then popped in the oven before the guests arrive and chat over glasses of chilled rosé. If tomatoes aren't in their prime, I might throw the best hamburgers I make (page 210) on the grill; the secret is ground brisket. In haste, I may assemble a pizza of mushrooms and Gruyère cheese on store-bought flour tortillas (page 106)—a tasty treat involving minimal time and almost no effort. And there are always eggs from the nearby farm in our fridge, ready to be deployed not only for breakfasts, but also as my secret lunch weapons in dishes like an herbed shrimp omelet (page 89) or eggs cooked in halved and hollowed-out poblano peppers with cheddar cheese and cilantro (page 100).

Predinner appetizers must be simple and full-flavored, but not filling; they should titillate the appetite, not satisfy it. I might serve a nice raw-milk French Camembert moistened with honey and covered with ground pistachios (page 18). My pantry is never without canned cannellini beans, which I often pour into the food processor, along with garlic, cumin, and Tabasco sauce, for a quick, tasty dip for toasts, tacos, or crackers (page 10).

The main course could be thick, juicy pork chops stuffed with spinach, Gruyère cheese, garlic, and nutmeg, topped by a fresh tomato sauce (page 216). Along with a simple salad, these chops make a meal. Or, if I see a nice-looking chuck roast in the market, I will rub it with hoisin sauce, roast it, and serve it with a sauce of red onion, chives, sage, garlic, and Dijon mustard (page 215). Any leftover sauce is also great on fish or even pasta. If I'm in the mood for chicken, I might do grilled tenders in an Argentinean chimichurri sauce with garlic, cilantro, and scallions (page 200)—ready in minutes and perfect for a summer night. In colder weather, I may be tempted to fall back on *poulet à la crème*, a traditional creamy chicken dish from my hometown in France that I've improved upon by adding white wine and mushrooms and using chicken thighs instead of a whole bird (page 199).

Cooking with offal has become popular among young chefs recently, a trend of which I wholeheartedly approve. Having grown up eating these "lesser meats," I'm happy to see that they are becoming more common in supermarkets. Don't be surprised if you find a dish prepared with them on my table. And don't be surprised either when you actually like it. That said, I recognize that many cooks are reluctant to prepare such ingredients. If that sounds like you, try my calves' liver with caramelized onions (page 260) just once. Gloria absolutely loves this preparation, and the quick-and-easy dish has brought many disbelievers to the offal fold.

Dessert at our house is reserved for when we have guests, and more often than not it means something built around fruit picked at its flavorful peak, such as perfect blueberries or peaches and a nibble of cheese, or rhubarb, honey, mint, and currant-flavored crème de cassis (page 383). Or it might be caramelized pear custard with maple syrup and rum (page 373). For those occasions that cry out for an ending on a chocolaty note, try my "instant" mini chocolate truffles with cognac, dark rum, or Grand Marnier—your call (page 409). They are fast, foolproof, and so addictive that I usually reserve my truffle making for the Christmas holidays, when excess is always forgiven.

Many of the dishes in this book date back to my childhood. Others were picked up as I learned about American food and traveled the world tasting Asian and Latin American cuisines. Whatever its origins, in my kitchen, a recipe is never carved in stone or static, but a living thing that will change subtly—or occasionally not so subtly—according to whim, new flavors that inspire me, the discovery of more expedient ways to arrive at the result I want, or simply what happens to be in my refrigerator.

I know that I will never make any recipe exactly the same way again. I will always be tinkering with the dish and thinking about new flavors and ingredients to substitute. Please feel free to do the same with these recipes. They will become all the more rewarding when they reflect *your* heart and soul.

Hors d'Oeuvres

||||||||||||||||||||||||||||||||||||||||||||||||

Cannellini Bean Dip

SERVES 4

DIP

One 1-pound can cannellini
  beans, drained (about
  1¾ cups)

1 large garlic clove, crushed

½ cup diced bread

¼ cup olive oil

1 tablespoon water

¼ teaspoon ground cumin

½ teaspoon salt

½ teaspoon Tabasco sauce

GARNISHES

⅓ cup reserved beans (from
  above)

2 teaspoons extra-virgin
  olive oil

¼ teaspoon paprika

½ teaspoon poppy seeds

1 teaspoon chopped fresh
  parsley

3 or 4 tostadas or hard taco
  shells, broken into wedges,
  or toasts or rice crackers

I LIKE TO OFFER GUESTS A LITTLE TREAT WHEN I'm serving drinks, and this dip is always welcome. My pantry is never without canned beans, from cannellini to black beans to large butter beans. The garnishes make the dish look more attractive—and more like a classic hummus made with chickpeas.

|||||||||||||||||||||||||||||||||||||||||||||||

FOR THE DIP: Reserve ⅓ cup of the beans for garnish. Put the remaining beans in a blender or food processor. Add all the remaining ingredients and process until very smooth, scraping the bowl with a rubber spatula a few times if need be to help combine the ingredients.

Transfer the dip (you should have about 2 cups) to a shallow serving dish and create a well in the center.

FOR THE GARNISHES: Put the reserved beans in the well in the dip and pour in the olive oil. Sprinkle with the paprika, poppy seeds, and parsley. Serve surrounded by the tostadas or tacos, toasts, or crackers.

Spicy Garbanzos

SERVES 4

One 15-ounce can chickpeas, drained

3 tablespoons mayonnaise

2 tablespoons sour cream

2 teaspoons hot chili sauce, such as Sriracha

¼ teaspoon salt

¼ cup (loosely packed) fresh tarragon leaves, plus an optional sprig for garnish

4 Boston lettuce leaves

1 tablespoon chopped fresh chives

I KEEP CANNED GARBANZO BEANS (ALSO KNOWN as chickpeas) on hand to use as a garnish for roasts or for a starter, as in this recipe. I like the hot chili sauce I find at my market, but if it is too hot for you, add only half as much as called for.

Mix together all the ingredients except the lettuce and chives in a bowl.

Arrange a lettuce leaf on each of four serving plates and fill with the chickpea mixture. Sprinkle with the chives and tarragon, if using, and serve.

Goat Cheese Tostadas

SERVES 4

I LOVE TO USE TOSTADAS, WHICH ARE TOASTED tortilla chips or tacos. In Mexico, they have both flat (plana) and rippled, wavy tostadas (ondulato); I use the flat ones for this recipe. I cover them with warmed goat cheese, sun-dried tomatoes, and chives.

Heat the goat cheese in a microwave oven for 30 seconds to soften it.

Spread the cheese on the tostadas and sprinkle the sun-dried tomatoes, pepper, chives, and olive oil on top. Break or cut into pieces and enjoy.

6 ounces fresh goat cheese

4 flat tostada shells (about 5 inches in diameter)

4 sun-dried tomatoes in oil, cut into 1/2-inch-wide strips

1/2 teaspoon freshly ground black pepper

1 tablespoon minced fresh chives

1 tablespoon extra-virgin olive oil

In the Beginning

WELL-MEANING COOKS FREQUENTLY SPOIL DINNER before the guests come to the table by serving a large, robust appetizer or too many smaller dishes. Ideally, an appetizer should titillate, not satisfy, the appetite. It should be a little morsel, well seasoned, so diners say, "Wow! That was really good. I wish I could have a little more." But there isn't any more. And that's the important part. Appetizers are all about expectations and leaving guests with exciting tastes in their mouths so they are primed to enjoy the courses that follow.

Appetizers should also be easy on the cook. I don't like to have to think about a first course in the hours just before a meal—I want to concentrate on the main dishes. And the less preparation, the better. In the winter, soup is a great starter, particularly because it can be made ahead of time and put back on the burner just before you're ready to serve. A soufflé can be mixed together in the afternoon and popped in the oven as guests arrive. One of my favorite fallbacks is to assemble a salad plate with eight or ten tidbits for guests to choose from: hard-cooked eggs, anchovies, smoked salmon, olives, cherry tomatoes. Often I open some oysters and serve a couple to each person. I'm not embarrassed to say that I frequently use the workers behind the deli counter at my supermarket as prep cooks—picking up mozzarella balls, a few different types of olives, and some sun-dried tomatoes leaves me with plenty of time and energy to devote to the main event.

Cheese and Tomato Towers

SERVES 4

THIS IS A TASTY AND BEAUTIFUL HORS D'OEUVRE or accompaniment to meat or fish. I use Campari tomatoes, which are the same size when sliced as the Ritz crackers that form the base of the towers. The mozzarella balls should be about the same diameter as well.

|||||||||||||||||||||||||||||||||||||||||||||||||||||||

Peel or do not peel the tomatoes, as you prefer. Cut each tomato crosswise into 6 slices.

Place a cracker in the center of each of four plates. Top each cracker with a slice of mozzarella and put a basil leaf on top, so it is sticking halfway out. Top with a slice of tomato and sprinkle some of the salt/pepper mixture on top. Repeat this process with the remaining crackers, mozzarella slices, basil leaves, tomatoes, and seasonings, creating "towers."

Sprinkle the towers with the olive oil and serve.

2 medium ripe tomatoes, such as Campari (14 ounces)

12 round buttery crackers (about 2½ inches in diameter)

3 small mozzarella balls (4 ounces each), cut into 4 slices each

12 fresh basil leaves

½ teaspoon each coarse salt and freshly ground black pepper, mixed together

2 tablespoons extra-virgin olive oil

Camembert with Pistachio Crust

SERVES 4 TO 6

½ cup pistachio nuts

1 Camembert cheese
round (about 9 ounces),
preferably from France and
made with raw milk

1 tablespoon honey

½ cup dried cranberries

Crackers, for serving

I HAVE ALWAYS ENJOYED A GOOD CAMEMBERT, especially the raw-milk varieties from France. To make this version a bit more elegant, I moisten the cheese with honey, cover it with chopped pistachios, and serve it garnished with dried cranberries.

||||||||||||||||||||||||||||||||||||||||||

Process the nuts in a food processor until pulverized but not ground into a powder—small pieces of nuts should still be visible.

Unwrap the cheese. If you object to the crust, you can scrape it lightly; I leave it on. Brush the top and sides of the cheese with the honey. Sprinkle a layer of nuts on top of the Camembert and, holding the cheese round in one hand, pat more nuts around the sides with the other hand, pressing lightly on the nuts so they stick.

Put the remaining nuts in the center of a serving platter and place the cheese on top. Sprinkle the cranberries around the cheese and serve at room temperature, with crackers.

Fontainebleau Cheese

MAKES ABOUT 2 CUPS

IN FRANCE, YOU FIND FRESH WHITE LOCAL cheeses served sometimes with sugar and fresh berries, other times in a savory version seasoned with herbs and garlic. Fontainebleau cheese, named after a town north of Paris, is usually sweetened and served with berries. In several restaurants where I worked, we made it with Petit Suisse, a type of creamy fresh cheese mixed with whipped fresh cream. My version of Fontainebleau is seasoned with salt and pepper, although it can also be sweetened and served with berries for a dessert. I use soft cream cheese, sometimes called "spread" or "whipped." I soften it further in a microwave oven to make it easy to combine with the cream. This recipe yields about 2 cups; I usually divide the mixture in half to make two cheeses.

One 8-ounce container soft cream cheese

½ cup plus 2 tablespoons heavy cream

¼ teaspoon salt

½ teaspoon freshly ground black pepper

Toasts or baguette slices, for serving

Place the cream cheese in a microwave oven and heat it for about 45 seconds to soften. Combine the cheese in a bowl with 2 tablespoons of the heavy cream, the salt, and pepper and mix well with a whisk.

Whip the remaining ½ cup cream until it is firm. Combine it with the cream cheese mixture.

Moisten the inside of two 1-cup bowls with water and line them with plastic wrap. (The water will make the plastic wrap adhere easily.) Fill the bowls with the cheese. Cover and refrigerate for at least a few hours, or overnight. *(Refrigerated, the cheese will keep for a couple of weeks.)*

To serve, invert one (or both) of the cheeses onto a plate and remove the plastic wrap. Spoon the cheese onto toasts or baguette slices.

Big Cheeses

THERE ARE TWO CHEESES THAT I VIEW AS MUST-HAVE kitchen staples, in the same league as salt, sugar, and flour. If you open my fridge, I guarantee that you will always find a piece of good Swiss cheese (the best being Beaufort, Comté, Emmenthaler, and Gruyère, although a really good Norwegian Jarlsberg can stand in) and a block of Parmesan. In addition, there will be a smelly cheese like Époisses, Pont l'Évêque, or Camembert, preferably made from unpasteurized milk.

I love to nibble on a piece of cheese at the end of a meal. But in my kitchen, cheese is as much an additive and flavor enhancer to other dishes as a stand-alone treat. I shred or grate it into soups, add it to gratins and soufflés, and crumble it atop green salads. Occasionally I gather all the tidbits of old dried-out cheese in my refrigerator, scrape any mold from them, and process them in the food processor with garlic, white wine, and black pepper to create a pungent paste called *fromage fort*. It is great spread on toasts for serving as an hors d'oeuvre or with a salad.

France's wealth of great cheese was one of the things I missed most when I arrived in the United States in 1959. With their Velveeta "cheese food" and bland blocks of "American" cheese, the grocery store dairy cases were forlorn places for a transplanted cheese aficionado. Salvation came when my friend Jean-Claude Szurdak found a shop in New York that stocked small bricks of a particularly pungent variety of

Limburger imported from Germany. We were happy, even though visitors occasionally recoiled when they opened our refrigerator. But pungency does have its limits. If you encounter a piece of cheese that gives off a smell of ammonia, it's a goner and, sadly, should be discarded.

One of the great benefits brought about by the revolution in American cuisine over the past few decades has been the explosion of artisanal cheese makers in this country. It seems like new brands are introduced every day—and they are winning international medals. To the uninitiated, the selection can be overwhelming, even intimidating. Fortunately there has been an equally large growth in the number of boutique cheesemongers who are more than happy to share their passion. Whole Foods Market also carries an impressive selection. If in doubt, put yourself in the hands of the person behind the counter. Pick up small pieces of several different cheeses, or select a cross section of one category, like blue cheeses. You may make some mistakes, but your exploits will be interesting and in the end rewarding.

Any cheese that I buy is a living organism. It changes color. It ages. And, if left long enough, it dies, like all living creatures. I don't trust a cheese that can stay in the supermarket case for a year with no detectable changes. That said, there is one exception. I still enjoy a charcoal-grilled hamburger topped with a melted slice of processed cheese a few times each summer. There's something quintessentially American about it.

Cucumber "Vases"

SERVES 4

THIS QUICK, UNUSUAL SALAD IS VERY ATTRAC-tive. You can vary the greens, selecting anything from watercress to romaine to mesclun. I like red oak leaf or ruby lettuce for its color and taste.

||||||||||||||||||||||||||||||||||||||||||||||||||||

Using a vegetable peeler, cut 9 long strips from the cucumber; discard the first one, which will be mostly skin, leaving you with 8 strips. (The rest of the cucumber can be used in another salad.) Cut 4 slices from the tomato, each about 1/2 inch thick.

Gather about 1 cup of the salad greens and a couple chives, if using, into a nice "bouquet" and wrap 2 of the cucumber slices around the stem ends of the leaves to make a "vase" to hold the greens. Repeat with the remaining greens and cucumber slices, creating 3 more bouquets.

Place a slice of tomato in the center of each of four plates. Arrange a cucumber vase of greens on top of each slice. Sprinkle the bouquets and vases with the salt, pepper, olive oil, and lemon juice. Serve.

1 seedless cucumber

1 medium ripe plum tomato

About 4 cups red oak leaf
   or mesclun salad greens,
   cleaned and spun dry

Fresh chives (optional)

1/2 teaspoon salt

1/2 teaspoon freshly ground
   black pepper

2 tablespoons extra-virgin
   olive oil

2 teaspoons fresh lemon juice

Carpaccio of Baby Bellas

SERVES 4

8 ounces baby bella mushrooms or large cremini mushrooms (about 8; you will use only the caps)

¾ teaspoon truffle salt or regular salt

½ teaspoon freshly ground black pepper

1½ teaspoons grated lemon rind

1 tablespoon fresh lemon juice

2 tablespoons extra-virgin olive oil

1 tablespoon grated Parmesan cheese

1 tablespoon finely minced scallion greens or fresh chives

Thin baguette slices, for serving

I HAD A FEW FRIENDS COMING FOR DRINKS and I didn't have anything for them to munch on except olives. So I decided to make a carpaccio of mushrooms. Only the caps of mushrooms are used; the rest can be pureed or sautéed and used in a soup or stew. The mushrooms become more flavorful after standing at room temperature for 1 hour. Truffle salt improves the taste, if available, but regular salt is fine.

|||||||||||||||||||||||||||||||||||||||||||||||||||

Holding a mushroom by the stem and on its side, slice the cap into ⅛-inch-thick slices. You should get about 5 slices. Repeat with all the mushrooms. You will have used about half the weight of the mushrooms; reserve the stems and gills for another recipe.

Arrange the mushroom slices on a platter so they overlap a little, like the tiles of a roof, starting with the biggest slices and finishing with the smallest. Sprinkle the salt, pepper, and lemon rind and juice on top, then sprinkle with the olive oil and cheese and finish with the scallions or chives. Let macerate for 1 hour at room temperature.

Serve the carpaccio with thin slices of baguette.

Tomato Tartine

SERVES 4

I LOVE TOMATOES RIGHT OUT OF THE GARDEN, in soups, salads, and gratins. I also like them as they are often served in Spain: split and rubbed on crunchy toasted bread. In this version, I serve a chunky tomato puree on soft crumpets.

||||||||||||||||||||||||||||||||||||||||||||||||

Split the crumpets horizontally, as you would English muffins. Cut the tomato crosswise in half and squeeze out the seeds and juice. Cut the tomato halves into chunks and pulse in a food processor until pureed but still a bit chunky.

Arrange the crumpets cut side up on a plate and cover with the pureed tomato. Sprinkle with the salt, olive oil, and chives. Serve.

2 crumpets (about 4 inches across)

1 large ripe tomato (about 8 ounces)

½ teaspoon fleur de sel or other coarse salt

3 tablespoons extra-virgin olive oil

1 tablespoon minced fresh chives

Gougères with Cheese

MAKES ABOUT 60 CHOUX

GOUGÈRES

1 cup milk

8 tablespoons (1 stick) unsalted butter

1 teaspoon sugar

¼ teaspoon salt

⅛ teaspoon cayenne pepper

1 cup all-purpose flour

4 large eggs

TOPPING AND FILLING

3 tablespoons grated Parmesan cheese

½ teaspoon paprika, preferably Spanish

1¾ cups coarsely chopped or grated Gruyère or Emmenthaler cheese

½ teaspoon fleur de sel or kosher salt

½ teaspoon freshly ground black pepper

GOUGÈRES, SMALL SAVORY PROFITEROLES FLAvored with cheese, are an ideal hors d'oeuvre for a big party. I usually make them ahead and freeze them, then transfer them directly from the freezer to a hot oven just before serving. In this recipe, I top the choux with Parmesan and paprika and fill them with seasoned chopped Gruyère. Sometimes I make a filling of béchamel sauce mixed with Gruyère, or I simply flavor the choux dough with grated Parmesan and Gruyère and don't stuff them at all. For large quantities, many cooks use a pastry bag fitted with a plain tip to pipe out the choux, but here, a spoon works just as well.

The recipe on page 28 fills the cooled puffs with a savory shrimp mixture. They can also be filled with guacamole or with sour cream and smoked salmon.

||||||||||||||||||||||||||||||||||||||||||||||||||

FOR THE GOUGÈRES: Preheat the oven to 400 degrees, with racks in the middle and upper third.

Bring the milk, butter, sugar, salt, and cayenne to a boil in a medium saucepan. Remove the pan from the heat and add the flour in one stroke. Mix thoroughly with a sturdy wooden spoon or spatula and then, after a few seconds, once the mixture is well combined, return the pan to the stove and stir for about 1 minute to dry the dough. Transfer the dough to a food processor and process for 5 or 6 seconds to cool slightly.

Meanwhile, break the eggs into a bowl and beat well with a fork or whisk. Set aside about 2 tablespoons of the beaten eggs in a small bowl, to brush the choux before baking. Add the rest of the eggs to the dough in the food processor and process until smooth and thick. Transfer to a bowl.

Line two baking sheets with aluminum foil. Using a teaspoon, scoop up about ½ teaspoon of the choux dough and push it off the teaspoon and onto one of the baking sheets with your index finger. Continue filling the pan with the choux, placing them about 1 inch apart, and then fill the second pan. (You will have about 60 choux.) Brush the tops of the choux with the reserved beaten egg.

FOR THE TOPPING: Mix together the Parmesan and paprika and sprinkle on top of the choux mounds. Bake for 15 minutes, then reduce the oven temperature to 350 degrees and continue cooking the gougères for another 15 minutes, or until they are puffy, brown, and dry to the touch. Cool in the oven with the door open for 10 to 15 minutes. (If the choux come out of the oven too fast, the humidity can make them soften.) Transfer to racks to cool completely.

FOR THE FILLING: Mix together the Gruyère cheese, salt, and pepper. When the gougères are cool, split them horizontally in half with a serrated knife, leaving them still attached on one side. Fill each one with about 1½ teaspoons of the Gruyère mixture. (*The filled puffs can be frozen for up to a month.*)

Preheat the oven to 400 degrees.

Place the choux on baking sheets and reheat in the oven for about 15 minutes, until they are warm and the cheese inside has melted. Serve right away.

Shrimp Gougères Provençal

5 tablespoons unsalted butter

3 tablespoons olive oil

½ cup chopped shallots

1 tablespoon chopped garlic

1 pound shrimp (any size), shelled and coarsely chopped into ¼-inch pieces (about 1¾ cups)

¾ teaspoon salt

1½ teaspoons freshly ground black pepper

⅓ cup coarsely chopped fresh cilantro or parsley

¼ recipe (15 gougères) gougères (see page 26), baked and cooled

THIS IS A GREAT HORS D'OEUVRE THAT I OFTEN feature at our boules parties. It can be served with the crab chips from the Crab Chips with Salmon Caviar recipe (page 38); in Chinese spoons, like the Egg and Herb Treats (page 29); or, as here, in gougère shells (page 26). Once cooked and cooled, the puffs are halved to create receptacles for the shrimp. The puffs can be made ahead and even frozen. The shrimp mixture should be cooked at the last moment, but it doesn't take more than a couple of minutes to prepare.

|||||||||||||||||||||||||||||||||||||||||||||||||||||

Heat the butter and oil in a large (12-inch) saucepan. When the mixture is foaming, add the shallots and garlic and cook for about 20 seconds. Add the shrimp and mix well. Cook for about 2 minutes, stirring to separate the shrimp, then add the salt, pepper, and cilantro or parsley and mix well. Transfer the shrimp mixture to a bowl.

With a serrated knife, cut the gougères horizontally in half. Fill each half with about a tablespoon of the shrimp mixture. Serve warm or at room temperature.

Egg and Herb Treats

SERVES 16

I SERVE THIS HORS D'OEUVRE OF HERBED EGGS lukewarm in Chinese spoons, which stand level and are the ideal size for a single mouthful. Fresh herbs and a dash of (optional) truffle oil on top make the dish special. Truffle oil is expensive, but a little of it goes a long way. It is available in specialty stores or online. Trout or salmon caviar adds a special accent and beautiful look.

|||||||||||||||||||||||||||||||||||||||||||||||||||||||||||||||

Break the eggs into a bowl and beat them well with the salt, pepper, and tarragon. Line up sixteen Chinese spoons on a platter.

Heat the butter in a small saucepan. Add the eggs and cook, stirring well with a small whisk for the smoothest possible mixture, for no more than a minute or so—remove the eggs from the heat while they are still quite runny, because the heat of the pan will continue to cook them. Whisk in the crème fraîche or cream and mix well.

Divide the eggs among the spoons (about 1 tablespoon per spoon). Scatter a few trout or salmon eggs on top of each one and sprinkle with some chives and a few drops of truffle oil, if desired. Serve.

4 large eggs, preferably organic

½ teaspoon salt

½ teaspoon freshly ground black pepper

2 teaspoons chopped fresh tarragon

1 tablespoon unsalted butter

3 tablespoons crème fraîche or heavy cream

2 tablespoons trout or salmon caviar

1 tablespoon chopped fresh chives

About 2 teaspoons truffle oil, for sprinkling (optional)

Tiny Fish

ON A RECENT VISIT TO SPAIN, I ENJOYED ONE OF THE finest fish dishes I can remember, far better than many I have been served in three-star restaurants. This wasn't even in a proper restaurant, but in a large tent-like structure on a fishing beach near Málaga. The proprietor had built an enormous bonfire with gnarled wood from nearby olive groves. He had acquired sardines right off the boats of the local fishermen and, without scaling or gutting them, he impaled the tiny silver fish eight abreast on wooden skewers and put them near, not in, the fire. Then the servers brought each customer a single skewer, along with some olive oil and coarse sea salt. Perfect!

In this country, cooks often have good reason to avoid sardines, anchovies, herring, and the like. Their high oil content causes these species to spoil rapidly and develop a strong, overly fishy flavor. As my Spanish host knew, with little oily fish, freshness is paramount. Although it is getting easier to find fresh sardines in high-quality seafood shops and restaurants in the United States, it is still difficult to get them very fresh.

Canned sardines, anchovies, or herring can be an excellent alternative, but they should be of the highest quality, preferably imported from France, Spain, or Portugal, and packed in olive oil. I love these small fish and often eat them straight from the can. For a more substantial lunch, I will put a bed of greens on a platter, add a few hard-cooked eggs, and put the fish, along with some of their oil, on top. Sometimes I'll add a dash of red wine vinegar. Sometimes not.

You can create a delicious meal in no time at all with a tin of these small fish and a can of beans. Puree white or black beans with some garlic in a food processor, scoop that onto a plate with a dab of sour cream and with the canned fish of your choice, or even smoked oysters or mussels, and finish with a sprinkling of cilantro leaves.

Bluefish and mackerel suffer from the same freshness issues as their little oily counterparts, and they sometimes receive additional insult when prepared with a heavy sauce that accentuates their fattiness, to the point where it becomes cloying. Fortunately, I have a few fishermen friends on the coast of Connecticut. I get their "lowly" bluefish, mackerel, porgy, or whiting just out of the water, and they are as good as the "nobler" fish like swordfish, salmon, or striped bass. I say turn the flesh's oiliness to your advantage by broiling the fish, or follow the example of that beachside *poissonnier* in Málaga and cook them fast in the dry heat of a hot fire. A backyard grill and lump charcoal will get the job done perfectly well.

Much is made of the omega-3 health benefits of eating oily fish. I'm a cook, not a doctor. I eat them because I like them, and if they happen to be good for me, all the better.

Black Bread and Butter Lattice

SERVES 4

3 tablespoons unsalted butter, softened

1 teaspoon drained bottled horseradish

¼ teaspoon freshly ground black pepper

12 slices cocktail pumpernickel bread (about 3 inches square)

THIS IS AN ELEGANT BUT EASY WAY OF PRE-senting buttered bread; I like it with clams and oysters on the half-shell or ceviche. Slices of thin cocktail pumpernickel bread are stacked together with a horseradish-flavored butter between the slices. Then the stack is cut into vertical "towers," with each one having a layered effect.

|||||||||||||||||||||||||||||||||||||||||||||||||

Mix together the butter, horseradish, and pepper in a small bowl. Using a spatula, spread about 1 teaspoon of the butter mixture on one slice of the bread and cover with another slice of bread. Butter this slice and continue with this process, using 4 additional bread slices; do not butter the top slice. Repeat with the remaining 6 slices and butter so you have 2 bread stacks. Refrigerate until the butter is very firm, so the slices are well glued together.

At serving time, cut each bread stack vertically into 6 slices.

Cheese and Anchovy Toasts

MAKES 12 TOASTS

1 tablespoon peanut oil

Twelve ¾-inch-thick oval
slices baguette

6 sun-dried tomatoes in oil,
halved

About 3 ounces Gorgonzola
cheese, cut into 12 pieces

12 small anchovy fillets

2 tablespoons pesto,
homemade (page 103) or
store-bought

1 tablespoon chopped fresh
chives

*I SERVE THIS HORS D'OEUVRE ON TOASTED
slices of baguette. I cut the baguette on an angle to get ovals
that are about ⅜ inch thick, drizzle peanut oil over them,
and toast them in the oven. I use homemade pesto or good
prepared pesto, tasty canned anchovy fillets in olive oil (the
best are from the Bay of Biscay in Spain and France), and
the Gorgonzola cheese at my market. But you can use another cheese—anything from Camembert to Gruyère. Be sure
to purchase soft, flavorful sun-dried tomatoes in oil.*

||||||||||||||||||||||||||||||||||||||||||||||||

Preheat the oven to 400 degrees.

Line a baking sheet with aluminum foil and spread the
oil on the foil. Lay the baguette slices on the sheet and then
turn them over, so they are lightly coated with oil on both
sides. Bake for about 12 minutes, until brown and crisp.

Arrange the toasts on a serving platter. Top each with a
sun-dried tomato half, a piece of cheese, and an anchovy fillet. Add a small dab of pesto to each, sprinkle with the chives,
and serve.

Salmon Tostadas

SERVES 4

WHEN I AM PRESSED FOR TIME OR SURPRISED by unexpected guests, I often serve this dish with drinks. I usually have smoked salmon in my refrigerator, and this sauce of mayonnaise, horseradish, and yogurt takes only a minute to put together. It is also great with poached fish. The splash of tequila lends a special touch.

|||||||||||||||||||||||||||||||||||||||||||||||||

Mix together the mayonnaise, yogurt, and horseradish in a small bowl. Spread equally on the tostadas. Arrange the salmon slices on top and sprinkle the olives over the salmon. Splash with the tequila and sprinkle on the chives.

Serve the tostadas whole or cut into pieces.

3 tablespoons mayonnaise

1 tablespoon plain yogurt

2 teaspoons grated fresh or bottled horseradish

4 flat tostada shells

4 ounces sliced smoked salmon

12 oil-cured black olives, halved and pitted

1 tablespoon tequila

1 tablespoon chopped fresh chives

Pressed Caviar Canapés

MAKES 8 CANAPÉS

WHEN GLORIA AND I DINE AT HOME, I LIKE TO prepare canapés with payusnaya, *pressed caviar, a very smooth, concentrated paste made from the eggs of domestic sturgeon such as paddlefish, hackleback, or shovelnose from the Mississippi River. Although it is expensive, the cost is a trifle compared to imported beluga, osetra, or sevruga sturgeon caviar and provides a good introduction to that delicious specialty.*

||||||||||||||||||||||||||||||||||||||||||||||||||

1 thin slice white bread

1 tablespoon pressed caviar (payusnaya; see headnote)

2 teaspoons finely chopped mild onion

1½ teaspoons unsalted butter, softened

Toast the bread. As soon as it comes out of the toaster, lay it on a work surface and lightly trim the sides to remove the crust. Then, holding your knife parallel to the work surface, insert the blade into the center of the bread and slice into 2 very thin toasts—replicating the original Melba toast.

Spoon the caviar onto a piece of plastic wrap and cover with another piece of plastic wrap. Press the mixture into a rectangle about the same size as the bread. Remove the top sheet of plastic wrap, invert the caviar onto the inside of one of the bread slices, and press it into place.

Rinse the chopped onion in a sieve under cool running water to remove the sulfuric acid and pat it dry with paper towels. Sprinkle the onion over the caviar.

Spread the inside of the other bread slice generously with the butter, place it buttered side down on top of the caviar, and press it into place. Cut into 8 canapés and serve.

Crab Chips with Salmon Caviar

MAKES 12 CHIPS

1 cup safflower or corn oil

12 crab chips

¼ cup crème fraîche

¼ cup salmon caviar

1 tablespoon finely minced
    fresh chives

GLORIA LIKES FISH AND, PARTICULARLY, FISH eggs in any form—sturgeon caviar, salmon or trout roe, shad roe, tobiko (flying fish roe)—and she loves this dish.

You can find dried crab and shrimp chips in Chinese markets. The size of half dollars, they keep for months in the pantry. Reconstituted in hot oil, they explode, tripling in size in about fifteen seconds. They can be filled with crème fraîche and caviar, as here, or salmon tartare, or cooked shrimp, or even guacamole or tomato salsa.

Heat the oil to 340 to 350 degrees in a large skillet. Drop 6 chips into the oil and cook for 15 to 20 seconds. They should be white or slightly golden at most. Remove with a slotted spoon and drain on paper towels. Cook the remaining chips. *(The chips can be fried hours, or even a day, ahead.)*

Fill the chips with the crème fraîche and top with the caviar and a sprinkling of chives. Serve.

Tuna Mascarpone Cream

SERVES 4

THIS MOUSSE IS EXCELLENT SERVED ON RICE crackers or toast as an hors d'oeuvre. It also makes a great first course when, as here, it is encircled in a ring of carrot (or cucumber) strips and topped with watercress. For the best results, use a blender or mini food processor. And make sure that you use tuna packed in olive oil; the quality is better and it is more flavorful than canned tuna in water.

||||||||||||||||||||||||||||||||||||||||||||||||||||

Process the tuna, mascarpone, lemon juice, salt, and pepper in a blender or mini food processor for 1 minute or so, until very smooth.

To serve, peel the carrot and then remove 4 long strips with the vegetable peeler. Form 1 strip into a ring. If the strip is too short to encircle the tuna, use several strips to make a neat ring. Use an ice cream scoop (or a spoon) to mound about ¼ cup of the tuna mixture in the center of each carrot ring. Repeat on three more plates.

Embed 2 or 3 sprigs of watercress in the top of the tuna on each plate. Serve with toasts or rice crackers.

One 6-ounce can tuna in olive oil

½ cup mascarpone cheese

1 tablespoon fresh lemon juice

¼ teaspoon salt

½ teaspoon freshly ground black pepper

1 carrot

8 to 12 sprigs watercress

Toast triangles or rice crackers, for serving

Salmon Rillettes

SERVES 6 TO 8

8 tablespoons (1 stick) unsalted butter, softened

3 tablespoons very finely chopped onion

6 ounces boneless, skinless salmon (the belly is best), cut into 1½-inch pieces

3 ounces sliced smoked salmon, finely chopped

½ teaspoon salt

½ teaspoon freshly ground black pepper

1 teaspoon bottled horseradish

SALMON RILLETTES MAKES A GREAT HORS d'oeuvre or first course, and it will keep for a couple of weeks refrigerated. Here I combine fresh salmon poached in butter with chopped smoked salmon and add a dash of bottled horseradish to the mixture. It is important that the butter used to poach the salmon doesn't get too hot, so the onions in it don't fry. I first heat the butter in a microwave oven until it clarifies—meaning the clear part of the butter separates from the milky part. Then some of the clear butter is reserved to coat and seal the little crocks of rillettes, and the rest of the butter, including the milky solids, is used to cook the fresh salmon.

Be sure you let the chilled rillettes temper for about an hour at room temperature before serving, or the mixture will be too hard. Serve with rice crackers or toast and a dry white wine.

||||||||||||||||||||||||||||||||||||||||||||||||||||

Heat the butter in a glass measuring cup or a small bowl in a microwave oven for 1 to 1½ minutes, until the clear part of the butter separates from the milky solids. Reserve ¼ cup of the clear melted butter to coat the rillettes.

Pour the rest of the melted butter, including the milky part, into a small saucepan. Add the chopped onion and cook gently over medium heat for about 2 minutes, until the onion has softened. Add the fresh salmon and mix well, then reduce the heat and cook, covered, for about 2 minutes. Mix again. The salmon should be barely cooked in the center and still a little pink. Transfer to a plate.

With a fork, crush the poached salmon into a coarse

mixture. Transfer to a bowl, add the chopped smoked salmon, salt, pepper, and horseradish, and mix well.

Divide the mixture among three small molds (I use ½-cup soufflé molds); the molds should be about three-quarters full. Smooth the top of each one with the back of a spoon. Pour the reserved melted butter on top. Refrigerate until ready to use. (*The rillettes will keep for a couple of weeks in your refrigerator.*)

To serve, let the rillettes warm up at room temperature for about 1 hour, so the salmon and butter soften a little. Then stir the top layer of butter into the rillettes and serve.

Play Boules!

ON THE SURFACE, NO GAME COULD BE SIMPLER THAN *boules*. A player from one team stands in a circle and tosses a ball, called a jack, onto the flat playing area. Then the teams take turns throwing other balls at the jack. The side that has thrown the ball closest to the jack at the end wins the round.

But for French people, *boules* is a deeply textured—and thoroughly enjoyable—social phenomenon. With no barriers in terms of age or gender, it's a chance for extended families to get together and have fun. Grandparents, parents, and children can all play. On Sunday afternoons all across France, town greens are transformed into *boules* courts that become hubs for people to visit, gossip, and flirt. My father maintained eight *boules* courts next to our family's restaurant near Lyons. On Sunday afternoons, he would shuttle between the kitchen and the wine cellar to keep the players refreshed. Between participants and spectators, those courts assured that the restaurant had a steady stream of customers.

Boules is as much a gastronomic pastime as it is a sport. No match would be complete without generous quantities of liquor (licorice-flavored Pernod and Ricard in France, white wine and rosé at our Connecticut home), which doesn't seem to affect the quality of play—or at least affects all players equally. We usually keep a supply of wine in a tub of ice outside, and guests begin helping themselves even before

we draw names from a hat to form the teams. Almost as important as something to slake the players' thirst is food, usually small items that they can eat with their hands. When we have our big *boules* gatherings, it's not unusual for me to prepare six or seven hors d'oeuvres to pass around: savory little profiteroles, or gougères (page 26); shrimp sautéed in butter with garlic; and merguez made with ground lamb shoulder, ground pork, and ground beef with a lot of cumin and hot peppers, which I serve on lettuce leaves, along with a tasty mushroom carpaccio (page 24).

During a game, we are very competitive, arguing and measuring, making suggestions to teammates. I consider myself to be a pretty good player, but I think almost everyone else feels the same way about their skills. No matter. By the next day, I will have forgotten the score and even who won but vividly remember the camaraderie and food. Sometimes the games continue informally until the wee hours. The only thing that finally makes us stop is when Paco, our aged miniature poodle, walks across the court and decides to curl up for a snooze among the balls.

Calamari and Shrimp Patties

SERVES 4 (MAKES 12 SMALL PATTIES)

THIS SEAFOOD MIXTURE CAN BE MADE INTO large patties and served in lettuce cups as a main course, or it can be formed, as it is here, into a bite-size hors d'oeuvre. Sometimes I wrap the patties in spring roll wrappers, which are available at Asian markets and some supermarkets.

||||||||||||||||||||||||||||||||||||||||||||||||||

Combine the squid and shrimp, salt, and pepper in a food processor and process for about 20 seconds. Scrape down the sides of the processor bowl with a rubber spatula, then add the sour cream and process for 20 seconds. Mix in the chives by hand.

To cook the patties, heat the oil and butter in a very large nonstick skillet over high heat. Working quickly, drop about 2 tablespoons of the mixture into the pan for each patty; you should have 12 patties. Cook for about 1½ minutes on each side, until the patties are nicely browned on both sides.

To serve, arrange the lettuce leaves on a platter, transfer the patties to the lettuce leaves, and add a sprig of cilantro to each. Let your guests wrap the lettuce leaves around the patties to make delicate finger food. Alternatively, moisten the spring roll wrappers with water to soften them. Place a patty on each softened wrapper, top with a lettuce leaf and a cilantro sprig, and bring the edges of the wrappers over to enclose the filling. Turn the packages over so the patties are visible through the wrappers, arrange on a platter, and serve.

12 ounces cleaned small squid (bodies and tentacles), cut into 1-inch pieces (1½ cups)

6 ounces shelled shrimp, cut into ½-inch pieces (½ cup)

½ teaspoon salt

½ teaspoon freshly ground black pepper

¼ cup sour cream

3 tablespoons minced fresh chives

1 tablespoon peanut oil

1 tablespoon unsalted butter

12 small leaves Boston or Bibb lettuce

12 fresh cilantro sprigs

Twelve 8-inch spring roll wrappers (optional)

Prosciutto Packages

MAKES 12 PACKAGES

12 small thin slices prosciutto (about 5 ounces); or 6 large ones, cut into halves

12 small mozzarella balls (about 1 inch in diameter)

12 kalamata olives, pitted

1 tablespoon extra-virgin olive oil

½ teaspoon freshly ground black pepper

1 tablespoon chopped fresh tarragon or parsley

YOU CAN VARY THESE BY USING CHEESE OTHER than mozzarella and mortadella instead of prosciutto. Have the prosciutto sliced thin but not too thin. The slices should be large enough to encase the cheese and olives. If you have very large slices, cut them in half.

||||||||||||||||||||||||||||||||||||||||||||||||||||

Lay out the prosciutto slices and place 1 mozzarella ball and 1 olive on each one. Roll up or fold over the prosciutto to create small packages and secure with toothpicks.

Arrange the packages on a platter and sprinkle with the oil, pepper, and herbs. Serve.

Duck Liver Mousse with Apples

MAKES 16 TO 18 HORS D'OEUVRES

WHEN I ROAST A WHOLE DUCK, I FREEZE THE rendered fat and livers for pâtés or mousses like this one. The apple gives it a wonderful sweetness and some acidity.

||||||||||||||||||||||||||||||||||||||||||||||||||||

Cut the fat into ½-inch pieces and put it in a skillet. Partially cover the pan to prevent spattering and cook over medium heat for about 8 minutes, or until the fat is rendered, with some cracklings.

Add the shallots, garlic, herbes de Provence, and apple and cook for 3 to 4 minutes. Add the livers, salt, and pepper and cook for about 3 minutes, turning the livers occasionally; the livers should still be pink inside. Set the pan to the side, off the heat, for 3 to 4 minutes, then drain the livers in a sieve set over a bowl, reserving the fat. Place the solids on a cutting board and finely chop with a big knife. Transfer to a bowl, add the reserved fat and Armagnac or Calvados, and mix well. Refrigerate for a couple of hours.

Stir the mixture well with a rubber spatula and refrigerate for another 2 to 3 hours. At this point, the mousse should be solid. Mix well to emulsify. Spoon the mousse into small (½- to ¾-cup) ramekins. Cover and refrigerate (or freeze, then thaw in the refrigerator to serve). Serve the mousse ice-cold from the refrigerator on toasts or crackers.

||||||||||||||||||||||||||||||||||||||||||||||||||||

NOTE: *This recipe can be made with chicken livers and chicken fat in the same way.*

6 ounces duck fat

⅓ cup sliced shallots

2 garlic cloves, crushed

½ teaspoon herbes de Provence

1 McIntosh or other apple (about 8 ounces), peeled, cored, and cut into ¾-inch cubes (about 1½ cups)

4 duck livers, separated into 2 pieces each, sinews removed (about 8 ounces)

1 teaspoon salt

1 teaspoon freshly ground black pepper

2 teaspoons Armagnac or Calvados

Toasts or crackers, for serving

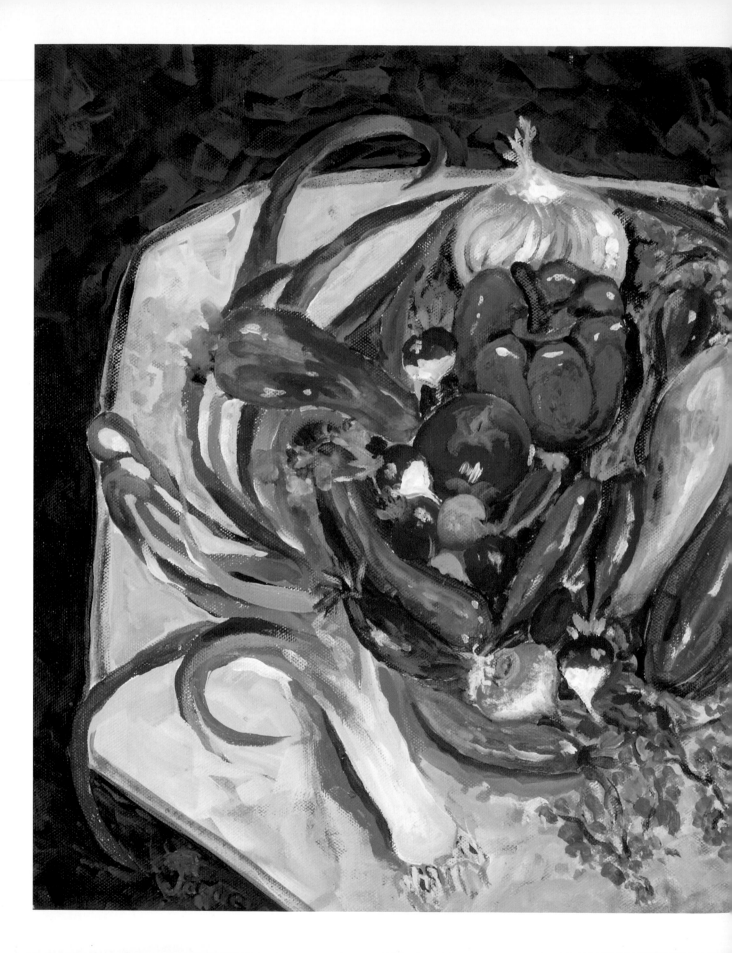

Soups and Salads

||||||||||||||||||||||||||||||||||||||||||||||||||||||

Parisian Potage

SERVES 4

1 tablespoon peanut oil

2 tablespoons unsalted butter

1 large leek, damaged outer leaves discarded, split, washed, and finely minced (3 cups)

1 pound Yukon Gold potatoes, peeled and held in cold water

4 cups homemade chicken stock or canned low-sodium chicken broth

1 cup water

½ teaspoon salt, or more to taste

½ teaspoon freshly ground black pepper

1 tablespoon chopped fresh parsley or chervil

½ cup grated Gruyère cheese or a dollop of softened unsalted butter (optional)

LEEKS AND POTATOES ARE COMMONLY MADE into creamy vichyssoise. For Parisian potage, the leeks and potatoes are cut into very small pieces, stewed in a little butter for a couple of minutes, and then cooked with chicken stock. This is one of my favorite soups. I serve it sprinkled with grated Gruyère cheese, but that is not essential.

||||||||||||||||||||||||||||||||||||||||||||||||

Heat the oil and butter in a large saucepan. Add the leeks and cook over medium heat for about 3 minutes, stirring occasionally.

Meanwhile, cut the potatoes into sticks about ¾ inch thick and slice the sticks crosswise into ⅛-inch slivers (you will have about 3½ cups). The potatoes should be kept in water after peeling, but they should not be washed after they are cut into slivers; this would wash away their starch, which helps make the soup smooth.

Add the stock, water, salt, and pepper to the leeks, then mix in the potato slivers. Bring to a boil, reduce the heat, and boil gently for about 12 minutes.

Serve the soup with a sprinkling of the parsley or chervil on top and, if you like, the grated cheese or a dollop of butter.

Broccoli Silk

SERVES 4 (MAKES ABOUT 5½ CUPS)

A SMOOTH, CREAMY BROCCOLI SOUP MAKES A great first course, and this one can be served cool or warm. While broccoli is usually combined with other vegetables and, sometimes, a white sauce, to make soup, in this recipe, the broccoli is simply boiled in salted water and then pureed and emulsified with a little butter (and Tabasco for heat). I use only broccoli crowns, to give the puree a beautiful green color. You can buy just the crowns, or cut them from the spears and use the spears for another recipe. Do not boil the broccoli in an unlined aluminum pot, or it will discolor.

1 pound broccoli crowns or tops, cut into 1-inch pieces

1 teaspoon salt

¼ teaspoon Tabasco sauce

2½ tablespoons unsalted butter

||||||||||||||||||||||||||||||||||||||||||||||||||||

Bring 3 cups water to a boil in a medium saucepan. Add the broccoli and salt, cover, and bring back to a strong boil (this will take about 2 minutes). Boil, covered, for another 4 minutes (for a total cooking time of about 6 minutes).

Drain the broccoli in a colander, reserving the liquid, and cool the crowns under cold water for 1 minute to stop the cooking and to keep them green.

Pour 2 cups of the reserved cooking liquid into a blender. Add the cooked crowns, Tabasco, and butter and process the mixture until very smooth. Let cool and serve, or reheat the soup and serve warm.

In Praise of Wilted Vegetables

I CAN'T BEAR THE THOUGHT OF FOOD BEING THROWN out. Ever. During my years as an itinerant cooking school instructor, Gloria would occasionally take advantage of one of my road trips to clean out the fridge. Consigning leftovers to the garbage was something I would never have countenanced had I been home. At first I would ask her questions like, "What happened to that chicken that we didn't finish last week?" But I quickly learned that I did not want to know the answer.

I use my soup pot, instead of the trash can, as a pretext for cleaning the fridge. Some cookbook authors claim that a great soup starts with only the freshest vegetables. Nonsense! Lettuce that has become wilted, a carrot or two that are slightly shriveled and limp, a halved onion that has begun to dry out where it was cut, all get tossed into a pot of chicken stock or, if I have no stock on hand, water with a chicken bouillon cube. I'll root around and discover a slice or two of ham hiding in the back of the refrigerator, or maybe a stub of sausage. They go into the pot too, and it is allowed to bubble away while I tend to other matters. The result is invariably good.

Every refrigerator seems to host an accumulation of leftover pieces of cheese biding their time until they become dry, hard, and moldy. I collect the tough, dried-out rinds from Parmesan cheese in a plastic bag and store them in the freezer. When enough have accumulated, I melt the chopped-up rinds into a big soup or a bean stew, adding body and flavor. Another of my tricks is to use one variety of cheese in a recipe that traditionally employs a different one. I typically use Gruyère in a cheese soufflé, but there is no law saying that a little Camembert that is getting on in age can't add its tanginess to the dish, and I'm not above incorporating blue cheese into my gougères batter.

My reluctance to get rid of scraps has nothing to do with economizing—I am simply congenitally incapable of throwing away food. It's a question of principle. I read somewhere that Americans waste more than 30 percent of the food they buy. There is something morally wrong about putting food in the garbage. I still carry the mental image of my father sadly kissing a morsel of bread that was furry with mold and muttering, "This is the staff of life," before tossing it into the chicken run.

Making use of ingredients that are beyond their prime, or at least what most North American cooks would view as having seen better days, has brought me unexpected rewards. When filming the first episode of *Today's Gourmet* in KQED's studios in San Francisco, Claudine and I found that we had come up three minutes short. Three minutes is valuable time in the television business. On a whim, I asked Claudine, who was in college at the time, what she had in her refrigerator at school. She rattled off a list of five or so items and admitted that they were all destined for the trash. I showed her how to do something wonderful with each one of those ingredients. Leftover food and what amounted to leftover time led to what was one of the most successful and talked-about episodes we ever made.

Tomato Velvet

SERVES 4 (MAKES 5 TO 6 CUPS)

2 tablespoons olive oil

1 cup coarsely chopped onion

2 teaspoons coarsely chopped
garlic

2 tablespoons all-purpose
flour

1½ pounds ripe tomatoes,
cut into 1-inch dice (about
4 cups)

⅓ cup sun-dried tomatoes in
oil, coarsely chopped

2 tablespoons tomato paste

1½ cups water

½ teaspoon salt

¾ teaspoon freshly ground
black pepper

1 teaspoon sugar

3 tablespoons unsalted butter

2 tablespoons fresh chervil
or tiny bush basil leaves or
shredded fresh regular basil
leaves

*HOT OR COLD, TOMATO SOUP IS ALWAYS WEL-
come at my house. I like it both chunky and smooth, as in
this version. To make it intensely tomatoey in taste, I use a
combination of fresh ripe tomatoes and sun-dried, as well as
concentrated tomato paste. The soup takes only minutes to
prepare and so can be made at the last moment or prepared
hours ahead and reheated before serving.*

||||||||||||||||||||||||||||||||||||||||||||||||||

H eat the oil in a large heavy saucepan. Add the onion
and sauté for 1 minute, then add the garlic and mix
well. Stir in the flour and let cook for a minute or two, stirring, then add all the tomatoes, the tomato paste, water, salt,
pepper, and sugar and bring to a boil. Stir well and boil gently,
covered, for 10 minutes.

Push the soup through a food mill or a sieve to remove the
tomato seeds and skin. Alternatively, you can emulsify the
soup in a food processor. (The recipe can be made ahead and
refrigerated for up to 2 days.)

At serving time, reheat the soup. Add the butter and emulsify with an immersion blender or in a standard blender so
the soup is creamy and smooth. Garnish with the chervil or
basil.

Garlic and Pasilla Soup

SERVES 4 (MAKES 8 CUPS)

4 to 5 dried pasilla chili
    peppers (about 2 ounces)

3 cups diced (1-inch) onions

2 heads garlic, peeled,
    separated into cloves, and
    crushed (about 20 cloves)

¼ cup olive oil

4 cups diced (1-inch) tomatoes
    (about 1½ pounds)

1 teaspoon dried oregano,
    preferably Mexican

Salt

GARNISHES

1 ripe avocado

¼ cup Mexican crema, if
    available, crème fraîche, or
    sour cream

4 fresh cilantro sprigs

1 cup croutons

THIS GARLIC SOUP IS SIMILAR TO ONE I EN-joyed in a restaurant in the town of Playa del Carmen, where we owned a vacation apartment for several years. The soup can be made with ancho or guajillo peppers, but I chose pasilla peppers, which are long black dried chilies with crinkled skin. (These are called chilaca peppers when fresh.) They have a complex taste and smell of chocolate, tobacco, and earth. Lots of garlic, onions, tomato, olive oil, and a bit of flavorful Mexican oregano complete the ingredient list.

The soup should be emulsified in a blender so it's smooth, and you can strain it if you object to eating tiny pieces of chili pepper skin. I garnish the soup with croutons and pieces of avocado and some thick Mexican crema (sour cream or crème fraîche is fine too) to help cut the fiery taste of the chilies.

Soak the chilies in 8 cups water for a couple of hours, until softened.

Remove the chilies from the water, reserving the soaking liquid. Remove and discard the stems and seeds and coarsely chop the chilies. (You should have a good cup.) Strain the soaking liquid and set it aside.

Sauté the onions and garlic in the olive oil in a large saucepan for 3 to 4 minutes, until blond in color. Add the chopped chili peppers and cook for about 1 minute, then add the tomatoes, reserved soaking liquid, oregano, and salt to taste. Bring to a boil, reduce the heat, partially cover, and boil gently for 30 minutes.

Transfer the soup to a blender, in batches, and blend for a full minute. Strain if desired. Taste for salt and add if needed.

To serve, cut the avocado in half and remove the pit. Using a teaspoon, scoop out pieces of avocado flesh about the size of an olive and put 6 to 8 pieces in each bowl. Pour the hot soup on top and garnish each serving with a tablespoon of crema (or crème fraîche or sour cream), a sprig of cilantro, and some croutons.

Oyster Chowder with Potatoes, Spinach, and Corn

SERVES 6 (MAKES ABOUT 10 CUPS)

1 pound medium potatoes
(about 4)

Salt

2 dozen large oysters, shucked
(¾ to 1 pound)

2 tablespoons olive oil

1 cup chopped onion

1 tablespoon chopped jalapeño
pepper

1 tablespoon chopped garlic

8 ounces baby spinach

4 cups milk

½ teaspoon freshly ground
black pepper

2 cups corn kernels (from
about 3 ears corn)

Crunchy bread, for serving

FOR THIS THICK CHOWDER, I PREFER LARGER oysters (3 or 4 to the pound). I like the chowder made with milk, which I find results in a more delicate and flavorful soup, but half-and-half can be substituted for a richer taste.

Opening oysters can be tricky, so to make it easier, I place them in a 400-degree oven until they start to open but are still basically raw. At this point, you can easily slide a paring knife inside and cut the adductor muscle to open the oysters. This can be done ahead, even the day before preparing the chowder. The potatoes can also be prepared ahead, and the corn cut off the cob, so the final recipe can be finished in 20 minutes or so.

||||||||||||||||||||||||||||||||||||||||||||||||

Preheat the oven to 400 degrees.

Put the potatoes in a saucepan, cover them with water, and add a dash of salt. Bring to a boil and boil gently for about 30 minutes, or until tender. Drain.

When the potatoes are cool enough to handle, peel them and cut into ¾-inch dice. (You should have about 3 cups.)

Meanwhile, arrange the oysters in a single layer on a large baking sheet and place in the oven for 12 minutes. They should open slightly, just enough so that a knife can be slid inside. Let cool for a few minutes, then cut through the adductor muscle to release each oyster from its shell. Put the oysters in a bowl, with their juice, and add any juice that collected on the baking sheet. Shake each oyster in the juice to get rid of any shell pieces and transfer to another bowl. Pour the juice slowly over the oysters, discarding any shell pieces

or sand at the bottom of the bowl. (You should have about 1½ cups oyster juice.) Cover and refrigerate.

At serving time, heat the oil in a large saucepan over high heat. Add the onion and jalapeño and cook for about 2 minutes. Add the garlic and spinach, stir, and cook for about 2 minutes, until the spinach wilts. Add the milk, 1½ teaspoons salt, the pepper, and potatoes, bring to a boil, and cook for about 2 minutes. Add the oysters, with their juice, and the corn, stir, and bring just to a boil, stirring occasionally.

Serve in large hot soup plates with crunchy bread.

Hanoi Chicken Soup

SERVES 6 TO 8 (MAKES ABOUT 3 QUARTS)

3 small shallots (unpeeled)

1 piece ginger, about 3 inches long, halved lengthwise

3 quarts homemade chicken stock, or canned low-sodium broth or 2 chicken bouillon cubes plus 3 quarts water

1 teaspoon salt (omit if using bouillon cubes), or to taste

3 star anise

1 whole chicken (3½ to 4 pounds)

1½ cups sliced red onions

3 cups (8 ounces) bean sprouts

½ cup (¾ ounce) dried tree ear mushrooms, reconstituted in 1½ cups warm water

2 small bundles (about 6 ounces) cellophane noodles (mung bean vermicelli)

3 cups shredded small bok choy (both green and white parts)

I ENJOY THE HANOI SOUP, OR PHO, *THAT MY wife makes at home in the conventional way, with boiled beef and noodles and some sliced raw beef added at the last moment. It is similar to a French pot-au-feu and a meal in itself.*

One day I decided to make a version with chicken. The stock, flavored with burnt shallots and ginger, as well as star anise, has a distinctive taste. First I simmer the charred shallots and ginger and anise in chicken stock (or chicken bouillon cubes in water). Then I poach a whole chicken in the stock. Once it is cooked, I pull the meat into pieces and finish the soup at the last moment with bean sprouts, shredded bok choy, tree ear mushrooms, and cellophane noodles (also called mung bean vermicelli).

The soup is served with an array of garnishes, including cilantro, red onion, chili peppers, quartered limes, scallions, and fish sauce, all of which guests can add at will to their hot soup. It is a complex dish, but most of it can be prepared ahead.

||||||||||||||||||||||||||||||||||||||||||||||||||

Impale the shallots and ginger on a metal skewer and burn over a gas flame for about 5 minutes, turning the skewer so the shallots and ginger are charred on all sides. Or run under a preheated broiler for a few minutes, until charred. Drop them into a stockpot (preferably narrow and tall, so the chicken will be immersed in the stock). Pour in the chicken stock and salt (or water and bouillon cubes) and add the star anise. Bring to a boil and boil gently, covered, for 10 minutes. Let the stock cool to lukewarm.

Add the chicken, breast side down, to the stockpot. (The chicken should be submerged in the stock; if need be, place an inverted plate or small pan lid on top to weight the chicken down.) Cover and bring to a strong boil, then reduce the heat and boil gently for 15 minutes. Shut off the heat and let the chicken, still covered, poach in the hot stock for about 1 hour.

Meanwhile, bring 3 cups water to a boil in a medium saucepan. Add the sliced onions and blanch for about 15 seconds. Using a skimmer, transfer the onions to a sieve and cool under cold running water, then drain and reserve for garnish. Add the bean sprouts to the water, bring the water back to a

GARNISHES

2 jalapeño peppers, seeded and finely diced

1½ cups fresh cilantro leaves

8 scallions, minced (¾ cup)

2 limes, quartered

Vietnamese fish sauce (*nuoc nam*)

strong boil, and cook for about 3 minutes. Drain in a sieve, cool the sprouts under cold water, and set aside in the sieve.

After the hour of poaching, remove the chicken from the stock and strain the stock. When the chicken is cool enough to handle, remove and discard the skin and bones and tear the meat into 2- to 3-inch pieces. Put the meat in a small bowl and set aside, covered with 1 cup of the hot stock to keep it warm.

Scoop off and discard some of the fat from the top of the stock. Add the reconstituted mushrooms and their liquid to the stock, bring to a boil, and boil for 10 minutes.

Meanwhile, put the noodles in a bowl, add 8 cups hot water, and set aside for 10 minutes to soften. Run hot tap water over the bean sprouts to heat them.

Add the bok choy to the boiling stock and boil for 2 minutes. Add salt if needed.

To serve, set out all the garnishes (including the red onions) on the table so your guests can add them as desired. Divide the noodles among six to eight large soup plates. Add the bean sprouts and chicken pieces and fill the bowls with the hot stock and bok choy. Serve.

Green Salad with Mustard Dressing

SERVES 4

A SALAD IS ALWAYS A PART OF OUR DINNER routine, whether as a first course or with the meal, or, for a more elaborate dinner, served after the meat course, often with cheeses. I probably make a dozen different salad dressings, but this one with mustard is one of my favorites, especially with tender Boston or Bibb lettuce.

The salad greens should be washed properly and well dried, preferably in a salad spinner, so as not to dilute the dressing. Take care that you don't bruise the leaves when washing and drying them. A green salad should be served cool but not ice cold, and it should not be tossed with the dressing more than 15 minutes ahead. When making a vinaigrette, be certain that you have the right proportion of vinegar to oil, and that both are of the best quality, and don't add too much salt. Attending to the small details is what makes a good salad.

MUSTARD DRESSING

2 teaspoons Dijon mustard

2 teaspoons red wine vinegar

1 teaspoon water

1/3 teaspoon salt

1/2 teaspoon freshly ground black pepper

2 tablespoons extra-virgin olive oil

8 to 9 cups torn Boston or Bibb lettuce, washed and spun dry

FOR THE DRESSING: Mix all the ingredients together in a salad bowl. Set aside at room temperature until ready to serve.

Just before serving, toss the salad greens thoroughly with the dressing.

Foraging

SOME OF MY EARLIEST MEMORIES ARE OF TAGGING along behind my parents and big brother across the fields surrounding Bourg-en-Bresse, my hometown, on family outings to forage for wild edibles. Our forays began in early spring, as soon as the grass started to turn green—the time of year when just-sprouted dandelion greens are at their most tender and least bitter. My father firmly believed that you had to eat dandelions at least three or four times every spring to clean your blood. For me, it was a treat to enjoy the first fresh salad of the season: the tender, whitish leaves from the plant when it is just beginning to emerge from under leaves. My mother dressed it with a vinaigrette made with garlic, croutons, a crushed anchovy, and a dash of mustard and finished it with a slightly runny boiled egg or smoked herring on top. It was a meal in itself.

As the summer wore on, my father hunted for wild mushrooms. He taught me to identify a few common easy-to-recognize and hard-to-mistake species, like meadow mushrooms, chanterelles, and cèpes. One of his favorite sources was a field where a farmer often allowed his bull to graze. This was both a good and bad thing: The bull's "pies" encouraged the growth of mushrooms, but the animal's disposition discouraged hunters from gathering them. On at least one occasion, my father was forced to flee from the charging animal, throwing his basket of mushrooms over the fence and diving after it.

Although money was tight in our family, we gathered wild food more out of tradition than of necessity. It was part of life; everybody in town did it. At dawn after a night of rain, the roadsides would be dotted with the parked cars of mushroom hunters. Even now when I go back to France, family members rise early after rains to beat the competition—and there is always a lot of it—to the dependable spots.

During one of her visits to the United States, we took my mother on a road trip to Monticello. We passed a field filled with rose mushrooms, and the sight of such plenty nearly drove her out of her mind. She wanted to stop the car immediately and start gathering them, certain that hordes of mushroom-starved Americans would soon descend. Gloria told her not to worry, that no one would take them. The mushrooms would still be there in the morning, and we wouldn't even have to get up early. She was right. Working at a leisurely pace after a good breakfast, we gathered more than thirty pounds of them.

I still love to forage. My wild plant menu includes dandelions, ramps (also called wild leeks), wild carrots, juniper berries, rose hips, rose petals, beach plums, berries, mint, wild asparagus, Concord grapes, borage, clover, nettles, acacia (locust) blossoms, violets, and tiger lily buds. Then there are the aquatic bounties of periwinkles, sand crabs, whitebait, blue crabs, mussels, clams, oysters, frogs, and escargots, as well as seaweed. But most of all, I forage for wild mushrooms. Each year I collect twenty to twenty-five pounds of about thirty different varieties: meadow mushrooms; boletus, chanterelles, morels, puff balls, and shaggy manes; and parasol, fairy ring, coral, cauliflower, hen-of-the-woods, chicken-of-the-woods, and oyster mushrooms. At least ten species of mushrooms grow on our own property. Keeping an eye out for them adds a sense of purpose to the daily walks I take with our dog, Paco.

Mushrooms are a fickle lot. You can never be certain that you will find them even during the right time of year in proven spots—especially if you are guiding someone new to mushroom hunting. On the other hand, there are days when mushrooms appear everywhere, almost like magic. When I find myself with a surplus, I clean my harvest, slice them, put them in a roasting pan, and cook them in the oven for about 40 minutes, until they are soaked in their own liquid. Then I bag and freeze the mushrooms and liquid for use in soups, sauces, and stews.

When newcomers ask me how to get started hunting mushrooms without taking the risk of harvesting poisonous varieties, I suggest they check for a mycology society or club in their area. Most places have one, and members are more than happy to introduce you to the hobby. It's best to start with one or two can't-fail varieties, then add more as you gain confidence.

I'm firmly convinced that being in tune with nature is a prerequisite for being a good cook, and a thorough understanding of the soil, the trees, the forest, the rivers, and the sea gives you the proper grounding to handle food with the respect and love it is due. Foraging is a fine way to keep your senses in tune while gathering terrific food that doesn't cost a cent.

Lyonnaise Pissenlit (Dandelion) Salad

SERVES 4

PISSENLIT, *AS THE COMMON DANDELION* (dent-de-lion) *is often called in Lyon, is a great early spring treat for our family. It's a tradition that started with my father and my two brothers. The leaves should be picked before the flowers start forming, while they are still small, white, and tender. There is no comparison between the wonderful wild dandelion greens you pick yourself and the ones found in markets.*

With a small paring knife, cut about an inch into the ground to get the dandelion plant out in one piece. Then cut away the bottom of the root and discard any damaged or darkened leaves. My recipe always includes lardons, small pieces of pancetta or pork belly; garlic-rubbed croutons; 7-minute boiled eggs, so the yolks are still runny inside; and a garlic, anchovy, and olive oil dressing. If you have smoked herring, a few slivers will make the salad even more authentic.

||||||||||||||||||||||||||||||||||||||||||||

Preheat the oven to 400 degrees.

FOR THE SALAD: Carefully lower the eggs into a saucepan of boiling water and cook them at a simmer for 7 minutes. Pour out the water and shake the pan to crack the eggshells, then fill the pan with ice water and let the eggs cool for at least 15 minutes.

Meanwhile, put the lardons in a saucepan, cover them with 2 cups water, and bring the water to a boil, then simmer for 10 minutes. Drain.

Put the lardons in a saucepan with 1 tablespoon of the olive

SALAD

4 large eggs

5 ounces pancetta, cut into lardons (strips about 1 inch long and 1/2 inch thick)

5 tablespoons extra-virgin olive oil

2 teaspoons finely chopped garlic

4 anchovy fillets, finely chopped

1 tablespoon red wine vinegar

1/2 teaspoon salt

1/2 teaspoon freshly ground black pepper

About 8 ounces (8 cups packed) young dandelion greens, washed two or three times and spun dry

(continued on page 71)

oil and cook gently for 5 minutes, or until crisp and lightly browned. Transfer the lardons, along with the rendered fat, to a salad bowl. Add the garlic, anchovies, vinegar, salt, pepper, and the remaining ¼ cup olive oil and mix well.

FOR THE CROUTONS: Spread the oil on a baking sheet. Press the croutons into the oil and then turn them over so they are oiled on the second side. Bake for 8 to 10 minutes, until nicely browned, then rub the croutons lightly with the garlic clove.

Peel the eggs under cold running water and set aside.

To serve: Add the greens to the salad bowl, along with the herring, if you have it, and toss with the dressing. Divide among four plates and top with the croutons. Cut each egg in half and place the eggs on top of the greens, so the runny yolks run into the salads.

(continued from page 69)

CROUTONS

1 tablespoon extra-virgin olive oil

A piece of baguette (about 3 ounces), cut into 16 croutons

1 large garlic clove, peeled

1 smoked herring fillet, cut into ½-inch-wide slivers (optional)

Cucumber, Onion, and Mint Salad

SERVES 4

FOR THIS WONDERFULLY REFRESHING SUM-mer salad, diced cucumber and onion are cured with salt for about 30 minutes, which draws moisture from the cucumber and makes it crunchy. I like to use mild white Vidalia or Maui onions, which give a good crunch but not a strong, sharp taste. I season the salad with sour cream and Tabasco, but it can also be dressed with oil and vinegar.

||||||||||||||||||||||||||||||||||||||||||||||||||||||

Peel the cucumber and cut it lengthwise in half. Using the tip of a teaspoon, scrape out the seeds. Cut the flesh into ½-inch dice. (You should have about 2½ cups.)

Combine the cucumber and diced onion in a bowl, sprinkle with the salt, and mix well. Let cure for 30 minutes.

Drain the cucumber mixture in a colander and pat dry with paper towels. Combine with the rest of the ingredients and serve.

1 large English (seedless) cucumber (about 1 pound)

1 cup diced (½-inch) mild onion

1½ teaspoons salt

2 tablespoons shredded fresh mint leaves

½ cup sour cream

½ teaspoon Tabasco sauce

Escarole with Tapenade Dressing

SERVES 4

12 oil-cured black olives,
   pitted

4 anchovy fillets

1 tablespoon drained capers

¼ teaspoon salt

½ teaspoon freshly ground
   black pepper

1½ tablespoons water

3 tablespoons extra-virgin
   olive oil

6 cups 2-inch pieces escarole,
   washed and spun dry

TAPENADE IS TRADITIONALLY A PASTE MADE of black olives, capers, anchovy fillets, and olive oil. In this recipe, I thin the tapenade with a little water and use it as a dressing on escarole; it's also good with curly endive (frisée).

Coarsely chop the olives, anchovies, and capers. Transfer to a small bowl, add the salt, pepper, water, and oil, and mix well.

At serving time, combine the escarole with the dressing and toss well. Serve.

Kohlrabi Salad

SERVES 4

A FARM CLOSE TO MY HOUSE GROWS KOHLRABI in early summer. Although it was relatively common when I was a child, this vegetable from the cabbage family, with a nutty, delicate taste similar to white turnips, is not very well known nowadays. I tend to like the green variety, which I find milder than the purple, but the taste of both is similar. Kohlrabi is excellent boiled, braised, or sautéed like potatoes. Here I serve it raw in a salad. Since the bottom is a bit tougher than the top, it should be more deeply peeled.

||||||||||||||||||||||||||||||||||||||||||||||||||

Peel the kohlrabi, making sure it is trimmed well on the root end so only the tender flesh remains. Using the slicing disk of a food processor or a mandoline, cut it into thin (about ⅛-inch) slices. Pile the slices together a few at a time and cut into ½-inch-wide strips. Keep in cold water to cover until ready to use.

At serving time, mix all the dressing ingredients together.

Drain the kohlrabi and dry the strips with paper towels. Mix with the dressing and serve on its own or on the lettuce leaves.

1 large green kohlrabi (about 1¼ pounds)

DRESSING

½ teaspoon salt

½ teaspoon freshly ground black pepper

1 tablespoon fresh lemon juice

3 tablespoons extra-virgin olive oil

2 tablespoons minced fresh chives

4 large lettuce leaves (optional)

Tomato and Potato Salad with Mustard Dressing

SERVES 4

1 potato (about 8 ounces)

Salt

1 pound tomatoes (2 to 3)

DRESSING

1 tablespoon Dijon mustard

1 tablespoon red wine vinegar

1 tablespoon water

½ teaspoon salt

½ teaspoon freshly ground
  black pepper

⅓ cup extra-virgin olive oil

¼ cup thinly sliced shallots

¼ cup sliced scallions

2 cups baby arugula

WHEN I MAKE TOMATO SALAD, I USUALLY PEEL and seed the tomatoes so the salad is more delicate and closer to my wife's tastes. I like this served at room temperature or cool, but not cold. All the ingredients except the arugula can be tossed together ahead and allowed to marinate for an hour or two. The assertive mustard dressing complements the creaminess of the potatoes and gives the proper acidity to the tomatoes—an excellent combination. I serve the salad on baby arugula, but you can use any other greens.

||||||||||||||||||||||||||||||||||||||||||||||||

Put the potato in a saucepan, add a dash of salt, and cover it with water. Bring the water to a boil and boil the potato gently for about 35 minutes, until tender.

Drain the potato and cool to lukewarm. Peel, then cut into ¾-inch dice.

Meanwhile, using a sharp or serrated vegetable peeler or a sharp knife, peel the tomatoes. Alternatively, drop them into a pot of boiling water for 20 to 30 seconds, then drain and peel. Cut the tomatoes in half and press out the seeds and juice (the skin and juice can be reserved for stock). Cut the tomatoes into ¾-inch dice (you will have about 3 cups).

FOR THE DRESSING: Mix all the ingredients together. Toss gently with the diced potatoes in a bowl. Add the diced tomatoes and mix gently.

At serving time, divide the arugula among four plates and spoon the salad on top. Serve.

Red Cabbage, Pistachio, and Cranberry Salad with Blue Cheese

SERVES 4

1½ pounds red cabbage (1 small to medium head), wilted leaves and big ribs removed and discarded (about 1 pound trimmed)

½ cup pistachio nuts

½ cup dried cranberries

1½ teaspoons salt

1 teaspoon Tabasco sauce

1 tablespoon cider vinegar

2 tablespoons peanut oil

1 tablespoon walnut oil

6 tablespoons crumbled blue cheese, such as Stilton or Roquefort

3 tablespoons chopped fresh chives

THE CRUNCHINESS OF THE CABBAGE AND NUTS in this substantial salad goes well with the chewiness of the sweet dried cranberries. A topping of crumbled blue cheese—I use Stilton or Roquefort—adds depth.

||||||||||||||||||||||||||||||||||||||||||||||

Shred the cabbage on a mandoline or cut it into thin strips with a sharp knife. Transfer to a bowl and add the pistachios, cranberries, salt, Tabasco, vinegar, and both oils. Mix well and let marinate for about 1 hour.

Divide the salad among four plates. Sprinkle with the blue cheese and chives and serve.

TOP: *Black Lentil Salad with Eggs, page 81;* BOTTOM: *Tabbouleh, page 82*

Black Lentil Salad with Eggs

SERVES 4

THERE ARE MANY TYPES OF LENTILS, INCLUD-ing red, yellow, Indian lentils, and French green lentils (du Puy). Here I use small black lentils called beluga lentils, which I can find cooked and vacuum-packed at my market. With soft-cooked eggs, the salad makes a wonderful first course. To serve it as an accompaniment to meat or fish, omit the eggs.

||||||||||||||||||||||||||||||||||||||||||||||||

FOR THE SALAD: Mix all the ingredients together in a bowl. Set aside.

FOR THE EGGS: Lower the eggs into a saucepan of boiling water to cover, then reduce the heat to low and simmer for 6 minutes. Drain off the water, add cold water and ice to the pan, and let the eggs cool for at least 15 minutes.

Shell the eggs (most easily done under cold running water).

At serving time, return the eggs to hot water for 1 minute to heat them to lukewarm. Divide the lentils among four plates and top each serving with an egg and a dash of coarse salt.

LENTIL SALAD

One 8-ounce package cooked beluga lentils or 2 cups other cooked lentils

½ cup chopped celery

⅓ cup chopped mild onion

¼ cup minced scallions

1 teaspoon finely chopped garlic

3 tablespoons extra-virgin olive oil

2 teaspoons Dijon mustard

2 teaspoons balsamic vinegar

½ teaspoon salt

½ teaspoon freshly ground black pepper

4 large eggs

Coarse salt

Tabbouleh

SERVES 4

1 cup coarse or medium-coarse bulgur

2 cups boiling water

1 teaspoon salt

2 teaspoons chopped jalapeño pepper

3 tablespoons fresh lime juice

¼ cup extra-virgin olive oil

½ cup diced (¼-inch) seeded (unpeeled) cucumber

½ cup diced (½-inch) tomato

½ cup thinly sliced scallions

½ cup julienned radishes

½ cup grated carrot

¼ cup coarsely chopped fresh mint

¼ cup coarsely chopped fresh cilantro

TABBOULEH IS MADE WITH BULGUR, WHICH IS presteamed cracked wheat. It can be found in health food stores and some supermarkets in coarse or medium-coarse forms. Either type is good here, but make certain you do not buy cracked wheat, which is uncooked. Many raw vegetables can be added to tabbouleh, and crumbled cheese, usually feta, is also good in it. The salad is always seasoned with mint, lemon or lime juice, and olive oil. (See photo, page 80.)

||||||||||||||||||||||||||||||||||||||||||||||||||

Put the bulgur in a saucepan or bowl and pour the boiling water over it. Set aside, covered, for 40 minutes.

Drain the bulgur in a sieve set over a bowl. To extract more moisture from the bulgur and make a fluffier, drier tabbouleh, press on the bulgur in the sieve with the back of a spoon, then transfer to a bowl to cool.

When the bulgur is cool, add the rest of the ingredients and stir well to combine. Serve cool or at room temperature.

Avocado, Tomato, and Crab Salad

SERVES 4

FOR THIS DISH, ALTERNATING SLICES OF AVO-cado and tomato are stacked on each plate, with crab salad spooned into the centers of the avocado slices. The salad is finished with black olives, coarse salt, and olive oil.

||||||||||||||||||||||||||||||||||||||||||||||

FOR THE CRABMEAT SALAD: Combine all the ingredients in a bowl.

Cut each avocado lengthwise in half, then twist and pull the halves apart and remove the pit. Peel off the skin, lay each half cut side down, and cut each half horizontally into 4 slices. Cut each tomato into 8 slices.

Place the largest slice from one of the avocado halves in the center of a plate and pack some crabmeat salad into the hollow in the center. Cover with a slice of tomato and add a dash of fleur de sel. Place another slice of avocado on top and fill the center with more crab salad. Continue alternating the tomato, avocado, and crab salad until the avocado half is reconstructed, finishing with the small rounded slice on top. Repeat the procedure on three more plates.

Scatter the olives around the salads, sprinkle with fleur de sel, and drizzle with the olive oil. Chill the salads slightly and serve cool but not cold.

CRABMEAT SALAD

¾ cup (12 ounces) crabmeat, picked over for shells and cartilage

2 tablespoons mayonnaise

1 tablespoon ketchup

2 tablespoons grated fresh or bottled horseradish

½ teaspoon Tabasco sauce

¼ teaspoon salt, preferably fleur de sel

2 ripe avocadoes

2 plum tomatoes (about the same diameter as the avocados)

Fleur de sel

16 oil-cured black olives, halved and pitted

About 2 tablespoons extra-virgin olive oil

Eggs, Cheese, and Bread

Omelet School

CHEFS CAN, AND OFTEN DO, ARGUE ALL DAY ABOUT HOW to turn out the perfect omelet. Allow me to settle the score: There is no single perfect omelet. Rather, there are three distinct ways the French prepare omelets. One method results in a smooth, pale yellow omelet that has no brown areas and is still quite wet. Another is a heartier dish in which large curds of egg are allowed to brown in butter. Finally, there is a Gallic take on Italy's frittata and Spain's tortilla, called an *omelette paysanne*, or peasant's omelet.

All three dishes begin with the same steps: Break eggs into a bowl, add salt and pepper, and whisk together with a fork. From this point on, though, the techniques diverge.

To make a classical French omelet of the type that might be served by a professional chef at a high-end restaurant, melt some butter in a skillet over high heat. Add the egg mixture and begin stirring with a fork, in much the same manner as you would when scrambling eggs. The idea is to move the eggs as soon as they begin to coagulate—this will give you the smallest-possible curd and a creamy texture. Shake the pan and then incline it so the eggs slide to one side. Using your fork, fold the edge of the omelet nearest you toward the center of the omelet. Bang on the handle of the pan so the first edge on the high side rises up above the rim of the pan, then fold it over so it meets the first edge in the center of the pan. Leave the omelet on the heat for 10 to 15 seconds, until it sets on top, then turn it out onto a plate. Cooking it too long will toughen it and cause it to brown.

But my mother, who cooked in her restaurants in France for more than half a century and prepared thousands of omelets, never made one like that in her life. She would pour the eggs into the hot butter and, with the tip of her fork, occasionally draw the sections that had coagulated around the edges back toward the center, allow them to settle while some of the liquid remaining on top flowed into the vacant spaces, and then repeat the process a few times until the whole thing had set into fairly large curds. At that point, she would lift one edge, tuck a couple of pats of butter underneath, and cook the omelet until it was nicely browned, then unmold it. It is the same as a standard omelet in an American diner.

To make an *omelette paysanne*, you slice some potatoes, onions, and perhaps mushrooms or pancetta and cook them in butter in a skillet, then pour the egg mixture on top, mix the pan's contents, and cook until the whole thing is solid. (You can put the pan under a broiler to finish the top if need be.) Slide the omelet onto a large plate. It will resemble a giant pancake. I usually drizzle a bit of olive oil on top and cut it into wedges to serve.

Is one style of omelet better than the other? Not really. Sometimes I'm in the mood for a hearty large-curd omelet. Sometimes my taste buds cry out for something more subtle. And when I want to get a substantial breakfast on the table for guests, I opt for an *omelette paysanne*. All three versions are delicious, unfussy, and ready in minutes. My type of food.

Herbed Omelet with Shrimp

SERVES 4

I LOVE EGGS ANY WAY THEY ARE PREPARED. I love shrimp as well, and this recipe combines them, plus asparagus and mushrooms. Perfect for lunch or brunch, the omelet also makes a nice first course for dinner or a light supper on its own.

||||||||||||||||||||||||||||||||||||||||||||||||

FOR THE GARNISH: Heat the oil in an 8- to 10-inch nonstick skillet. Add the mushrooms, asparagus, and shallots and sauté over high heat for 1½ minutes. Add the salt, pepper, and shrimp and cook, tossing occasionally, for 1½ to 2 minutes. Transfer to a bowl.

FOR THE OMELET: Melt the butter in the same skillet over high heat. Beat the eggs with the salt and pepper, mix in the herbs, and add to the foaming butter. Cook, stirring and mixing, over high heat for about 2 minutes, until most of the mixture is set but still moist.

Roll up the omelet and invert it onto a platter. Sprinkle the garnish on top and serve.

GARNISH

2 tablespoons canola oil

1 cup diced (1-inch) mushrooms

1 cup sliced (1-inch) asparagus

½ cup sliced shallots

¼ teaspoon salt

¼ teaspoon freshly ground black pepper

8 ounces shrimp, shelled and cut into 1-inch pieces

OMELET

2 tablespoons unsalted butter

8 large eggs, preferably organic

½ teaspoon salt

½ teaspoon freshly ground black pepper

3 tablespoons chopped assorted fresh herbs (such as chives, parsley, tarragon, and/or chervil)

Spanish Tortilla

SERVES 4

MANY BARS IN SPAIN HAVE A COLD POTATO tortilla, *or omelet, on their tapas menu; these have nothing in common with Mexican tortillas. I love them and often make my own version containing chorizo, scallions, mushrooms, and herbs. It is great as a first course for dinner or as a main course for lunch or a light dinner.*

|||||||||||||||||||||||||||||||||||||||||||||||

Heat the olive oil in a 9- to 10-inch nonstick skillet. Add the potatoes and chorizo and cook, covered, over medium-high heat for 2 to 3 minutes, until the potatoes start browning and becoming tender. Add the mushrooms, scallions, and garlic and sauté over high heat, uncovered, for about 2 minutes. Set aside in the skillet.

Preheat the broiler. Beat together the eggs, salt, pepper, and chives in a bowl. Add the eggs to the potatoes and cook over high heat, stirring with a fork, until the eggs are mostly set, about 1 minute. (It is okay if some of the egg mixture is still wet.) Sprinkle the cheese over the tortilla and place the skillet under the hot broiler for about 2 minutes to set the top.

Slide the tortilla onto a plate (pour a little oil around it to release it if it sticks to the pan). Cut into wedges and serve.

3 tablespoons olive oil, plus a little additional if needed

2 potatoes (about 12 ounces), peeled and thinly sliced

1 small Spanish chorizo sausage (about 2 ounces), skinned and thinly sliced (about ½ cup)

1 cup sliced mushrooms

1 cup sliced scallions

1 tablespoon chopped garlic

8 large eggs, preferably organic

¾ teaspoon salt

¾ teaspoon freshly ground black pepper

2 tablespoons chopped fresh chives

2 tablespoons grated Parmesan cheese

Morel and Shrimp Eggs en Cocotte

SERVES 4

½ cup (½ ounce) dried morel mushrooms (about 12 small)

3 tablespoons chopped shallots

1½ cups diced (½-inch) white mushrooms (about 4 ounces)

¾ cup heavy cream

¾ cup diced (½-inch) shrimp (about 4 large shrimp)

½ teaspoon salt

½ teaspoon freshly ground black pepper

1 teaspoon potato starch, dissolved in 2 tablespoons dry Madeira (Sercial)

4 jumbo eggs, preferably organic

2 teaspoons chopped fresh chives

4 slices toast

FOR THIS CLASSIC RECIPE, MORELS AND WHITE mushrooms (although any mushrooms will work) and shrimp are combined in a cream sauce flavored with sherry, poured over eggs in small soufflé molds or bowls, and cooked in a double boiler. The dish makes a very elegant starter for a fancy dinner. The sauce can be made ahead and the eggs cooked just before serving.

||||||||||||||||||||||||||||||||||||||||||||||||||

Drop the morels into a bowl and pour 1 cup lukewarm water over them. Let soak for 1 hour.

Lift the morels out of the soaking liquid and cut them in half. (You will have about ¾ cup.)

Put the shallots, reconstituted morels, and white mushrooms in a medium saucepan and add ½ cup of the mushroom soaking water (discard the sandy residue in the bottom of the bowl). Bring to a boil and boil until most of the liquid has evaporated, 6 to 8 minutes. Add the cream, diced shrimp, salt, and pepper and bring back to a boil. Add the potato starch–Madeira mixture, mix well, and bring to a boil. Remove from the heat. *(This can be done up to an hour ahead.)*

At serving time, divide the mushroom mixture among four ½-cup soufflé molds or small heatproof bowls. Crack 1 egg into each mold. Arrange the molds, leaving some space between them, in a large saucepan deep enough that there will be at least 1 inch above them when the pan is covered with the lid, so the eggs can steam. Surround the molds with about

1 inch of water. Cover the pan and bring the water to a boil, then reduce the heat and boil gently for 5 to 6 minutes, until the egg whites are set but the yolks are still soft and runny.

Place a cocotte on each of four plates. Sprinkle the chives on top and serve immediately, with the toast. Eat with a teaspoon.

Egg and Swiss Chard Gratin

SERVES 4

8 large eggs, preferably organic

1 small bunch red or white Swiss chard (about 12 ounces)

1 teaspoon salt

1 teaspoon freshly ground black pepper

1 tablespoon peanut oil

1½ cups sliced mushrooms

1½ tablespoons unsalted butter

1½ tablespoons all-purpose flour

1½ cups milk

1 cup grated Swiss cheese, preferably Gruyère or Emmenthaler

A GRATIN OF EGGS WAS A FAVORITE AT OUR house when I was a kid. Sometimes plain, sometimes with leftover meat or poultry, it made a great first or main course. This version with Swiss chard is close to the one my mother usually served.

|||||||||||||||||||||||||||||||||||||||||||||||||||||

Bring 3 cups water to a boil in a large saucepan. Add the eggs and bring the water back to a boil, then reduce the heat and cook the eggs at a very gentle boil for 10 minutes.

Pour out the hot water and shake the pan to crack the eggshells. Fill the pan with cold water and ice and let the eggs cool thoroughly in the water.

Preheat the oven to 400 degrees.

Wash the Swiss chard and cut the ribs and leaves into 2-inch pieces. Pile them, still wet, into a skillet, cover, and cook over high heat for about 6 minutes, just until the chard wilts. Uncover and cook over high heat for 1½ to 2 minutes to evaporate most of the moisture. Add ¼ teaspoon each of the salt and pepper and mix well.

Spread the chard in the bottom of a 5- to 6-cup gratin dish (set the skillet aside). Peel and slice the cooled eggs and arrange them on top of the chard.

Heat the oil in the skillet you used to cook the chard. Add the mushrooms and ¼ teaspoon each of the salt and pepper and cook for about 2 minutes, until most of the moisture has evaporated. Spread the mushrooms on top of the eggs.

Melt the butter in a medium saucepan. Add the flour, mix

with a whisk, and cook for 30 seconds. Add the milk and the remaining ½ teaspoon each salt and pepper and bring to a strong boil, stirring occasionally until the mixture thickens. Boil for 10 seconds, then pour over the eggs and mushrooms and spread evenly over them. Top with the grated cheese.

Place the dish on a baking sheet and bake for 30 minutes, or until the gratin is beautifully browned on top. (If needed, run under a hot broiler for a minute or so to brown it.) Serve hot.

Good Eggs

IF I HAD TO CHOOSE ONE INGREDIENT THAT I COULD not do without, it would probably be eggs. Gloria and I eat a lot of them—scrambled, hard-cooked, *en cocotte* (in ramekins), in omelets, you name it. Lunch or dinner might begin with a poached egg on top of a simple salad. I also have a weakness for soufflés and eggy gratins.

Like many French people of my generation, I am unapologetically frugal (some would say miserly) when it comes to parting with money at the grocery store. If the organic greens in the produce section cost two or three times as much as the conventional lettuces stacked nearby, I'll probably put my organic preferences aside. I may not line up for $15-a-pound biodynamic pork chops, though I will buy delicious, inexpensive offal and cuts that are often shunned by the home cook. But when it comes to eggs, I splurge. And so should you.

Seeking out high-quality eggs is worth every extra penny. I am lucky in this regard: A Jamaican woman who lives right down the road from us maintains a mixed flock of a few dozen laying hens. Hers are not industrial birds, bred for maximum output and life in cramped cages on a factory farm. They are the same breeds you'd find scratching around any northeastern barnyard a century ago: Rhode Island Reds, Barred Rocks, White Giants. And they spend their days much as their ancestors did, pecking for seeds and insects in the open air, flapping their wings, basking in the sun. In addition to commercial poultry feed, there

is a bag of cracked corn and a bucket of bread and vegetable scraps in the corner of the barn. So I know what these chickens are eating, and I know that they live happy lives. I am convinced that that makes a huge difference in my kitchen.

You don't have to have a friendly hen-keeping neighbor to enjoy great eggs. These days, every farmers' market has at least one stall selling eggs from pastured hens. (I'm always leery about claims such as "cage-free" and "free-range" on cartons of supermarket eggs. Such descriptions are often misleading.) Sure, these eggs will cost more. Regular grocery store eggs sell for about $2 a dozen. I pay my neighbor $4, and that is money well spent.

The difference is easy to see: Crack a supermarket egg onto a plate, and you will be greeted with a flat, pale yellow yolk. The clear albumen (white) will flow outward in a thin, runny puddle. Perform the same test with a "real" egg, and a deep yellow or fiery-orange yolk will all but stand up and salute you. You will also be able to clearly distinguish two types of egg white. One is thick, viscous, and clinging in an elevated circle close to the yolk. It is clearly different from the thinner albumen that spreads out toward the edges of the egg. These whites mean my neighbor's eggs deliver far more volume than factory-farmed eggs and have a beautiful texture. When I make a soufflé, pastry cream, custard, or other such mixture that needs to thicken, I've found that I can achieve the same results using fewer fresh country eggs, which contain more lecithin, a thickening agent, than store-bought. And then there's the taste. My neighbor's eggs have a rich, rounded flavor that varies subtly as what the chickens forage for changes with the seasons. In comparison, store-bought eggs are bland and tasteless.

I first visited Chez Panisse, Alice Waters' famous Berkeley restaurant, with James Beard in 1976. He'd spoken highly of the young restaurateur, but I withheld judgment until the arrival of our first course, a salad of mixed greens bordered by halved hard-cooked eggs. The eggs were perfectly cooked, their yolks still slightly creamy, with no trace of the green border that is a sure sign of a improperly prepared egg. Someone had gone to the trouble of securing good eggs and cooked them conscientiously. I knew then that I was in for a great meal.

Eggs in Pepper Boats

SERVES 4

2 cubanelle, poblano, or
banana peppers (about
4 ounces each)

1 tablespoon olive oil

4 tablespoons water

½ teaspoon salt

6 tablespoons grated cheddar
cheese

4 extra-large eggs, preferably
organic

¼ teaspoon freshly ground
black pepper

About 2 tablespoons fresh
cilantro leaves

ONE DAY I DECIDED TO COOK EGGS IN SWEET peppers with a bit of cheese and cilantro. It made a great lunch dish. I used the long, pale green peppers sometimes called banana peppers. Poblano and cubanelle peppers also work, especially if you want to add a little heat.

|||||||||||||||||||||||||||||||||||||||||||||||||||

Split the peppers lengthwise in half and remove the seeds and the stems if you want. Arrange them cut side down in a large skillet and add the oil, water, and ¼ teaspoon of the salt and cook, covered, over medium heat, turning occasionally, for about 4 minutes, or until the peppers are softened somewhat but still firm.

Remove the skillet from the heat and, if necessary, turn the peppers over so they are hollow side up. Place the cheese in the peppers. Break an egg into each one and sprinkle the eggs with the remaining ¼ teaspoon salt and the pepper.

Return the skillet to the stove, cover, and cook over medium heat for 3 to 4 minutes, until the egg whites are set but the yolks are still runny. Transfer to plates, sprinkle with the cilantro, and serve immediately.

Fondue with Pesto

SERVES 4

8 ounces Gruyère, Emmenthaler, or Beaufort cheese, grated

⅓ cup dry white wine

¼ teaspoon salt

½ teaspoon freshly ground black pepper

¼ cup pesto, homemade (page 103) or store-bought

Toasted bread strips (from a baguette), for serving

ONE OF THE DISHES MY DAUGHTER, CLAUDINE, has eaten since she was an infant, and still loves, is cheese fondue. I don't make mine like the Swiss, who thicken their fondues with arrowroot. Instead, I make it as my mother and aunts did in the Lyonnaise area of France, using Gruyère or Emmenthaler cheese, white wine, and garlic. When I decided to make this fondue as an hors d'oeuvre, I added some basil pesto I had on hand and served the dish with toasted bread strips for dipping.

The fondue can be prepared in a couple of minutes, and, while it is somewhat messy to eat, it is delicious. (A pair of scissors comes in handy to cut off hanging cheese strings.) Any good melting cheese will work well here.

||||||||||||||||||||||||||||||||||||||||||

Combine the cheese, wine, salt, and pepper in an attractive heatproof serving bowl and heat in a microwave oven on high for 1 minute. Stir the mixture and, if need be, microwave for another 20 or 30 seconds to melt the cheese completely. Stir again until well mixed.

Spoon the pesto on top of the fondue and serve with toast strips. Dip the toasts in the hot cheese mixture, cutting off hanging strings with scissors, if desired, and enjoy. Remelt the fondue if the mixture becomes too thick for dipping.

Baguette with Pesto

SERVES 4

IT IS ALWAYS NICE TO HAVE VARIETY IN THE bread basket. Since baguettes get a bit stale after a day or so, I extend their life by spreading toasted chunks of the bread with my own pesto or pesto I buy at the supermarket.

||||||||||||||||||||||||||||||||||||||||||||||

Preheat the oven to 400 degrees.

Cut the baguette crosswise in half and then cut each piece lengthwise in half so you have 4 long strips of baguette. Cut each one into 3 pieces, for a total of 12 pieces.

Line a baking sheet with aluminum foil and pour the olive oil on top. Dip all sides of the bread pieces in the oil, then spread them out and bake for about 15 minutes, until nicely browned.

Spread the pesto on the bread, arrange in a bread basket, and serve.

||||||||||||||||||||||||||||||||||||||||||||||

HOMEMADE PESTO MAKES ABOUT 1 CUP

||||||||||||||||||||||||||||||||||||||||||||||

Place all the ingredients in a blender and process, pushing the basil down a few times if necessary, until you have a light green puree. Cover and refrigerate until ready to use. It will keep, covered, for 1 week.

Half a baguette (6 to 7 ounces), about 10 inches long

2 tablespoons extra-virgin olive oil

2 tablespoons pesto, homemade (recipe follows) or store-bought

PESTO

2 cups lightly packed fresh basil leaves, washed and still wet

1 tablespoon grated Parmesan cheese

2 tablespoons whole hazelnuts

3 garlic cloves, crushed

¼ teaspoon salt

⅓ cup extra-virgin olive oil

Ricotta Quenelles

SERVES 4 AS AN APPETIZER

A QUENELLE IS A FOOTBALL-SHAPED DUMP-ling. These light and delicate quenelles take only a few seconds to prepare in a food processor (or in a bowl by hand), and they can be made a couple of days ahead of serving. Be sure to use good whole-milk ricotta cheese. The quenelles can be sautéed, as they are here, or baked in a cream sauce. They are a great accompaniment for grilled meat, poultry, or fish.

||||||||||||||||||||||||||||||||||||||||||||||||||

FOR THE QUENELLES: Combine all the ingredients in a food processor and process for 10 seconds, or mix in a bowl with a whisk.

Bring about 1½ inches of water to about 190 degrees (just under a boil) in a large saucepan. Using two large spoons or a ¼-cup metal measuring cup, scoop up and form 8 oval-shaped quenelles (about 3 tablespoons each), dropping them into the simmering water as you go. Poach for about 10 minutes, rolling the quenelles over in the water halfway through the cooking so they cook on both sides. Remove with a slotted spoon and drop into a bowl of ice water. When the quenelles are cold, drain and refrigerate until ready to serve.

At serving time, heat the butter and oil in a large nonstick skillet. Add the quenelles and sauté, covered, over medium heat for 3½ to 4 minutes. Turn them over, sprinkle with the cheese, cover, and cook for about 4 minutes longer. Sprinkle with the chives, if using, and serve.

QUENELLES

1 cup whole-milk ricotta cheese

½ cup all-purpose flour

1 large egg

½ teaspoon salt

½ teaspoon freshly ground black pepper

2 tablespoons grated Parmesan cheese

2 tablespoons shredded fresh basil leaves

3 tablespoons unsalted butter

1 tablespoon olive oil

1½ tablespoons grated Parmesan cheese

Minced fresh chives (optional)

Mushroom and Gruyère Pizza

SERVES 2 FOR LUNCH, 2 TO 4 AS AN HORS D'OEUVRE

2 tablespoons peanut oil

2 flour tortillas (8 inches across)

1 cup diced (½-inch) Gruyère cheese (about 5 ounces)

3 cups sliced (1-inch pieces) portobello mushrooms (about 6 ounces)

2 scallions, cut into 1-inch pieces

¼ teaspoon salt

¼ teaspoon freshly ground black pepper

I ALWAYS HAVE FLOUR TORTILLAS IN MY RE-frigerator, and I often make pizzas with them to serve with lunch or for drinks. This pizza, topped with a puree of mushrooms and Gruyère, is unusual and tasty.

Preheat the oven to 425 degrees.

Rub 1 teaspoon of the oil on each tortilla and arrange them oiled side down on a baking sheet lined with aluminum foil.

Combine the cheese, mushrooms, scallions, salt, and pepper in a food processor and process until you have a coarse puree. Spread the puree on the tortillas, covering the entire surface of each one. Sprinkle the remaining 4 teaspoons oil on top.

Bake the pizzas for 12 to 14 minutes, until hot, bubbling, and browned underneath. Cut into quarters and serve.

Roasted Garlic

SERVES 4

WHOLE HEADS OF ROASTED GARLIC ARE A WON-derful accompaniment to fresh white cheese, or squeeze out the soft garlic and spread it on bread. In this recipe, the garlic heads are split almost completely through horizontally, leaving them with a "hinge," so they can be presented open or closed. They are baked en papillote, wrapped in aluminum foil, so they stay moist.

4 large garlic heads (2½ to 3 ounces each)

½ teaspoon salt

½ teaspoon freshly ground black pepper

2½ tablespoons olive oil

||||||||||||||||||||||||||||||||||||||||||||||||

Preheat the oven to 450 degrees.

Using a sharp knife, cut through each garlic head horizontally one third of the way down until almost sliced in half, leaving a "hinge" on one side.

Tear off a 12-inch square of aluminum foil and put the garlic heads side by side in the center of the foil. Open each head and sprinkle the cut sides of the garlic with the salt, pepper, and oil. Press the halves back together to re-form the heads. Bring the edges of the foil together and pinch them together to enclose the garlic in a packet.

Place the foil package on a baking sheet and bake for 45 minutes. Let the package rest for a few minutes before unwrapping the garlic; it should be soft and lightly browned. Serve at room temperature.

Fast Fougasse

MAKES 1 OVAL LOAF

1 pound prepared pizza dough

2 tablespoons cornmeal or polenta

2 tablespoons extra-virgin olive oil

1 teaspoon fleur de sel or other coarse salt

½ teaspoon herbes de Provence or Italian seasoning

FOUGASSE IS A FLATBREAD FROM THE SOUTH of France. Slits cut into the shaped dough create openings as it bakes and make the bread very crusty. Olive oil and herbes de Provence are usually part of the recipe. I make this fougasse with pizza dough that I buy in my supermarket, so it takes only a few minutes to prepare, and the result is great!

Place the dough on a 12-by-18-inch baking sheet lined with aluminum foil and spread it into an oval about 8 by 14 inches. Sprinkle the cornmeal or polenta on top. Cut four parallel slits through the dough with a blunt knife (so you don't damage the pan), spaced about 1 inch from the edges. Lift and separate the dough so that the slits are opened up and the oval is expanded to about 9 by 16 inches. Brush the oil (which will help to brown the dough) over the dough and into the openings and sprinkle with the salt and herbes de Provence or Italian seasoning.

Cover the dough with a large baking pan and let rise in a warm place for about 30 minutes.

Preheat the oven to 450 degrees.

Bake the loaf for 20 to 25 minutes, until it is dark brown, dry, and crusty. Cool on a rack for a few minutes, then break into pieces and serve.

Country Bread

MAKES 1 LARGE LOAF

3 cups plus 1 tablespoon
unbleached bread flour,
preferably organic

1 cup unbleached whole wheat
flour, preferably organic

1 envelope (2¼ teaspoons)
active dry yeast

2 teaspoons salt

2 cups tepid water
(100 degrees)

*THIS IS THE ALL-PURPOSE BREAD THAT WE MAKE
often at our house. When it has cooled, I slice it, freeze it, well
wrapped, and use the slices as needed right out of the freezer.*

Place 3 cups of the bread flour, the whole wheat flour, yeast, and salt in a food processor. Turn the processor on and, with the motor running, add the water. Process for 15 to 20 seconds. The dough will be soft. Transfer it to a large bowl, cover, and let rise at room temperature for about 3 hours until doubled in size.

Push the dough down, bringing the edges toward the center to create a compact ball. Place seam side down on a baking sheet lined with aluminum foil. Press into a roundish shape 7 to 8 inches in diameter. Cover with a large bowl and let rise again for a couple of hours, until almost doubled in size.

Preheat the oven to 425 degrees.

When the bread has risen, sprinkle the remaining 1 table-spoon bread flour on top of the loaf and, using a serrated knife, cut a few parallel slashes about ¼ inch deep in the surface of the bread. Place in the oven and mist with water from a spray bottle. After 5 minutes, spray the loaf again with water. Bake for about 50 minutes total, until deeply browned and puffy. Cool on a rack before serving.

Pain Farci (Stuffed Bread)

SERVES 4

THE DELICATESSEN AT MY SUPERMARKET FEA-
*tures at least five types of olives, miniature mozzarella balls,
sun-dried tomatoes in oil, marinated mushrooms, pimientos,
roasted garlic, and more. For this recipe, I fill a plastic container with an assortment of these tidbits directly from the
salad bar to create a salad that I use to fill hollowed-out hard
rolls. They make a great lunch.*

‖‖

Slice off the tops of the rolls and reserve. Pull out the soft
insides, which can be used for bread crumbs.

Mix all the remaining ingredients together in a bowl. Spoon
into the roll shells. Serve with the roll tops on the side or use
them as caps.

4 hard rolls (ciabatta type,
   2 ounces each), about
   3½ inches across and
   3 inches high

8 small marinated mushrooms

8 small mozzarella balls

8 sun-dried tomatoes in oil

8 kalamata olives, pitted

8 oil-cured black olives, pitted

8 green olives, pitted

1 small pimiento, cut into
   ½-inch pieces (about
   ⅓ cup)

⅓ cup shredded or whole
   fresh basil leaves

3 tablespoons extra-virgin
   olive oil

½ teaspoon freshly ground
   black pepper

Fresh Butter

MAKES 8 OUNCES

2 cups heavy cream

¼ teaspoon fleur de sel
(optional)

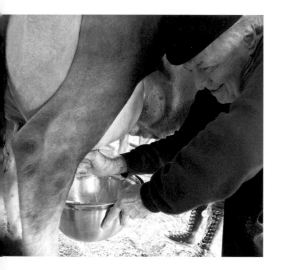

I REMEMBER MAKING BUTTER AS A CHILD ON the farms where I used to spend my summers. The farms used a wooden baratte, or churn, with a paddle inside and a handle on the outside to turn the paddle and churn the cream into butter. It was my job to turn the handle, and it always seemed to take forever for that cream to turn into butter.

When we have leftover cream at home from a party or special dinner, my wife, Gloria, has gotten into the habit of making butter with it before it spoils. She "churns" it in the food processor, and it only takes a few minutes. (Sometimes the process takes longer than other times—3 to 4 minutes. (If it seems to be taking too long, let the processor cool down for a few minutes before continuing.) One quart of heavy cream yields about 1 pound butter and 2 cups of delicious real buttermilk. Once the butter is made, she presses it between paper towels to absorb excess liquid. She sometimes salts it, but most of the time she leaves it unsalted. We use it or freeze it in 4-ounce portions.

Pour the cream into the food processor and process until the cream breaks down and separates into butter and liquid (buttermilk). At first the cream will become like whipped cream; keep processing, and it will break down and turn into butter. Pour the contents of the processor bowl into a sieve set over a bowl to separate the solids and liquid. You will have about 1 cup buttermilk. Transfer the butter to a paper towel and knead in the salt if you prefer salted butter.

Put more paper towels on top of the butter and blot out additional liquid.

Divide the butter in half and roll each half into a small log. Wrap in plastic wrap and use as needed, or freeze.

les chefs

Jacques 8Y

Fish and Seafood

Blackfish Beignets with Spicy Sauce

SERVES 4 AS A FIRST COURSE

SAUCE

½ cup mayonnaise

¼ cup sour cream

2 tablespoons ketchup

1 tablespoon Sriracha or other
hot chili sauce

2 tablespoons chopped fresh
chives

1 tablespoon fresh lemon juice

BATTER

¾ cup all-purpose flour

½ teaspoon baking powder

1 large egg yolk

1 cup soda water

2 tablespoons minced fresh
chives

⅔ cup canola oil

1 pound blackfish (tautog) or
other firm white fish fillets,
cut into ½-inch slices
(about 12)

Salt

BEIGNETS ARE FRITTERS, AND I PREPARE THEM often with vegetables, fruits, meat, shellfish, or finfish. The batter can be made with beer, milk, and eggs; whipped egg whites; just flour and water; or, as in this recipe, with egg yolk, flour, baking powder, and soda water. You can prepare the batter a few hours ahead. After they are fried, it is important to keep the beignets on a wire rack so air can circulate around them and the bottoms don't get soggy. The sooner you serve them, the better. The spicy sauce, a favorite of Gloria's, is good with any fried fish or shellfish or with steamed or poached fish. Blackfish (tautog) is plentiful in summer on the coast in Connecticut. Firm and moist, it is excellent grilled, poached, or fried.

||||||||||||||||||||||||||||||||||||||||||||||||||||||

FOR THE SAUCE: Mix all the ingredients thoroughly in a bowl. Cover and refrigerate until needed.

FOR THE BATTER: Put the flour, baking powder, egg yolk, and half the soda water in a bowl and mix until smooth with a whisk. Add the rest of the soda water and the chives and mix well. *(The batter can be made up to a few hours ahead and refrigerated.)*

FOR THE BEIGNETS: Preheat the oven to 175 degrees.

Heat half the oil in a large skillet, preferably nonstick, until hot. Dip 4 pieces of the fish into the batter until coated on all sides and place in the hot oil. Cook for 2½ to 3 minutes

on each side. Transfer to a wire rack set over a baking sheet, sprinkle with salt, and keep warm in the oven. Repeat with the remaining fish, adding more oil to the skillet as needed.

Serve with the sauce.

‖‖‖‖‖‖‖‖‖‖‖‖‖‖‖‖‖‖‖‖‖‖‖‖‖‖‖‖‖‖‖‖‖‖‖‖‖

NOTE: *If making the beignets ahead, reheat them under a hot broiler for a couple of minutes on each side before serving.*

Smoked Salmon on Corn Fritters

SERVES 4 AS A FIRST COURSE, ABOUT 12 AS AN HORS D'OEUVRE

SMOKED SALMON SERVED ON CORN FRITTERS is a delicious first course as well as a fine hors d'oeuvre. The salmon can be a commercial smoked variety. Or you can use thin slices of fresh salmon: Sprinkle them with salt and pepper and cure them in the refrigerator for 15 to 20 minutes to make a quick gravlax.

The corn fritters are good as a garnish for most grilled meats or fish. They are best served right after cooking, but they can be made ahead, cooled on a wire rack (so they don't get soggy underneath), and reheated in the oven as needed. The corn kernels could be replaced with other vegetables, from chopped spinach to peas to diced zucchini. The flour-and-beer batter could not be easier to make.

1 cup all-purpose flour

¾ cup beer

¼ teaspoon salt

2 ears sweet corn, husked and kernels cut off (about 2 cups)

¼ cup canola oil

About 6 ounces (about 8 slices) thinly sliced smoked salmon or gravlax (see headnote)

3 tablespoons whipped cream cheese or sour cream

2 tablespoons shredded fresh basil leaves

Put the flour, half the beer, and the salt in a bowl and mix with a whisk until smooth. Add the rest of the beer and the corn kernels and mix well.

Heat 2 tablespoons of the oil in a 12-inch nonstick skillet over high heat. When it is hot, use a ¼-cup measuring cup to make 4 fritters. Cook for about 4 minutes, then flip over with a spatula and cook for 4 minutes on the other side, or until cooked through. Transfer the fritters to a wire rack. Repeat with the remaining oil and fritter batter.

Arrange 2 or 3 fritters on each plate and cover each one with a slice of smoked salmon or gravlax. Drop about 1 teaspoon of the whipped cream cheese or sour cream onto the center of each topped fritter and sprinkle on some basil. Serve.

Teaching

IT MAY COME AS A SURPRISE THAT ALTHOUGH I AM A professional chef, I consider myself first and foremost a cooking teacher. For the past four decades, I have made a living instructing cooking students. Yet I came to teaching by accident—literally. In 1974, I barely survived a car wreck that left me with fractures to my back, pelvis, arm, and leg. At one point, a doctor told Gloria that my left arm would have to be amputated, provided I even survived and gained sufficient strength to undergo the surgery. I kept my arm, but my recovery was slow and painful. Even the most optimistic prognosis made it clear that putting in grueling shifts in commercial kitchens was a thing of the past. But cooking was all I had ever done. How was I to earn a living?

As serious as it was, my accident could not have happened at a better time. In the mid-seventies, a new culinary trend was sweeping the United States. Specialty kitchen stores were opening across the country, especially in California, that bellwether of all things American. Many of these included teaching kitchens where patrons could learn how to use the novel equipment the stores offered for sale. And those kitchens needed to be overseen by competent cooks who could also teach. Within a few years, I was on the road giving cooking lessons for thirty-five or forty weeks a year and was booked for more than a year in advance.

I discovered that I loved teaching. My mind has always worked in a linear manner; I like to look at dishes and break them down into simpler and simpler steps as I go along until I've bored down to the essential steps of the recipe. And that is what teaching is all about—allowing students to see and understand the essentials. I soon found that I thrived on the excitement of my students when they discovered that they could do something they'd never attempted before.

My students have also taught me a great deal. Because I have spent nearly all my life in and around kitchens, much of my cooking is instinctive. In my early years as an instructor, I assumed that everybody had similar innate culinary know-how. So I was shocked when I'd do something as simple as skim a stock, and people in the class would open their eyes in amazement and say, "So *that's* how you do it." When I got that type of reaction, I would jot down a few notes to myself so that I would remember to carefully explain a particular technique in my next class. Gradually those reminders began to take shape and formed the basis for my book *La Technique*, published more than forty years ago and still in print—a tribute to the lasting value of what my students taught me. Recipe styles come and go, but the underlying techniques, what I teach my students, remain the same. They enable novice cooks to go beyond the printed recipe and understand the food.

My television career has been an extension of my teaching and writing. My book *La Technique* has formed the basis of shows that I have done at KQED in San Francisco, and my cookbooks and television series have always been produced to complement one another.

My long and rewarding teaching career is not without irony. After getting a master's degree in French literature from Columbia University

in New York, I proposed that I do my PhD on the role of food in French literature. I could well have spent the second half of my career as a professor lecturing students and writing learned journal articles had the head of the department not dismissed my suggestion outright, as "not a serious subject." The importance of food has changed in our life. Today I am a dean at New York City's International Culinary Center and teach courses at the Department of Gastronomy at Boston University—which, in 2011, awarded me, *a cook,* with an honorary Doctor of Humane Letters.

Instant Gravlax with Cream Cheese–Horseradish Sauce

SERVES 4 AS A FIRST COURSE

2 teaspoons kosher salt (see headnote)

1½ teaspoons light brown sugar

1 teaspoon 5-spice powder

½ teaspoon freshly ground black pepper

One 1-pound salmon fillet, cut from the head end, totally cleaned of skin, pin bones, and any sinews (about 12 ounces cleaned)

SAUCE

⅓ cup whipped cream cheese

1 tablespoon grated fresh or bottled horseradish

1 teaspoon Tabasco sauce

2 tablespoons minced fresh chives

2 tablespoons crushed roasted peanuts

TO MAKE THIS CURED SALMON DISH, BUY A fillet of the best salmon (preferably wild and not too large) cut from the head end, rather than the tail end. Then slice the fillet crosswise from back to belly. The resulting slices will be wider at the top and long and narrow at the bottom, and they will resemble the petals of a flower when arranged on the plates at serving time.

The salmon will cure in 15 to 20 minutes, but it can be prepared a day or two ahead. Kosher salt has larger crystals than table salt and cures the fish faster and better. If using table salt, use only 1¼ teaspoons instead of the 2 teaspoons called for.

Combine the salt, brown sugar, 5-spice powder, and pepper in a small bowl. Cut the salmon into 8 slices. Arrange the slices side by side on a large plate and sprinkle them on both sides with the salt mixture. Cover with plastic wrap and refrigerate for at least 15 to 20 minutes, or as long as 48 hours.

FOR THE SAUCE: Mix the cream cheese, horseradish, and Tabasco together in a small bowl.

At serving time, spoon a good tablespoon of the sauce into the center of each of four dinner plates. Arrange 2 slices of salmon on top, with the thin ends of the slices meeting in the center. Sprinkle with the chives and peanuts and serve.

Yucatán Ceviche

SERVES 4 AS A FIRST COURSE

I HAVE AT LEAST HALF A DOZEN RECIPES FOR ceviche, the raw fish salad so popular in South America, but this one—closest to what we usually ate in our apartment in Mexico—is a favorite. Made without any oil, it relies on the flavors of red onion, cilantro, tomato, and lime juice. I often use blackfish, one of the best fish of the summer—firm, white fleshed, juicy, and tasty—in this ceviche. Enjoy it as a first course for dinner or main course for lunch.

||||||||||||||||||||||||||||||||||||||||||||||||||||

Trim the fish of any sinews or pin bones, so it is totally clean. Cut the fish into ¾-inch pieces.

Combine the fish with the remaining ingredients except the lettuce.

Arrange the lettuce on four plates or fit the leaves into martini glasses. Divide the ceviche among the plates or glasses. Serve immediately.

1 pound white fish fillets

¾ teaspoon salt

¾ cup coarsely chopped red onion

1 tablespoon finely chopped garlic

3 tablespoons fresh lime juice

1½ cups diced (½-inch) ripe tomatoes

¼ cup coarsely chopped fresh cilantro

1½ teaspoons finely chopped jalapeño pepper, or to taste

Lettuce leaves, for serving

Tuna Tartare with Bagel Chips and Radishes

SERVES 4 AS A FIRST COURSE

TUNA

One 8-ounce cleaned tuna steak, cut into ½-inch pieces (about 2 cups)

½ teaspoon salt

½ Tabasco sauce

¼ cup finely chopped mild onion

2 tablespoons minced scallions

3 or 4 large radishes, trimmed

⅛ teaspoon salt

⅛ teaspoon freshly ground black pepper

16 bagel chips

12 oil-cured black olives, halved and pitted

1½ tablespoons walnut oil

1½ tablespoons chopped fresh chives

FOR THIS STARTER, I SEASON DICED RAW TUNA and serve with shredded radishes and bagel chips. Walnut oil gives the dish a wonderful taste, but you can use olive oil if you prefer.

||||||||||||||||||||||||||||||||||||||||||||||||||

FOR THE TUNA: Combine the tuna, salt, Tabasco, onion, and scallions in a bowl. Cover and refrigerate.

At serving time, grate enough radishes on the large holes of a box grater to measure 2½ cups. Season the grated radishes with the salt and pepper. Divide the radishes among four plates and spread them out to create a ring on each plate.

Spoon the tuna mixture into the radish rings. Stand 4 bagel chips around the tuna on each plate, scatter the olives over the radishes, and sprinkle with the oil and chives. Serve.

Tuna à la Minute

SERVES 4 AS A FIRST COURSE

IT TAKES ONLY A FEW MINUTES TO COOK VERY thin slices of tuna in a 250-degree oven. The slices can be arranged on dinner plates and refrigerated, ready for the oven, hours ahead. At serving time, cook the garnish while the tuna is warmed on the plates (the low cooking temperature makes this safe for most plates) just until the edges of the fish turn gray. The hot garnish that is then spooned on top finishes the cooking.

||||||||||||||||||||||||||||||||||||||||||||||||

Cut the tuna crosswise in half and then in half again, to make 4 pieces. Then cut each piece in half horizontally through the center so you have 8 slices, each about ½ inch thick. (This is easier than cutting a single piece in half horizontally.) Arrange 2 tuna slices on each of four dinner plates, cover, and refrigerate.

At serving time, preheat the oven to 250 degrees.

Heat the oil in a large skillet. Add the scallions and zucchini, sprinkle with ¼ teaspoon each of the salt and pepper, and sauté for 2 to 3 minutes. Add the olives, tomatoes, and butter and heat until very hot.

Meanwhile, sprinkle the remaining ¼ teaspoon each salt and pepper on the tuna slices and place them in the oven for 5 minutes, or just until the edges of the tuna turn pale gray.

Remove the plates from the oven, spread the tomato garnish on top of the tuna slices, and sprinkle with the chives, if using. Serve.

One 12-ounce cleaned tuna steak (about 1 inch thick)

2 tablespoons olive oil

⅓ cup minced scallions

1 cup diced (½-inch) zucchini

½ teaspoon salt

½ teaspoon freshly ground black pepper

¼ cup diced (¼-inch) oil-cured black olives

1½ cups diced (½-inch) seeded peeled tomatoes

2 tablespoons unsalted butter

1 tablespoon minced fresh chives (optional)

Fluke Tartare

SERVES 4 AS A FIRST COURSE

1 teaspoon grated lemon rind

2 teaspoons fresh lemon juice

2 teaspoons wasabi paste or
powder

3 tablespoons finely chopped
mild onion

2 tablespoons mayonnaise

2 tablespoons sour cream

¾ teaspoon salt

12 ounces very fresh fluke
fillets (see headnote), cut
into ¼-inch dice

3 cups mesclun salad greens,
cleaned and spun dry

20 kettle-style potato chips or
12 Melba toasts

4 fresh dill or tarragon sprigs
or thinly sliced lemon rind

I OFTEN GRILL OR SAUTÉ FLUKE, BUT WHEN IT is super fresh, I use it in tartare. Seasoned with wasabi paste, mayonnaise, and sour cream, the tartare makes a nice first course served on a mesclun salad with crunchy potato chips or Melba toast. Other flatfish, such as lemon or gray sole or flounder, can be substituted.

||||||||||||||||||||||||||||||||||||||||||||||||

Whisk together the lemon rind and juice, wasabi, onion, mayonnaise, sour cream, and salt in a bowl until well combined. Add the fish and mix it in well. (*The tartare can be served right away or refrigerated for a couple of hours.*)

At serving time, divide the salad greens among four plates. If serving with the potato chips, place one chip in the center of the salad on each plate, mound the fish on top, and stand 4 more chips around the tartare, pressing them into it to create a box or frame. If using Melba toast, mound the fish on the plates and push 3 toasts into the tartare on each plate to make a decorative triangular box. Top each serving with a sprig of dill or tarragon or lemon rind.

Spicy Shrimp with Cocktail Sauce

SERVES 4

SHRIMP

2 cups water

¼ cup red wine vinegar

⅓ cup sliced scallions

⅔ cup chopped onion

1 teaspoon dried oregano,
    preferably Greek or
    Mexican

½ teaspoon hot pepper flakes

1½ teaspoons salt

1 pound large shrimp
    (16–20 count) in the shell

COCKTAIL SAUCE

½ cup mayonnaise

3 tablespoons ketchup

1 teaspoon hot mustard,
    preferably a grainy variety

½ teaspoon Tabasco sauce

⅓ cup coarsely chopped
    scallions

COOKING SHRIMP IN THE SHELL MAXIMIZES its flavor. This stock is quite spicy, and the shrimp should be cooked at least 2 hours ahead and left in the liquid. Eat them at room temperature, sucking out the juices from the shells. You can enjoy the shrimp as is, but I usually serve it with this piquant cocktail sauce, which includes the unusual addition of julienned radishes. The sauce is also excellent with poached fish or cold meat.

The spicy shrimp stock is also delicious and should be drunk while eating the shrimp. I prepare a cocktail like one Craig Claiborne used to make with clam juice and vodka, substituting the spicy broth for the clam juice. For each cocktail, pour 2 tablespoons vodka into a small glass and top with ⅓ cup of the cold stock. Stir and enjoy.

||||||||||||||||||||||||||||||||||||||||||||||||

FOR THE SHRIMP: Bring all the ingredients except the shrimp to a boil in a medium saucepan and boil gently for about 5 minutes. Add the shrimp, stir, bring to a light boil, and stir again. Set the shrimp aside, uncovered, in the cooking stock to cool to room temperature. Refrigerate for at least 2 hours, or until ready to serve. *(The shrimp can be made up to 24 hours ahead.)*

FOR THE COCKTAIL SAUCE: Mix all the ingredients together in a bowl. Refrigerate until needed.

Serve the shrimp with the sauce for dipping and the cocktails (see headnote), if desired.

||||||||||||||||||||||||||||||||||||||||||

VARIATION: *If you don't want to serve your guests unshelled shrimp, shell the shrimp, reserving the shells. Add the shells only to the water and vinegar and boil gently for 5 minutes. Strain the mixture into a bowl and discard the shells. Return to the saucepan, add the shrimp, scallions, and onion and bring to a light boil. Set the shrimp aside, uncovered, in the cooking stock and cool to room temperature. Refrigerate until ready to serve.*

½ teaspoon finely chopped garlic

3 tablespoons julienned radishes

2 tablespoons chopped fresh cilantro

¼ teaspoon salt

Top Neck Clams with Vinegar and Scallion Sauce

SERVES 4 AS A FIRST COURSE

24 top neck or cherrystone clams, washed

3 tablespoons unsalted butter

2 tablespoons olive oil

⅓ cup minced scallions

2 tablespoons balsamic vinegar

1 teaspoon freshly ground black pepper

Minced fresh chives (optional)

Buttered black bread, for serving

I AM LUCKY TO HAVE A FRIEND WHO IS A PROfessional fisherwoman, so I get bags of shellfish for the best possible price. Gloria likes littleneck clams, but I prefer the larger top neck or cherrystone clams. Occasionally I use the large quahog clams in pasta or soup.

I open clams with a paring knife, which can be difficult and dangerous; a good alternative is to put the clams on a baking sheet and place them in a 350-degree oven. After 7 or 8 minutes, they will pop slightly open but will still be completely raw. Then it is easy to slide a knife inside, sever the adductor muscle, and open the clams. (Another way to open clams is to place them in the freezer on a baking sheet for 20 to 30 minutes. They will not be frozen inside, but it will be easier to slide the knife between the shells.)

After chilling the clams in the refrigerator, we often enjoy them cold on the half-shell with horseradish sauce or fresh lemon juice. Other times, we eat them lukewarm with pesto or garlic butter or, as in this recipe, scallions and balsamic vinegar.

||||||||||||||||||||||||||||||||||||||||||||||||||

Preheat the oven to 350 degrees.

Arrange the clams in one layer on an aluminum foil–lined baking sheet and place in the oven for about 8 minutes, or just until they open. Remove from the oven and let cool for 3 to 4 minutes.

Slide your knife inside each clam and sever the muscle

connecting it to the shell. Remove the top shell, being careful to save the juice, leaving the clam in the other half shell. Arrange on a platter.

Heat the butter and oil in a small skillet. Add the scallions and cook for 2 to 3 minutes, until the butter starts browning lightly and the scallions soften. Add the vinegar and cook for 10 to 20 seconds.

Divide the mixture among the open clams, still lukewarm from the oven, and sprinkle the pepper on top. Garnish with chives, if using. Enjoy with buttered black bread.

Sautéed Shad Roe with Shallots

SERVES 4 AS A FIRST COURSE

MY WIFE IS ALWAYS WAITING FOR SPRING TO get her fix of shad roe. I prepare shad roe several ways, but Gloria likes it simply sautéed and still rare in the center. Be careful to sauté it over low heat, or the roe may burst and splatter, landing on the cook as well as the stove. Half a sac of roe is enough for a first course. You can double the recipe to serve as a main course.

||||||||||||||||||||||||||||||||||||||||||||||||

Preheat the oven to 150 degrees.

Heat the oil in a large skillet, preferably nonstick. Sprinkle the roe with the salt and pepper. Place the roe in the skillet in one layer, reduce the heat to low, cover, and cook for about 2 minutes. Turn the roe carefully, as it may burst and splatter, and cook, covered, for another 2 minutes. Transfer the roe to four warm plates and keep warm in the oven.

Add the shallots and butter to the pan and cook for about 1 minute. Add the celery leaves or parsley and lemon juice and stir well.

Pour the sauce over the roe and serve immediately.

2 tablespoons olive oil

2 pairs shad roe (about 1¼ pounds), separated into halves (discard the membrane that holds the halves together)

¾ teaspoon salt

¾ teaspoon freshly ground black pepper

⅓ cup finely chopped shallots

3 tablespoons unsalted butter

¼ cup coarsely chopped celery leaves or fresh parsley

2 tablespoons fresh lemon juice

Escargots in Baked Potatoes

SERVES 4 AS A FIRST COURSE

GARLIC-HERB BUTTER

4 garlic cloves, crushed (about 1 tablespoon)

2 tablespoons skinned or unskinned whole almonds, preferably Marcona

½ teaspoon salt

½ teaspoon freshly ground black pepper

½ cup (loosely packed) fresh parsley leaves

2 tablespoons dry white wine

5 tablespoons unsalted butter, softened

3 tablespoons olive oil

2 baking potatoes (about 12 ounces each)

¼ teaspoon salt

¼ teaspoon freshly ground black pepper

2 dozen canned snails from France

1½ slices white bread, coarsely chopped (1 cup)

WHEN I AM IN A HURRY, I COOK BAKED POTA-toes in my microwave and finish them in a very hot regular oven to get a crust on them. It takes 10 minutes for my oven to reach 450 degrees and about the same time for the potatoes to be almost cooked through in the microwave. In this recipe, I cook the potatoes in the microwave, stuff them with escargots and a garlic-and-herb butter, and finish them in the hot oven. The escargots can be replaced with shrimp or scallops for a variation.

Cooked escargots in cans are available at specialty stores, some supermarkets, and online. Make sure that you buy good snails from France. Do not buy Achate or Achatina snails, which usually come from Taiwan or China—they are cheap, but they taste like mud.

||||||||||||||||||||||||||||||||||||||||||||||

FOR THE BUTTER: Put the garlic, almonds, salt, pepper, parsley, and wine in a mini food processor or a blender and process for about 10 seconds. Add the soft butter and oil and process for about 30 seconds, until you have a smooth, creamy mixture. *(The butter can be made several days ahead and refrigerated or even frozen.)*

Preheat the oven to 450 degrees.

Meanwhile, microwave the potatoes on high for 10 minutes. Cut the cooked potatoes lengthwise in half. Scoop out most of the potato flesh, put it in a bowl, and season it with the salt and pepper.

Spread a total of about 1½ tablespoons of the garlic and

herb butter in the bottom of the potato shells. Pile the sea-soned potato flesh and the snails on top and dot the remaining garlic and herb butter randomly on top of the stuffed potatoes. Sprinkle on the coarsely chopped bread.

Arrange the potato halves on a baking sheet and bake for 10 to 12 minutes, until heated through and browned on top. Serve.

Simple Seafood Salad

SERVES 4

DRESSING

One 2-ounce can anchovy fillets in oil, coarsely chopped, with their oil

2 teaspoons finely chopped garlic

1½ tablespoons fresh lemon juice

¼ cup olive oil

1 teaspoon salt

1 teaspoon freshly ground black pepper

THE DRESSING FOR THIS SALAD—MADE WITH anchovies, garlic, and lemon juice—can be prepared ahead, then combined with the butter beans and left at room temperature for an hour or so, and the shellfish can be sliced beforehand and refrigerated. That way, it takes only a couple of minutes to finish the dish, which should be served just warm, with plenty of bread to soak up the dressing. The canned beans are drained but not rinsed, because the liquid left on them helps thicken the dressing.

||||||||||||||||||||||||||||||||||||||||||||||||||

FOR THE DRESSING: Mix all the ingredients, including the oil from the anchovies, together in a medium bowl.

Add the beans, almonds, and onion to the dressing and mix well. Set aside.

About 15 minutes before serving time, bring 6 cups water to a boil in a medium saucepan over high heat. Drop the scallops, shrimp, and squid into a large sieve, lower them into the boiling water, stirring well, and cook for 2 minutes (the water will not come back to a boil). Drain and add to the ingredients in the bowl, along with the chives and tarragon.

Spread the lettuce leaves on a serving plate or individual plates and spoon the seafood mixture on top. Let cool slightly, and serve with the bread.

SALAD

1 can (about 1 pound) butter beans, habas grandes, or cannellini beans, drained but not rinsed

⅓ cup unskinned whole almonds, cut in half

3 tablespoon coarsely chopped red onion

8 ounces sea scallops (about 8), cut in half

8 ounces shelled shrimp (about 8), cut into 3 pieces each

8 ounces cleaned small to medium squid, tentacles removed and left whole, bodies cut into 1½-inch pieces

2 tablespoons chopped fresh chives

1 tablespoon chopped fresh tarragon

8 leaves butter or Bibb lettuce

1 baguette or crusty loaf, for serving

Sailing the Open Sea (2010)

Tilapia

MANY COOKS TURN UP THEIR NOSES AT TILAPIA, BUT if more people tried it, they would be pleasantly surprised. If you've been stung by off-tasting or muddy tilapia in the past, aquaculture has solved those problems. Today the flesh is mild and unassertive. Because all the tilapia in this country is farmed, it arrives at the seafood counter fresh and is never in short supply. It is also relatively inexpensive. And, unlike farmed salmon and shrimp, it is raised in what most environmentalists would agree is a sustainable manner.

The single-serving-sized fillets are ready in minutes, no matter how you prepare them. My favorite way is simply to give them a dash of oil, salt, and pepper and stick them under the broiler. When they come out, I might mix fresh thyme or tarragon with some lemon juice and good olive oil, especially in the summer, and top them with that. Or I will sauté onion and tomato and add a bit of white wine. My preference is something simple so I can still taste the fish.

That said, tilapia can also accommodate strong-tasting sauces. I sometimes make a glaze by mixing miso with soy, honey, and rice vinegar. I brush the fillets with that and they are table-ready after 5 minutes at most under the broiler. A fish that can deliver so much with so little time, cost, and effort should get more respect.

Sautéed Tilapia

SERVES 4

MY FISH MARKET ALWAYS HAS FRESH TILAPIA; *it is a reliable, mild-flavored fish. The mushroom, scallion, and white bean garnish can be made a couple of hours ahead, but the fish should be sautéed and combined with the garnish just before serving.*

||||||||||||||||||||||||||||||||||||||||||||||||||||

FOR THE GARNISH: Heat the olive oil in a 12-inch non-stick skillet. Add the mushrooms and cook over high heat for about 1½ minutes until softened. Add the scallions, beans, salt, and pepper and stir well. Transfer to a bowl and set aside.

Heat the butter and oil in the same skillet. Sprinkle the salt on the fish fillets. When the butter and oil are hot, add the fish fillets in one layer, without overlapping, and cook for 1 to 1½ minutes on each side, depending on the thickness. The fish should be barely cooked through.

Transfer the fish to a serving plate and add the garnish to the drippings in the pan. Sauté for 1 minute, or until hot.

Spoon the garnish over the fish and sprinkle on the lemon juice. Serve.

GARNISH

1 tablespoon olive oil

1 small portobello mushroom, cut into ¾-inch pieces (1¼ cups)

½ cup sliced (½-inch) scallions

½ cup canned Boston or navy beans, drained

¼ teaspoon salt

¼ teaspoon freshly ground black pepper

1 tablespoon unsalted butter

1 tablespoon canola oil

½ teaspoon salt

4 skinless tilapia fillets (about 5 ounces each and ½ inch thick)

Juice of ½ lemon

Broiled Black Sea Bass with Cottage Cheese and Tarragon Sauce

SERVES 4

SAUCE

½ cup large-curd cottage cheese

¼ cup sour cream

1½ tablespoons chopped fresh tarragon

2 teaspoons grated fresh or bottled horseradish

⅛ teaspoon salt

⅛ teaspoon freshly ground black pepper

1½ cups pieces (½-inch) country bread

1 tablespoon olive oil

½ cup minced scallions

¾ teaspoon salt

¾ teaspoon freshly ground black pepper

4 skinless black sea bass or bluefish fillets (about 6 ounces each)

1 tablespoon canola oil

IN THE SUMMER, I PREPARE THIS DISH WITH bluefish. When just out of the water, bluefish is excellent, but it doesn't age well. If you are lucky enough to live on the East Coast and have access to truly fresh bluefish, use it here; if not, use black sea bass or another firm white-fleshed fish. The cottage cheese–horseradish sauce is excellent with any broiled, grilled, or poached fish.

||||||||||||||||||||||||||||||||||||||||||||||||||||

FOR THE SAUCE: Mix all the ingredients together in a bowl. Cover and refrigerate.

Preheat the oven to 400 degrees.

Toss the bread pieces well with the olive oil and spread out on a baking sheet. Bake for about 10 minutes, until nicely browned. Toss with the minced scallions and set aside.

At serving time, preheat the broiler. Line a baking sheet with aluminum foil. Combine the salt and pepper and sprinkle evenly on both sides of the fish fillets. Using a sharp knife, make a few ½-inch-deep cuts in each fillet so the heat from the broiler can penetrate the fish.

Brush the fillets with the canola oil and arrange them on the lined baking sheet. Broil 3 to 4 inches from the heat, without turning, for about 4 minutes. The fish should still be slightly underdone in the center.

Arrange the fillets on four plates and sprinkle the bread and scallion mixture on top. Serve immediately, with the sauce on the side.

Striped Bass in Yellow Pepper Sauce

SERVES 4

STRIPED BASS ARE PLENTIFUL ON THE CON-
necticut coast in the summer, and I am fortunate to have fish-
ermen friends who occasionally bring fresh fish to my house.
The yellow pepper sauce appears very rich, because it looks
like a classic butter sauce, but it has a fraction of the calories.

||||||||||||||||||||||||||||||||||||||||||||||||||

Heat the olive oil in a medium saucepan. Add the onion and sauté for 1 minute. Add the diced yellow pepper and ¾ cup of the water, bring to a boil, cover, and cook for 5 minutes.

Add ¼ teaspoon each of the salt and black pepper to the bell pepper mixture and emulsify the mixture with an immersion blender or in a standard blender until smooth. Add the butter and emulsify for another 10 to 15 seconds. (You will have about 1¾ cups sauce.) Set aside.

Toss the zucchini julienne with the pinch of salt in a microwavable bowl. Cover and heat in a microwave oven for about 45 seconds, just long enough to wilt the zucchini.

Sprinkle the remaining ½ teaspoon salt and ¼ teaspoon black pepper on the fish fillets. Arrange them in a single layer in a skillet and pour the remaining ½ cup water around them. Bring to a boil, turn the fish over, cover, and cook for about 2 minutes. The fish should still be pink inside. (Increase the cooking time, if needed.)

Reheat the sauce in the microwave oven and divide it among four warm plates. Place a piece of drained fish on top of the sauce on each plate and spoon some of the zucchini julienne on top. Sprinkle the chives over the sauce and serve.

2 tablespoons olive oil

½ cup chopped onion

1 yellow bell pepper (about 8 ounces), cored, seeded, and cut into ½-inch dice (1½ cups)

1¼ cups water

¾ teaspoon salt, plus a pinch

½ teaspoon freshly ground black pepper

2 tablespoons unsalted butter

1 small zucchini, cut lengthwise into ¼-inch slices and julienned (1½ cups)

4 skinless striped bass fillets (about 6 ounces each and 1 inch thick)

1 tablespoon minced fresh chives

An Embarrassment of Fishes

EVERYONE APPRECIATES IT WHEN A GUEST BRINGS A host or hostess gift, but I was particularly grateful one recent summer afternoon when Jacques Torres, the well-known New York chocolatier and confectioner, who also happens to be an accomplished fisherman, showed up at our house holding a just-caught ten-pound striped bass. Friends have a habit of turning up on my doorstep when they catch a fish too big for their families, and I'm more than happy to help solve their problem. I wasted no time cleaning Jacques's bass (outside, in order to avoid a divorce), and then I faced a pleasant quandary: How would I prepare a fish that was as long as my legs?

A whole fish is a great main course that is guaranteed to make a big impression at any large gathering. It being Sunday when Jacques came by, a day when many friends gather with us to play *boules*, I chose a preparation that may sound daunting but is actually straightfor-ward, requires minimal time in the kitchen away from guests (and the action-packed *boules* court), and all but guarantees perfectly cooked flesh: I mixed 3 pounds kosher salt with egg whites and a little flour to form a paste that I pressed onto the fish as one would a pastry crust. Then I popped it into the oven at 450 degrees for about 45 minutes—just enough time for me to assemble a few sauces: a mayonnaise with

capers, a warm butter sauce with tarragon, and another one with hard-cooked eggs and herbs. I brought the whole fish to the table and cracked off the crust. What remained was skinless, moist, and, though it may seem counterintuitive, not particularly salty fish.

Other times I fillet a large fish to feed the multitudes. Once I have the fillets, I can go in many directions. At the peak of summer, I'll simply toss them on the grill and serve them with any vegetables that are ripe in the garden—tomatoes, eggplant, zucchini, peppers. If I'm cooking inside, I often simply slide the fillets under the broiler and cook until the skin becomes a kind of crackling on top. Or I'll shred some potatoes and mix in some leeks and garlic. I put a patty of that for each serving into a nonstick skillet and top it with a piece of fillet and then with another fistful of the potato mixture. When the bottoms brown, I turn the "sandwiches" and brown the other side. The fish is nice and moist in the center, and the potatoes make a crunchy crust.

The joys of being in possession of a large fish continue long after the last diner has left the table. The bones can become the base for a sauce if I brown them in oil, then add wine and water and cook the stock for 20 minutes. I strain the liquid and freeze it for later use. Or I might do soup by making the same base but adding onion, tomatoes, garlic, and some leek to it. Everything goes into the stock, even the head—provided Gloria, who loves the meat found on a fish head, hasn't gotten to it first and nibbled off every morsel.

Steamed Fish with Provençal Vegetable Stew

SERVES 4

THE ZUCCHINI-BASED STEW IN THIS DISH, FLA-vored with poblano and jalapeño peppers, garlic, and tomatoes, is also delicious on its own. It can be made ahead, but the fish should be cooked just before serving. The beauty of this recipe is that you use one pan for the vegetables and then steam the fish in the same pan. The fish fillets (or steaks) are placed in the hot vegetable stew and steamed for 2 to 5 minutes, depending on how thick the fish is and how well-done you like it; I steam them for 3 minutes, which results in a slightly rare interior.

The fish you use can be anything from mahi-mahi (my first choice here) to cod or tuna to amberjack. The fillets or boneless steaks should weigh about 4 ounces and measure 1¼ to 1½ inches thick.

||||||||||||||||||||||||||||||||||||||||||||||||||

FOR THE STEW: Put all the ingredients except the olives and fish in a large saucepan and cook, covered, over high heat for 5 minutes. Reduce the heat to low and cook for 10 minutes longer. *(The stew can be made several hours ahead.)*

At serving time, bring the stew to a boil. Put the fish in the stew, burying the fillets or steaks about ½ inch deep, and sprinkle the olives on top. Cover and cook over high heat for 2 to 5 minutes, depending on how you like your fish cooked.

Arrange the fish on four plates and spoon the vegetable stew on top. Serve immediately.

STEW

¼ cup extra-virgin olive oil

2 cups diced (½-inch) onions

1½ cups diced (½-inch) seeded poblano pepper (1 large)

4 cups diced (1-inch) small firm zucchini

2½ cups diced (1-inch) tomatoes

1 tablespoon chopped jalapeño pepper, or to taste

2 tablespoons chopped garlic

1 teaspoon crushed fresh thyme leaves

2 teaspoons salt

⅓ cup pitted oil-cured black olives

4 fish fillets or steaks (see headnote; about 4 ounces each and 1½ inches thick)

Fillet of Sole Riviera with Pico de Gallo

SERVES 4

8 small or 4 large skinless lemon sole fillets (about 1½ pounds total), cleaned of any sinew

½ cup dry white wine

½ teaspoon salt

⅓ cup pico de gallo, homemade (recipe follows) or store-bought

1 cup diced (½-inch) peeled, seeded cucumber

⅓ cup heavy cream

3 tablespoons chopped fresh chives

PICO DE GALLO

1 cup diced (½-inch) plum tomatoes

3 tablespoons chopped mild onion

1 tablespoon finely chopped jalapeño pepper

1 tablespoon fresh lime juice

3 tablespoons coarsely chopped fresh cilantro

ON THE YUCATÁN RIVIERA IN MEXICO, GLORIA and I always kept pico de gallo, also called salsa fresca, on hand. We could buy it fresh at the supermarket, but it is easy to make your own. One night I used it to create this simple fish recipe, with superlative results.

||||||||||||||||||||||||||||||||||||||||||||||

Place the fillets in a large skillet in one layer and add the wine, salt, pico de gallo, and cucumber. Shake the pan so everything is loose, then cover, bring to a boil, and boil for about 30 seconds. The fillets are thin and should be barely cooked; if they are thicker, increase the cooking time. Transfer the fillets to four warm plates.

Bring the cooking liquid to a boil. Add the cream, bring back to a boil, and boil over high heat for 30 seconds to reduce the liquid and concentrate the flavor. Pour any juice that has accumulated around the fillets into the saucepan.

Coat the fish generously with the sauce, sprinkle on the chives, and serve.

||||||||||||||||||||||||||||||||||||||||||||||

PICO DE GALLO MAKES 1¼ CUPS

||||||||||||||||||||||||||||||||||||||||||||||

Combine all the ingredients in a bowl.

Sole Vin Blanc

SERVES 4

FISH STOCK

Reserved fish bones and skin (from below)

⅓ cup coarsely chopped onion

¼ cup coarsely chopped celery

1 garlic clove, crushed

1 bay leaf

1 fresh thyme sprig

¾ cup fruity dry white wine

2 cups water

FISH AND SAUCE

1 fluke or other sole (about 2 pounds), gutted, boned, cut into 4 fillets, and skin removed; bones and skin reserved

¼ cup finely chopped shallots

⅓ cup dry white wine

Reserved ½ cup fish stock (from above)

⅓ teaspoon salt

TO GIVE THIS CLASSIC DISH A MODERN TWIST, I do not make a traditional velouté, a roux-thickened fish fumet or stock, for the sauce. Instead, I just poach the fish in wine and fish stock and add fresh butter at the end.

The best sole for this recipe would be real Dover sole (the market can fillet it for you), but since it is not always available and it is expensive, you can substitute fluke or another sole.

||||||||||||||||||||||||||||||||||||||||||||||||||

FOR THE STOCK: Put the fish bones and skin into a large saucepan and add the remaining stock ingredients. Bring to a boil over high heat, then stir well and boil over medium heat for 15 to 18 minutes.

Strain the stock (you should have about 1½ cups stock). Set aside ½ cup of the stock for the sauce and freeze the remaining cup to use in a soup or sauce. (When cold, the fish stock will be like aspic because of the gelatin in the fish bones.)

FOR THE FISH: Preheat the oven to 150 degrees.

Fold each fluke fillet into thirds, with the whiter side on the outside. The bundles should be about 2 inches thick. Place the bundles in one layer in a saucepan and add the shallots, wine, reserved fish stock, salt, and pepper. Bring to a boil, cover, reduce the heat, and boil gently for about 1½ minutes. Turn the fish bundles over, cover again, and cook for an additional 1½ minutes. Transfer the fish to an ovenproof plate and keep warm in the oven.

Boil the cooking liquid over high heat for 2 to 3 minutes, until you have reduced it to about ½ cup. Reduce the heat to medium and, using a whisk, add the butter about ½ tablespoon at a time, whisking well to incorporate it and create a creamy sauce.

Divide the fish among four warm plates and coat with the sauce. Sprinkle with the chives and serve immediately.

⅓ teaspoon freshly ground black pepper

4 tablespoons unsalted butter, softened

1 tablespoon chopped fresh chives

French-Mex Cuisine

MOST AMERICANS CONSIDER ME TO BE THE QUINTES-sential French chef, but don't try to tell that to the person who taught me how to cook—my mother.

I will never forget the dinner we had when she came over to visit Gloria and me about fifteen years after I had arrived in this country. At the end of the meal, *Maman* turned to me and said, "This was very good, Tati [my nickname], but it is not French at all."

I replied, "But at least you say it's good."

I had never given the question of my cooking's Frenchness or lack thereof any thought. When it comes to food, I am open and eager to absorb anything I encounter, wherever I go and whoever I eat with. There is only one constant for me if adopting a new ingredient, presentation, or flavor into my repertoire: It must be good.

One of the biggest influences on how I have cooked over the past decade and a half has been Mexico. Through a series of fortunate coincidences, Gloria and I found our way to Playa del Carmen, then a sleepy, affordable town on the Yucatán Peninsula. We fell in love with the area—the weather, the beach, the water, the restaurants, the markets, and the food stalls—and purchased an apartment where we spent a month or more every winter. The town has little traffic and is delightfully walkable.

Typically, my friend Jean-Claude Szurdak, who also vacations there,

and I would meander down to the beach, which was only a few hundred feet from our terrace, at about eleven in the morning. It was no accident that this is the time that the fishermen usually return from sea and haul their small motorboats onto the sand. Using our broken Spanish and plenty of finger-pointing and gesticulating, we would secure a whole snapper or grouper, which the fishermen weighed on antique hanging scales and presented to us as is. To avoid a verbal scolding when we returned to the apartment, we cleaned our purchase on the beach.

For a change of pace, we detoured to the market for fresh local calamari or shrimp—or a pig's tongue to stew—and to supplement our larder of hot peppers. There were always hundreds of varieties to choose from—red, yellow, orange, green, purple; some bigger and longer than bananas, some smaller than cherries—with an exciting palate of different flavors and heat.

Generally we cooked one meal a day at home and went out for the other one. Because of the town's numerous restaurants and food carts, the most difficult part of dining out in Playa del Carmen was deciding where to eat and what to have. The decision was made that much harder because I love spicy food. So we might stop for tacos, or enjoy any of the numerous styles of fresh-out-of-the-water ceviche on offer. Usually the day ended with Jean-Claude and me playing a game or two of *boules* on the hard-packed sand of a floodlit parking lot.

Sadly, we recently sold our Mexican apartment. Great medical services are one of the few things Playa del Carmen lacks, and as I looked toward my eighties, that became a concern. But we'd had a great run, and we wanted to say good-bye to Playa del Carmen while all our Mexican memories were still wonderful.

Now in my kitchen, I frequently practice what could be called "French-Mex" cuisine. I might fillet a nice white-fleshed fish, drizzle a little white wine on it, and add a dash of salt and pepper (a classically French first step), then put four or five tablespoons of pico de gallo on it (as Mexican as you can get) and poach it, adding a couple of tablespoons of cream until it reduces a bit, then finish the dish with a sprinkle of cilantro. French techniques certainly, but applied to local ingredients.

Broiled Sole with Chive Butter

SERVES 4

OFTEN THE SIMPLEST WAY OF COOKING FOOD is the best, and that applies especially to fish. Seasoned, oiled, and placed close under the broiler, sole takes only a couple of minutes to cook. Here I coat it with a mixture of chives, butter, and lemon juice to serve.

||||||||||||||||||||||||||||||||||||||||||||||||||||

Line a baking sheet with aluminum foil. Spread the oil over it and sprinkle with the salt and pepper. Arrange the fillets on the pan and then turn them over so they are seasoned on both sides. *(This can be done an hour or so ahead of cooking; keep the fish refrigerated.)*

When ready to cook, melt the butter with the chives in a saucepan, or melt the butter with the chives in a small bowl in the microwave oven. Mix in the lemon juice. Keep warm.

Place the sole under the broiler, 2 to 3 inches from the heat source, and broil for about 2½ minutes, until barely cooked.

Arrange the fish on warm plates and top with the chive butter. Serve immediately.

1½ tablespoons olive oil

¾ teaspoon salt

¾ teaspoon freshly ground black pepper

4 lemon sole fillets (about 6 ounces each and ½ inch thick)

2½ tablespoons unsalted butter

3 tablespoons minced fresh chives

1 tablespoon fresh lemon juice

Grilled Snapper with Olive Topping

SERVES 4

TOPPING

1 cup mixed pitted olives, coarsely cut into ¼-inch pieces

1 small tomato, halved, seeded, and cut into ½-inch pieces (½ cup)

2 tablespoons olive oil

1 tablespoon chopped fresh parsley

4 skinless snapper fillets (about 6 ounces each)

1 tablespoon olive oil

¾ teaspoon salt

I LIKE TO GRILL THICK FILLETS OF SNAPPER cut from the back, as opposed to the belly. Adjust the grilling time if your fillets are thinner or thicker, or if you like your fish well-cooked instead of medium-rare, as we prefer it.

The topping is made with an array of pitted olives that I get at my supermarket—kalamata, green, oil-cured black, spicy green—the more the better.

||||||||||||||||||||||||||||||||||||||||||||||||||||||

Preheat the oven to 145 degrees for warming the plates and resting the grilled fish, which always seems to improve its texture. *(The fish can be cooked up to 20 minutes ahead and kept warm in the oven.)*

Heat a grill to high.

FOR THE TOPPING: Mix all the ingredients together. Set aside.

Pat the fish dry with paper towels and rub on both sides with the oil. Sprinkle with the salt.

Place the fish on the hot grill and cook for about 3 minutes on each side for medium-rare, or longer if you like your fish well cooked. Transfer the fish to a platter and let rest in the oven for up to 20 minutes, until ready to serve.

Serve on warm plates, sprinkled with the olive topping.

Poached Grouper with Black Bean Sauce

SERVES 4

THIS MEXICAN-INSPIRED DISH IS MADE WITH grouper, a firm-fleshed white fish called meru *in Spanish; you can substitute black sea bass or striped bass. I first sauté diced jicama—that wonderful, crunchy vegetable we use raw in salads—in olive oil with poblano chili peppers, tomato, and wine, then stew the fish in that mixture.*

||||||||||||||||||||||||||||||||||||||||||||

Pour the oil into a large stainless steel saucepan or skillet, add the wine, poblano, scallions, tomatoes, jicama, and salt and pepper to taste, and boil for 2 minutes over high heat. Arrange the fish fillets on top, salt lightly, cover, and bring to a boil. Reduce the heat and simmer for 3 to 4 minutes.

MEANWHILE, FOR THE SAUCE: Put the beans, with their liquid, into a food processor or blender and add the olive oil, cilantro sprigs, and a dash each of salt and pepper. Process or blend until pureed.

When the fish is cooked, using a slotted spatula, transfer the fillets and all the solids to a platter. If you have more than ¼ cup cooking liquid, reduce it as necessary. Add to the pureed black beans, then transfer the sauce to a saucepan and heat, stirring, until hot.

Divide the sauce among four dinner plates and place the cooked fish on top. Spoon the cooked vegetables on top of the fillets, garnish with cilantro, and serve.

1 tablespoon olive oil

¼ cup dry white wine

3 tablespoons diced (½-inch) poblano pepper

3 tablespoons sliced (½-inch) scallions

1 cup diced (1-inch) tomatoes

1½ cups diced (½-inch) peeled jicama

Salt and freshly ground black pepper

4 skinless grouper, striped bass, or black sea bass fillets (5 to 6 ounces each and about 1 inch thick)

SAUCE

¾ cup cooked or canned black beans, with their liquid

1½ tablespoons olive oil

2 fresh cilantro sprigs

Salt and freshly ground black pepper

Fresh cilantro leaves, for garnish

Flounder with Lemon Butter

SERVES 4

⅓ cup all-purpose flour

1 large egg, beaten

2 tablespoons peanut oil

4 flounder fillets (about
5 ounces each)

¾ teaspoon salt

¾ teaspoon freshly ground
black pepper

2 tablespoons unsalted butter

2 tablespoons fresh lemon
juice

2 tablespoons chopped fresh
chives

ONE OF THE MOST DELICATE OF THE FLATFISH family is the flounder. It is plentiful during the spring and summer and its soft, buttery flesh is good sautéed, poached, or broiled. Make sure to pat the fillets dry with paper towels so they won't be coated with too much flour. The dish is finished with hot lemon butter and chives.

||||||||||||||||||||||||||||||||||||||||||||||||

Spread the flour on a plate and the beaten egg on another plate. Heat the oil in one very large (at least 12-inch) nonstick skillet or two smaller nonstick skillets over high heat.

Meanwhile, pat the fillets dry with paper towels and sprinkle with the salt and pepper. Dip the fillets lightly in the flour to coat them on both sides, tap off any excess flour, then dip in the beaten egg, coating them on both sides, and arrange side by side in the skillet(s). Cook the fillets for about 1½ minutes, then turn them over with a large spatula and cook them for 1½ minutes on the other side.

Transfer the fillets to four hot plates. Add the butter to the large skillet or one of the smaller skillets and when it has melted and is hot, add the lemon juice. Shake the pan to combine the ingredients, and pour the sauce over the fish. Sprinkle with the chives and serve.

Cod in Light Cream Sauce

SERVES 4

WHEN IT IS REALLY FRESH, COD IS BEST SIM- ply poached in salted water and served with the sauce on the side. To get the true taste of the fish, salted water is a better medium than stock with wine and aromatic vegetables. Here the sauce is made with lightly whipped cream, salt, pepper, and red wine vinegar and finished with a bit of mayonnaise to stabilize it and prevent it from melting when spooned over the hot fish.

|||||||||||||||||||||||||||||||||||||||||||||||

FOR THE SAUCE: Using a whisk, beat the cream gently in a small bowl for 20 to 30 seconds, just until it starts to get frothy. Add the salt, pepper, and vinegar and stir briefly; the cream will thicken. Mix in the mayonnaise and chives and refrigerate until ready to serve.

In a deep skillet, combine 4 cups water with the salt and bring to a boil over high heat. Lower the fish into the water and bring the water back to a boil (this will probably take about 2 minutes). Reduce the heat and cook the fish at a very gentle boil for about 2 minutes (for slightly undercooked fillets), or longer if you prefer your fish more cooked.

Using a skimmer, lift the fish from the water, blot gently with paper towels, and place a fillet on each of four hot plates. Sprinkle with a few grains of fleur de sel and serve immediately, with the sauce.

SAUCE

½ cup heavy cream

¼ teaspoon salt

¼ teaspoon freshly ground
    black pepper

1 tablespoon red wine vinegar

¼ cup mayonnaise

2 tablespoons chopped fresh
    chives

1 teaspoon salt

4 skinless cod fillets,
    preferably back fillets
    (about 6 ounces each and
    ¾ inch thick)

Fleur de sel

Grilled Bacalao (Salt Cod) Steaks with Olive Sauce

SERVES 4

One 1¼-pound center-cut salt cod fillet (1½ inches thick)

4 teaspoons olive oil

SAUCE

½ cup mixed pitted olives (black, green, kalamata, etc.), cut into ½-inch pieces

¾ cup diced (¼-inch) tomatoes

2 tablespoons olive oil

¾ teaspoon freshly ground black pepper

2 tablespoons fresh thyme leaves (I use lemon thyme from my garden)

Salt (optional)

I HAVE ENJOYED GRILLED BACALAO, OR SALTED codfish, steaks in Portuguese restaurants, but it can only be done properly when you can get a very thick fillet of salt cod. I cut steaks about 1½ inches thick from the thick center of the fillet to grill and use the thinner belly or tail portions in stews or brandade. Thick salt cod has to be soaked for 48 hours to desalt it and the water changed three or four times along the way. It is always difficult to know for sure if the fish is de-salted enough; I tend to soak it for a longer time rather than not enough, as salt can always be added to the recipe you are making. To test it, make a small incision in the thicker part of the fish with the blade of a knife and taste it to be certain that it is desalted enough. About 1¼ pounds thick center-cut salt cod will weigh about 1½ pounds after soaking and can be cut into 4 steaks of about 6 ounces each. When the fish is rehydrated, it will feel soft but never as soft as fresh cod; it has an intense taste that we love.

|||||||||||||||||||||||||||||||||||||||||||||||

Desalt the salt cod by soaking it in plenty of cold water in the refrigerator for 48 hours, changing the water at least 2 to 3 times per day.

When ready to cook, heat a grill until very hot and preheat the oven to 175 degrees.

Drain the codfish and pat dry with paper towels. Cut into 4 equal steaks and coat each steak with 1 teaspoon of the olive oil. Place on the hot grill and cook for about 10 minutes, turning once, until well marked.

Transfer the cod to a baking sheet and place in the oven to finish cooking and rest, 10 to 20 minutes. The fish should be flaky but still a bit underdone inside.

MEANWHILE, FOR THE SAUCE: Mix together the olives, tomatoes, olive oil, and pepper.

To serve, place a steak on each of four warm plates. Coat with the sauce and sprinkle on the fresh thyme. Taste and season before serving if necessary.

Broiled Salmon with Miso Glaze

SERVES 4

I HAVE BOTH BAKED AND GRILLED MISO-GLAZED salmon, but I find that broiling it gives a great result and is also the easiest way to cook it. I make the marinade with red miso paste, maple syrup, soy sauce, hot chili sauce, and rice vinegar. The salmon can be marinated for as long as overnight.

Miso paste has a deep taste, and the maple syrup, soy, and vinegar give it great complexity. Extra miso glaze can be served with the cooked fish, if you like. Miso keeps forever in the refrigerator and can be used in salad dressings or with poultry or fish.

|||||||||||||||||||||||||||||||||||||||||||||||||

FOR THE MARINADE: Mix all the ingredients together until smooth.

Line a baking sheet with aluminum foil, preferably non stick. Put the salmon on a plate and, using a spoon, spread the marinade all over the fillets. Place the fillets on the lined baking sheet, cover, and refrigerate for at least 1 hour, and up to overnight.

At cooking time, position an oven rack so it is 5 to 6 inches from the broiler and preheat the broiler. Place the pan of salmon on the rack and broil for about 4 minutes, until the salmon is nicely browned but still pink inside.

Serve the salmon on warm plates, drizzling any juices over it.

MARINADE

2 tablespoons red miso paste

1 tablespoon maple syrup

2 teaspoons tamari or dark soy sauce

2 teaspoons rice vinegar

1 teaspoon hot chili sauce, such as Sriracha

4 skinless salmon fillets (about 6 ounces each and about 1¼ inches thick)

Salmon Fillets Poached in Oil with Pimiento and Tomato Sauce

SERVES 4

4 boneless, skinless salmon
    fillets (about 6 ounces each)

½ teaspoon salt

½ cup peanut oil, or as needed

½ cup olive oil, or as needed

SAUCE

½ cup pimientos, cut into
    ½-inch pieces

½ cup sun-dried tomatoes in
    oil, cut into ½-inch pieces

1 cup water

¼ teaspoon salt

⅛ teaspoon Tabasco sauce

1 tablespoon unsalted butter

1 tablespoon chopped fresh
    chives

POACHING FISH IN OIL KEEPS IT VERY MOIST and tender. The secret is to fit the fillets snugly into a saucepan to minimize the oil required to cover them. The oil is brought to a low temperature (180 to 190 degrees) and the fish cooks in the warm oil in minutes. The fish absorbs very little of the oil, and you will have about the same amount of oil after cooking. It can be strained and reused.

The sauce, made of pimientos and sun-dried tomatoes in oil from the supermarket deli counter, is a cinch to put together.

Sprinkle the salmon fillets on both sides with the salt and put them in a saucepan that holds them snugly. Pour the oil over them. It should cover the salmon; if it doesn't, add a little more. Heat the oil to 180 to 190 degrees (it will start to boil) and then turn the fish over with a fork. The outside of the fish will turn white. Cover and set aside.

FOR THE SAUCE: Put the pimientos, tomatoes, water, salt, and Tabasco in a blender and process until smooth. (You will have about 1¼ cups.) Transfer to a microwavable bowl or a saucepan, drop in the butter, and heat in the microwave oven or on top of the stove until warmed through. Stir in the butter until the butter has completely melted.

Drain the fish. Divide the sauce among four warmed plates and place the fish on top. Sprinkle with the chives and serve.

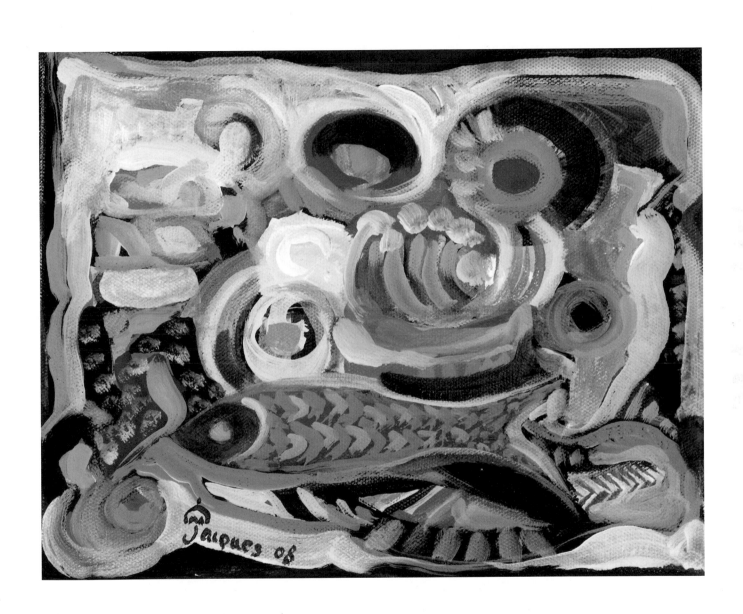

Salmon Scaloppine with Sorrel Sauce

SERVES 4

About 2 ounces sorrel leaves
(3 loosely packed cups)

½ cup heavy cream

½ teaspoon salt

½ teaspoon freshly ground
black pepper

8 (skinless, boneless) salmon
scaloppine (about 3 ounces
each and ½ inch thick),
cleaned of all sinew

I USE SORREL FROM MY GARDEN IN THIS CLASsic recipe. The acidity of the herb cuts the richness of the sauce and the salmon. Sorrel, which cooks very quickly and becomes very soft, always turns a brownish color. A less astringent version of this dish can be made with a chiffonade of spinach instead of sorrel.

Remove any stems from the larger sorrel leaves. Gather the leaves into a bundle and slice them crosswise into 2-inch-wide pieces.

Combine the sorrel, cream, and ¼ teaspoon each of the salt and pepper in a 12-inch nonstick skillet (use two smaller skillets if you don't have a large one). Bring to a boil, stirring occasionally, and boil for about 30 seconds, until the sorrel "melts" into a soft puree. Transfer the mixture to a bowl and keep warm.

Clean the skillet with a paper towel and heat it for about 1 minute. When it is hot, add the salmon scaloppine in one layer, sprinkle with the remaining ¼ teaspoon each salt and pepper, and cook for 30 to 45 seconds on each side; the salmon should still be rare in the center.

Arrange 2 scaloppine on each of four warm plates. Coat with the sorrel sauce and serve immediately.

Red Snapper with Two Sauces

SERVES 4

FOR THIS DISH, SMALL FILLETS OF RED SNAP-per are sautéed skin side down, covered, for just a couple of minutes and served with two fresh tomato sauces, one red and one yellow. The sauces take almost no time and can be made ahead. To serve, half of each plate is covered with the red sauce and the other half with the yellow sauce, the fillets are placed on top, and a sprinkling of herbs completes the dish.

||||||||||||||||||||||||||||||||||||||||||||||||||

Drop the red tomato pieces into a 4-cup glass measuring cup or a bowl and heat in the microwave oven on high for 1½ to 2 minutes. Add ½ teaspoon each of the salt and pepper and process with an immersion blender or in a regular blender until smooth. Add the butter and process for 10 seconds. Strain through a sieve.

Repeat with the yellow tomatoes, using 1 tablespoon of the oil instead of butter. Set the sauces aside.

At serving time, cut two or three slits in the skin of each snapper fillet. Heat the 1 remaining tablespoon oil in a large nonstick skillet over high heat. When it is hot, place the fillets skin side down in the pan and sprinkle them with the remaining ½ teaspoon each salt and pepper. Cook, covered, for about 3 minutes, without turning. (Because the pan is covered, the fish will cook on top as well; it should be slightly undercooked.)

Cover half of each of four hot plates with red tomato sauce and half with yellow tomato sauce. Place a fillet skin side up in the middle of each plate, sprinkle with the chives, and serve immediately.

2 cups diced (1-inch) red tomatoes

1½ teaspoons salt

1½ teaspoons freshly ground black pepper

1 tablespoon unsalted butter

2 cups diced (1-inch) yellow tomatoes

2 tablespoons walnut or olive oil

4 skin-on red snapper fillets (5 to 6 ounces each)

2 tablespoons chopped fresh chives

Chirashi Sushi

SERVES 4

THIS JAPANESE DISH IS EASIER TO MAKE THAN conventional sushi and strikingly beautiful. Sushi rice is spread on a platter and the fish, shellfish, and vegetables are scattered on top. Then the platter is brought to the table so guests can help themselves.

There are many versions of chirashi. Here I use sea urchin roe (uni), salmon or trout caviar, tuna, salmon, and scallops, along with avocado, scallions, tree ear mushrooms, and toasted sesame seeds. The sushi rice is made ahead, then the whole dish assembled at the last moment and served with wasabi paste and soy sauce.

||||||||||||||||||||||||||||||||||||||||||||||||

FOR THE RICE: Put the rice in a bowl, cover with cold water, and stir for a few seconds, then drain. The water will be cloudy. Repeat several times, until the water runs clear.

Transfer the rice to a saucepan, add the 3½ cups cold water, and bring to a boil, uncovered, stirring a couple of times. Cover, reduce the heat to very low, and cook for 15 minutes. Turn off the heat and let the rice rest, still covered, for 15 minutes.

MEANWHILE, FOR THE VINEGAR SEASONING: Combine the ingredients in a glass bowl and heat in the microwave oven for 1 minute. Stir to make sure that the sugar and salt are dissolved.

After the rice has rested for 15 minutes, spread it out in a

RICE

2½ cups sushi rice

3½ cups cold water

VINEGAR SEASONING

⅓ cup rice vinegar

3 tablespoons mirin (sweet rice wine)

1 tablespoon sugar

1 teaspoon salt

TOPPINGS

2 ounces salmon or trout caviar

2 teaspoons corn or sunflower oil

¼ cup (about ⅓ ounce) dried small tree ear mushrooms, soaked in 1 cup cold water for 20 minutes

8 large tiger shrimp (10 ounces), shelled and cut into 1-inch pieces

One 8-ounce tuna steak, cut into 1-inch cubes

(continued on page 176)

(continued from page 175)

One 8-ounce skinless salmon fillet, cut into 1-inch cubes

8 ounces tiny bay scallops, or 8 ounces large sea scallops, cut into ¾-inch pieces

4 ounces (about ⅔ cup) sea urchin roe (uni)

¼ cup minced scallions

1 large avocado, halved, pitted, peeled, cut into 1-inch cubes (1½ cups), and sprinkled with 1 tablespoon fresh lemon juice to prevent discoloration

3 tablespoons toasted sesame seeds

A few fennel sprigs, for decoration

WASABI PASTE

¼ cup wasabi powder

3 tablespoons water

Soy sauce, for serving

large gratin or other baking dish. Pour the vinegar seasoning over the top and mix it in gently. Cover until ready to serve. (The rice is served at room temperature.)

FOR THE TOPPINGS: Mix the salmon or trout caviar with the corn oil in a small bowl, so it is loose and will be easy to sprinkle on the dish.

Drain the tree ear mushrooms and place them in a saucepan. Cover with 2 cups water and bring to a boil, then boil gently for 15 minutes; drain. (The mushroom cooking liquid can be kept for soup.)

Combine the shrimp pieces with ½ cup hot water in a skillet and cook for 45 seconds to 1 minute; the water will barely come to a boil, so the shrimp will still be somewhat translucent in the center. Drain and set aside.

FOR THE WASABI PASTE: Mix the wasabi powder with the water in a small bowl, stirring to create a paste. Let sit for at least 15 minutes.

At serving time, spread the rice on a serving platter so that it is 1 to 1½ inches deep. Scatter the shrimp, tuna, salmon, scallops, uni, and caviar over the top, along with the scallions, avocado, and tree ear mushrooms. Sprinkle the sesame seeds and fennel sprigs on top and serve with the wasabi and soy sauce.

A Recipe Is Born

PEOPLE OFTEN WONDER HOW RECIPES ARE CREATED. In my case, there is no single answer. I can be inspired by something I saw in a magazine or encountered in a market. Often it is a dish I've eaten in a restaurant or at a friend's or while traveling abroad. Something plants a fragmentary idea that I begin to explore mentally, tasting it in my mind as I progress. How would it be if I paired it with this? What if I substituted that? How about putting an Asian or African spin on it?

When I cooked at an event in California's Napa Valley, one of my fellow chefs, who was Japanese, prepared *chirashi sushi*—a large tray of sushi rice with pieces of raw fish arranged on top of it, rather than the bite-size pieces of sushi familiar to most diners. It struck me as a great dish, big enough for gatherings of sushi devotees but nowhere near as nitpicky as fashioning individual pieces for each guest. Gloria loves sushi, so I decided I would do a take on *chirashi* when I got home.

The preparation I tasted in Napa was topped with tuna and uni (sea urchin roe). My mind began to churn. The nice thing about the early stages of a recipe is that there are no constrictions: I am free to do anything I want. The uni was definitely going to stay, as it's one of Gloria's favorites. She has a weakness for salmon too, so I envisioned pink cubes of salmon and bright-red cubes of tuna on top of the rice. As I thought about tastes, I decided that salmon caviar would bring something more than the raw salmon alone and would give the sushi an attractive color contrast. In the same vein, I thought the dish would be improved by the addition of a small dice of avocado. And tree ear mushrooms. Why? Because I love their taste and figured that they would add a delightful crunch and great color to the sushi. Serendipity landed one final ingredient on the version I served Gloria: When I opened the refrigerator, I saw that she had bought a beautiful bunch of scallions. I sliced a few and sprinkled them on top. If it had been a bunch of fresh cilantro in the fridge rather than scallions, that probably would have topped the sushi instead.

When I'm formulating a recipe, taste trumps texture and color in every case. But once I have the taste I want nailed, I allow my visual sense to step in. In my mind, I saw the orange-red of the caviar and the blood red of the tuna, the black of the tree ear, and the vibrant green of the scallions. Visually stunning and great tasting. I'd hit the bull's-eye.

But even before I got my take on chirashi to the table, my mind was wandering, considering other possibilities. If I hadn't been able to find uni, fine. I could have done without it and produced something not the same but still delectable. No salmon caviar? What about beautiful ultrafresh mackerel, or eel, or flounder? Then I thought, I could do a similar dish using cooked meat instead of fish. Or I could sauté cubes of chicken with a lot of onion and mushrooms. Maybe put some sliced hard-cooked eggs on top.

At some point, the recipe I had encountered stopped being the Japanese chef's and became mine. I owned it, and I could do whatever I wanted. And that's what I always hope readers will do with the recipes I write down and put into my books. Try them exactly as written once or twice, until you understand the basic principles, then let your taste buds—and the contents of your refrigerator—take them in directions that are all your own. Eventually you may forget where you got the idea for *your* special dish. I won't object a bit—rather, I will feel flattered.

Shrimp Burgers on Zucchini

SERVES 4

I HAD A DISH SIMILAR TO THIS IN A SMALL restaurant in Mexico, and at Gloria's request, I created my own version at home. I use medium-size raw shrimp and puree the tails in a food processor, then combine the puree with pieces of the shrimp to form thick burgers.

|||||||||||||||||||||||||||||||||||||||||||||||||||||

Cut the shrimp crosswise in half. Process the tail pieces into a puree in a food processor and transfer to a bowl.

Cut the remaining shrimp into ½-inch pieces and add them to the bowl. Add the chives and mix well. Divide the mixture into 4 equal parts and form each one into a burger about 1 inch thick. *(These can be made a few hours ahead and refrigerated.)*

When ready to cook, heat the oil in a large skillet. Add the zucchini with ¼ teaspoon each of the salt and pepper and sauté over high heat for 4 to 5 minutes.

Meanwhile, melt the butter in another large skillet with a lid. Sprinkle the remaining ¼ teaspoon each salt and pepper on the shrimp patties and place them carefully in the hot butter. Cook for about 1½ minutes over high heat, then gently turn the burgers over. Cover, reduce the heat to medium, and cook for 2 to 2½ minutes, until the burgers are barely cooked through.

Arrange the zucchini on four warm plates. Place the shrimp burgers on top, sprinkle with the chives, and serve.

1¼ pounds shelled and deveined medium shrimp

3 tablespoons chopped fresh chives

2 tablespoons olive oil

2 firm zucchini (about 1 pound), cut into ⅜-inch slices (about 3½ cups)

½ teaspoon salt

½ teaspoon freshly ground black pepper

2 tablespoons unsalted butter

Minced fresh chives

Sautéed Calamari with Tiny Croutons and Hot Peppers

SERVES 4

1 pound cleaned small to medium squid (bodies and tentacles)

2 tablespoons unsalted butter

¼ cup peanut oil

¼ teaspoon salt

¼ teaspoon freshly ground black pepper

½ cup Wondra flour

1 cup diced (½-inch) country-style bread

3 tablespoons chopped fresh parsley

¼ cup chopped onion

1 tablespoon chopped garlic

2 tablespoons diced (½-inch) drained pickled peperoncini or jalapeño peppers

I USE SMALL TO MEDIUM SQUID FOR THIS RECipe. The tiny bread croutons and hot pepper give the dish added texture and taste. Bottled peperoncini or jalapeños in brine are always on hand in my pantry. Preserved in water and vinegar, the mildly hot peperoncini or hot jalapeños are great additions to salads and sandwiches.

||||||||||||||||||||||||||||||||||||||||||||||

Remove the tentacles from the squid and cut the bodies into ¾-inch-wide strips. Dry all the pieces with paper towels.

Heat the butter and oil in a 12-inch skillet (or use two smaller skillets). Meanwhile, sprinkle the squid with the salt and pepper, toss it with the flour, and tap off any excess flour.

Add the squid to the hot skillet(s), along with the bread pieces, and sauté over high heat for 2 minutes. Add the parsley, onion, and garlic and sauté for 1 minute. Add the diced hot peppers and toss for a few seconds.

Serve.

Calamari Stew with Saffron and Cilantro Rice

SERVES 4

1 pound fresh or frozen squid (bodies and tentacles), defrosted if frozen

½ teaspoon saffron threads

4 tablespoons olive oil

1 cup chopped onion

¼ cup diced (½-inch) celery

2 teaspoons chopped garlic

One 14½-ounce can diced tomatoes

¼ teaspoon herbes de Provence

½ teaspoon salt

½ teaspoon freshly ground black pepper

Cilantro Rice (recipe follows)

1 tablespoon chopped fresh chives

THE CALAMARI STEW AND THE SAFFRON RICE go well together, but each could also be served on its own. Saffron (the dried pistils of crocuses) is very expensive but worth it. Make certain that you buy real saffron, the best of which comes from Spain or Iran.

Fresh or frozen calamari can be used in this dish. I often use frozen cilantro in the rice: When I get a bunch of fresh cilantro, I usually use the leaves and freeze the stems. Then, when I need cilantro, I chop the frozen stems, which break easily into small pieces.

||||||||||||||||||||||||||||||||||||||||||||||||

Cut the calamari into 2-inch pieces and wash thoroughly under cool water. Drain and pat dry with paper towels.

Put the calamari in a bowl and sprinkle the saffron on top, crushing it between your index finger and thumb as you add it. Add 2 tablespoons of the olive oil and mix well. Cover and refrigerate until needed. *(This can be done hours ahead.)*

Heat the remaining 2 tablespoons olive oil in a large saucepan. Add the onion, celery, and garlic and sauté for 2 minutes. Add the tomatoes, herbes de Provence, salt, and pepper, bring to a boil, and cook for 5 minutes. Set aside until serving time. *(This can be done a couple of hours ahead.)*

At serving time, add the calamari to the saucepan and bring to a boil, then simmer at just under a boil for 10 minutes.

Divide the rice among four soup plates, making a well in the center of each serving. Spoon the calamari stew into the wells, sprinkle with the chives, and serve.

CILANTRO RICE SERVES 4

Heat the oil in a medium saucepan. Add the onion and cilantro and cook for 1 to 2 minutes. Add the rice and mix well, then add the stock, salt, and pepper and bring to a boil. Stir, cover, reduce the heat to low, and cook the rice for 20 minutes, or until tender. Fluff the rice with a fork and serve.

CILANTRO RICE

1½ tablespoons olive oil

½ cup chopped onion

¼ cup chopped cilantro (see headnote)

1 cup Carolina long-grain white rice

2 cups homemade chicken stock or canned low-sodium chicken broth

¼ teaspoon salt

¼ teaspoon freshly ground black pepper

Octopus Stew with Onions, Paprika, and Wine

SERVES 4

TO PREPARE FRESH OCTOPUS, I FIRST DROP IT into boiling water for a few minutes. The water doesn't even come back to a boil, but this is long enough to stiffen the octopus, which makes it easier to cut. Then, for this stew, I cut it into chunks and cook it with wine, vegetables, and seasonings in a low oven for a couple of hours, until very tender and flavorful. It can be served on rice, couscous, pasta, polenta, or potatoes.

||||||||||||||||||||||||||||||||||||||||||||||||

Bring 10 cups water to a boil in a large saucepan. Drop the whole octopus into the boiling water and stir it around for 3 minutes. (The water will not have returned to a boil.) Transfer the octopus to a plate and let it cool enough so you can handle it.

Remove the beak, if any, from the octopus and discard. Cut the octopus into 2- to 3-inch chunks.

Preheat the oven to 275 degrees.

Heat the oil in a large ovenproof saucepan or a Dutch oven. Add the octopus pieces and salt and cook for 2 minutes. Add the wine and bring to a boil. Cover the pan and place in the oven for 1 hour.

Remove the pan from the oven (leave the oven on) and add the onions, carrots, celery, scallions, garlic, paprika, jalapeño peppers, and tomatoes. Bring to a strong boil on top of the stove, then mix well, cover, and place back in the oven for 1 hour, or until the octopus is very tender.

Sprinkle with the chives and serve.

1 fresh or frozen cleaned octopus (about 2 pounds), defrosted if frozen

3 tablespoons olive oil

1½ teaspoons salt

½ cup dry white wine

1½ cups diced (1-inch) onions

1 cup diced (1-inch) carrots

1 cup diced (1-inch) celery

¾ cup sliced (1-inch) scallions

2 tablespoons coarsely chopped garlic

1 teaspoon Spanish paprika

1 tablespoon chopped jalapeño peppers, or more to taste

1 cup diced (½-inch) fresh or canned tomatoes

2 tablespoons minced fresh chives

Mussels with Cream and Chives on Soft Polenta

SERVES 4

4 pounds medium mussels (about 8 dozen), washed, debearded if necessary

1¼ cups fruity dry white wine

2 tablespoons olive oil

½ cup chopped shallots

2½ cups diced (½-inch) mushrooms (about 6 ounces)

2 tablespoons all-purpose flour

¾ teaspoon salt, or to taste

¾ teaspoon freshly ground black pepper

½ cup heavy cream or sour cream

POLENTA

4 cups water

½ teaspoon salt

1 cup instant polenta

⅓ cup minced fresh chives

SPRING IS THE BEST SEASON FOR MUSSELS IN the Northeast, when they are full, plump, juicy, and tender. I like to serve about 1 pound per person—about 2 dozen medium-size mussels.

The classic way to cook mussels is with white wine, onion, garlic, and parsley. In this recipe, I steam the mussels in wine until they open, then discard the empty half shells and finish the sauce with shallots, mushrooms, cream, and chives. Heavy cream is best, but sour cream also works well for a lighter dish.

|||||||||||||||||||||||||||||||||||||||||||||||||||

Combine the mussels with the wine in a large saucepan, cover, place over high heat, and cook for about 5 minutes, tossing the mussels or stirring with a spoon a couple of times; the mussels should be open at this point.

Let the mussels cool for a few minutes, then remove the empty half shell from each and discard. Put the mussels in the half shells in a dish. You should have about 2 cups mussel cooking liquid; add water if needed.

Heat the oil in a medium saucepan. Add the shallots and mushrooms and cook over medium-high heat for 3 to 4 minutes. Sprinkle the flour on top and mix it in well, then cook for 30 seconds. Add the reserved 2 cups cooking liquid and bring to a boil, stirring occasionally with a whisk until the mixture thickens. Mix in the salt and pepper. Cook for about 2 minutes, then add the cream and bring to a boil. Add salt if necessary and set aside until ready to serve.

FOR THE POLENTA: Bring the water and salt to a boil in a medium saucepan. Sprinkle the polenta into the water, stirring it in vigorously with a whisk. Bring to a boil and cook, stirring often, for about 3 minutes over medium heat, until thick and creamy. (*Note:* If it is prepared ahead, the polenta will thicken; add water when reheating to bring it to the desired creamy consistency.)

Meanwhile, combine the mussels with the sauce and bring to a boil. Simmer for 1 minute.

Serve the mussels, sprinkled with the chives, over the polenta or with the polenta on the side.

Mussel and Clam Stew

SERVES 4

¼ cup olive oil

1 cup coarsely chopped onion

½ cup coarsely minced
    scallions (about 4)

¼ cup sliced garlic (about
    8 cloves)

1½ tablespoons all-purpose
    flour

1 cup fruity dry white wine

½ teaspoon salt

1 teaspoon freshly ground
    black pepper

2 pounds littleneck clams
    (about 2 dozen), washed

2 pounds medium mussels
    (about 5 dozen), washed,
    debearded if necessary

French bread, for serving

MUSSELS AND CLAMS COMPLEMENT EACH OTHER in this lusty stew. The secret to this congenial mixture is frying the garlic, onions, and scallions in olive oil just long enough so that they are lightly browned but not burnt—this gives vigor to the finished dish. A bit of flour lends viscosity to the sauce, which you will want to mop up with French bread.

Heat the olive oil in a large saucepan. Add the onion, scallions, and garlic and cook over high heat, stirring occasionally, for about 7 minutes, or until the vegetables are lightly browned.

Sprinkle the flour on top and mix it in well, then stir in the wine, salt, and pepper. Add the clams and mussels and mix well. Bring to a boil, then mix well, cover, and cook, stirring occasionally, until all the clams and mussels have opened, about 8 minutes.

Mix well again and serve in soup plates, with plenty of bread to soak up the sauce.

The Seaweed Solution

I SPENT MY EARLY CAREER IN LANDLOCKED KITCHENS in southeastern France and Paris, but even in the days of rudimentary refrigeration and slow transportation, we always had fresh oysters and clams. They arrived from the coast packed in wooden boxes, sandwiched between layers of moist seaweed, and were always clean and fresh.

I still use that trick. I find seaweed on the rocky beach in my town, or I substitute layers of moistened paper towels or even newspaper for it.

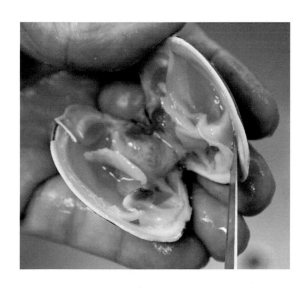

We live near Long Island Sound, so I buy my shellfish directly from the purveyors, typically in lots of a hundred or more. Packed between layers of seaweed and kept in the refrigerator or on the porch during the cool months, they survive quite nicely for a couple of weeks, ready and waiting for us to enjoy a dozen on the half-shell any evening before dinner, should the whim strike us.

Steamers in Hot Broth

SERVES 4

4 pounds steamers (about
   5 dozen)

¾ cup chopped onion

1 tablespoon chopped garlic

1 cup dry white wine

2 teaspoons Sriracha or other
   hot chili sauce

3 tablespoons olive oil

3 tablespoons chopped fresh
   parsley

Thick slices crusty bread, for
   serving

*STEAMER CLAMS ARE PLENTIFUL AND INEXPEN-
sive along the New England coast in summer. My wife introduced me to this dish when we first met. The clams have
long necks sticking out of their shells, and when the shells are
pressed together, the necks squirt water and sand. As a result,
they are sometimes called "piss clams" by locals; they are
also known as soft-shell or long neck clams. During cooking,
they produce a flavorful broth that is then consumed with the
clams.*

*Steamers are sandy and should be washed several times in
clean water while rubbing them against one another to remove as much mud and sand as possible. To eat, remove the
cooked clams from the shells and, using your fingers, pull off
and discard the black skin from the neck, the best part of the
clam; the skin should slide off easily.*

Drop the clams into a bowl of cold water and rub them
together to clean the mud and sand from the shells. Repeat this process 2 or 3 times, or until the water remains clear.

Drain off the water and put the clams in a large saucepan
with all the remaining ingredients except the parsley (and
bread). Cover and bring to a boil over high heat (this will take
4 to 5 minutes). Stir the clams and cook for another 4 minutes
or so, stirring occasionally, until all the clams have opened.

Spoon into soup bowls with the broth, sprinkle with the
parsley, and serve with crusty bread. Guests can remove
the clams from their shells and pull off the black skin from
the neck to enjoy it with the hot broth.

Poultry and Meat

Poussins (or Cornish Hens) à la Russe

SERVES 4

2 poussins or Cornish hens
(about 1½ pounds each)

2 teaspoons paprika,
preferably Spanish

1 teaspoon salt

1 teaspoon ground cumin

1 teaspoon cayenne pepper

1 tablespoon olive oil

1 tablespoon chopped fresh
chives

POUSSINS, BABY CHICKENS WEIGHING ABOUT 1½ pounds each, are very similar to Cornish hens. Juicy and tender, they can be roasted whole, stewed, or grilled. If poussins are not available, use Cornish hens of about the same weight. I prepare the birds à la Russe, or in the Russian style: The poussins are halved and cooked mostly skin side down in a skillet with a weight on top to make them very crusty outside while remaining juicy inside. I use two bricks wrapped in aluminum foil as weights; you can place a skillet with a weight inside it on top of the birds to get the same result.

||||||||||||||||||||||||||||||||||||||||||||||||

Cut the poussins (or Cornish hens) lengthwise in half and press on the halves with your hands to flatten them. Make an incision about ½ inch deep at the junction of the thighs and drumsticks to help the birds cook more evenly.

Mix together the paprika, salt, cumin, and cayenne and spread onto the skin and inside the halved poussins.

Heat the olive oil in a saucepan large enough to hold the 4 halves without overlapping. When the oil is hot, arrange the chicken halves skin side up in the pan and cook over medium-high heat, uncovered, for about 8 minutes.

Turn the halves skin side down and place two foil-wrapped bricks (or a heavy skillet with a weight in it) on top to press down on the meat. Cook over medium-low heat for about 20 minutes, or until the chicken skin is crusty and dark brown and the meat is cooked through.

Serve with the natural juices and a sprinkling of the chives.

Poulet à la Crème

SERVES 4

CHICKEN IN CREAM SAUCE IS A SPECIALTY OF *the town where I was born, Bourg-en-Bresse. My mother's simple recipe included a whole cut-up chicken with water, a dash of flour, and a bit of cream to finish. I have added white wine and mushrooms to make the dish a bit more sophisticated, and used chicken thighs, which are the best part of the chicken (1½ thighs per person should be a generous serving for a main course). A sprinkling of chopped tarragon at the end makes it more special, but it is optional. I am not sure my mother would approve of my changes, but this is easy, fast, and good. Most of the time, my mother served hers with rice pilaf.*

|||||||||||||||||||||||||||||||||||||||||||||||||||||

Melt the butter in a large saucepan. Add the chicken thighs to the pan in one layer and brown over high heat for about 2½ minutes on each side.

Add the mushrooms to the pan and sprinkle on the flour. Turn the chicken pieces with tongs so the flour is dispersed evenly. Stir in the wine and water and mix well. Bring to a boil and add the salt and pepper. Cover, reduce the heat, and cook gently for 25 minutes.

Add the cream, bring to a boil, and boil, uncovered, for about 1 minute.

Serve sprinkled with the chopped tarragon, if desired.

2 tablespoons unsalted butter

6 chicken thighs (about 3 pounds), skin removed (about 2½ pounds skinned)

8 mushrooms (about 6 ounces), washed and sliced

1½ tablespoons all-purpose flour

½ cup dry white wine

¼ cup water

¾ teaspoon salt

¾ teaspoon freshly ground black pepper

½ cup heavy cream

1 tablespoon coarsely chopped fresh tarragon (optional)

Grilled Chicken Tenders with Chimichurri

SERVES 4

1¼ pounds chicken tenders (about 16)

½ teaspoon salt

1 tablespoon olive oil

CHIMICHURRI SAUCE

½ cup coarsely chopped fresh cilantro

⅓ cup minced scallions

1 tablespoon chopped garlic

½ cup julienned radishes

1 teaspoon dried oregano, preferably Mexican

½ teaspoon hot pepper flakes

½ teaspoon salt

2 tablespoons fresh lime juice

⅓ cup olive oil

CHIMICHURRI SAUCE, ORIGINALLY FROM ARGENtina, is a finely chopped mixture of garlic, parsley, oil, and vinegar, usually served with beefsteak. In Mexico, it is made with cilantro and lime juice, and my version contains cilantro, scallions, radishes, and Mexican oregano. If chicken tenders are not available, cut up boneless, skinless chicken breasts for this recipe.

||||||||||||||||||||||||||||||||||||||||||||||

Preheat the oven to 140 degrees. Heat a grill to hot (or heat a nonstick skillet until very hot).

Put the tenders in a bowl, sprinkle with the salt and oil, and stir until well coated.

Arrange the chicken tenders on the hot grill (or in the hot skillet) and cook for about 1½ minutes. Turn and cook for 1 minute on the other side, until just cooked through. Transfer to a platter and keep warm in the oven while you prepare the sauce.

FOR THE CHIMICHURRI SAUCE: Mix all the ingredients together in a bowl.

Serve the chicken coated with the sauce.

Chicken Jardinière

SERVES 4

2½ ounces lean pancetta, cut into lardons (strips about 1 inch long and ½ inch thick)

1½ tablespoons peanut oil

4 chicken legs (about 2¾ pounds), left whole or cut into 2 pieces each, ends of the drumsticks and skin removed (about 2¼ pounds trimmed)

MY MOTHER MADE THIS TYPE OF STEW FROM the carcass of a raw chicken and its gizzards; I use pancetta instead of gizzards for additional flavor and chicken legs, which stay moist during the cooking. Jardinière means "gardener" in French, and the vegetables change according to what is in season or in my garden. The stew is easy to put together, and it gets better every time you reheat it.

||||||||||||||||||||||||||||||||||||||||||||||||||

Sauté the lardons in the oil in a large saucepan or a Dutch oven (the pan should be wide enough to hold the chicken

in a single layer) over high heat for 2 minutes. Add the chicken pieces and sauté them, turning once, for about 8 minutes, until lightly browned. Sprinkle with the flour, salt, and pepper and move the chicken around to distribute the flour evenly. Cook for 1 minute, then add the wine and water and mix well.

Add the potatoes, mushrooms, onions, carrots, garlic, and thyme and mix well. Bring to a full boil, making sure that the stew is boiling throughout, then cover, reduce the heat to low, and cook for 45 minutes. *(The stew can be prepared ahead to this point and reheated to serve.)*

At serving time, add the peas to the stew, bring to a boil, and boil for 2 minutes.

Transfer the stew to individual plates or a large platter, sprinkle with the parsley, and serve.

1½ tablespoons all-purpose flour

1 teaspoon salt

1 teaspoon freshly ground black pepper

¾ cup fruity dry white wine

¾ cup water

12 small red potatoes (about 8 ounces), peeled

8 small baby bella or cremini mushrooms (about 5 ounces), washed

12 small pearl onions (about 4 ounces)

1¼ cups diced (1-inch) carrots

1½ tablespoons coarsely chopped garlic

1 fresh thyme branch

1 cup frozen baby peas

2 tablespoons chopped fresh parsley

Chicken with Chili Sauce and Achiote Rice

SERVES 4

3 dried mulato or ancho chili peppers

2 chayote (about 12 ounces each)

4 chicken thighs (about 1½ pounds)

1 cup coarsely chopped onion

½ cup coarsely chopped scallions

¼ cup diced (½-inch) chorizo sausage (Mexican, Spanish, or domestic)

1 tablespoon coarsely chopped garlic

1 teaspoon dried oregano, preferably Mexican

1¼ cup diced (1-inch) tomatoes

¼ cup dry white wine

Salt

Achiote Rice (recipe follows)

CHICKEN THIGHS ARE COMBINED WITH DRIED mulato or ancho peppers, scallions, chorizo sausage, and Mexican oregano and garnished with chayote, sometimes called squash pears or mirliton. The thighs are served on a bed of rice mixed with onions sautéed in some of the chicken fat and flavored with achiote (also called annatto) paste.

||||||||||||||||||||||||||||||||||||||||||||||

Soak the chili peppers in water to cover for about 1½ hours.

Remove the chilies from the soaking liquid; reserve ½ cup of the liquid. Break the peppers open, discard the stems and seeds, and chop the peppers very coarsely. (You should have about ¾ cup.)

Peel the chayote, cut it in half, and remove and discard the seeds. Cut each chayote half into 4 wedges.

Arrange the chicken thighs skin side down in a large non-stick skillet and cook, partially covered, over medium-high heat for about 15 minutes, until nicely browned. Remove all but about 2 tablespoons of the fat from the pan; reserve the 2 tablespoons fat for the rice.

Turn the chicken so the browned skin side is up, scatter the onion, scallions, chorizo, and garlic around the chicken, and cook for 3 minutes. Add the oregano, tomatoes, wine, chopped chilies, reserved soaking liquid, and chayote. Season with salt to taste, cover, and boil gently for 10 minutes.

Serve the chicken with the rice on the side, or serve the rice

1 cup very coarsely chopped
onion

2 tablespoons chicken fat
(reserved from Chicken
with Chili Sauce)

2 teaspoons achiote (annatto)
paste

2 cups water

1 cup short-grain white rice
(or another rice of your
choosing)

½ teaspoon salt

as a base under the chicken, placing a chicken thigh on top of each portion of rice, and arrange the chayote wedges around the chicken. Spoon on the sauce and serve.

|||||||||||||||||||||||||||||||||||||||||||||||

ACHIOTE RICE SERVES 4

|||||||||||||||||||||||||||||||||||||||||||||||

Cook the onion in the chicken fat in a saucepan over low heat for 3 to 4 minutes. Mix the achiote paste well with the water to dissolve, then add to the onion, along with the rice and salt, and stir well. Bring to a boil, cover, reduce the heat, and cook gently for 20 minutes, or until the rice is tender. Serve.

Chicken and Rice with Cumin and Cilantro

SERVES 6 TO 8

CHICKEN WITH RICE, OR ARROZ CON POLLO, *IS a staple at our house. We like it best when it is made with chicken wings. In this version, the dish is highly seasoned with cumin, ginger, garlic, and a great deal of cilantro. Whole chicken wings have three sections. If you buy whole wings, remove the tips and save them for stock; cut the remaining sections apart so you have two meaty pieces. In my market, I can usually buy my wings already trimmed and cut into pieces.*

|||||||||||||||||||||||||||||||||||||||||||||||||||

Heat the olive oil in a 12- to 14-inch skillet or a pot large enough to hold the chicken wings in one layer. Dry the wings with paper towels, place them in the hot oil, and brown over high heat, uncovered, for about 8 minutes. Turn the wings over with tongs and brown them on the other side for 8 minutes. Using the tongs, transfer the browned wings to a bowl.

Add the onions, garlic, and ginger to the drippings in the skillet and cook for 2 to 3 minutes. Add the rice and cumin and mix well, then add the tomatoes, salt, Sriracha, water, and chopped cilantro stems and mix well.

Return the wings to the pan and bring to a strong boil. Cover, reduce the heat to low, and cook for about 30 minutes, until the wings are cooked through.

Serve the stew garnished with the chopped cilantro, if desired.

2 tablespoons olive oil

3 pounds chicken wings (about 20), tips (if any) removed, remaining sections separated into 2 pieces each

2½ cups coarsely chopped onions

¼ cup coarsely chopped garlic

¼ cup coarsely chopped peeled ginger

2 cups (about 13 ounces) Carolina long-grain white rice

1½ tablespoons ground cumin

One 14½-ounce can diced tomatoes

2½ teaspoons salt

1 tablespoon Sriracha or other hot chili sauce

2½ cups water

1½ cups chopped fresh cilantro stems, plus (optional) ½ cup chopped fresh cilantro for garnish

Sautéed Duck Breast with Arugula Salad and Cracklings

SERVES 4

CRACKLINGS

4 boneless duck breasts
(about 6 ounces each)

¼ teaspoon salt

SALAD

½ teaspoon finely chopped
garlic

¼ teaspoon salt

½ teaspoon freshly ground
black pepper

1½ tablespoons red wine
vinegar

1½ tablespoons extra-virgin
olive oil

1½ tablespoons toasted
sesame or hazelnut oil

DUCK

2 tablespoons unsalted butter

¼ teaspoon salt

¼ teaspoon freshly ground
black pepper

¼ cup dry red wine

2 tablespoons water

AT THE BEGINNING OF MY CAREER, AND FOR many years afterward, there were only a couple of ways of cooking duck: roasted whole or in a stew. In the 1970s, nouvelle cuisine brought us boneless breast of duck sautéed or grilled and served rare, with or without a sauce. Conventionally, the skin is scored and the breast is sautéed skin side down until a great deal of fat is rendered and the skin is richly browned and caramelized. The meat will be rare and juicy, but the skin will still be quite fatty and somewhat soft inside, and most people leave it on their plates. In my version of this dish, I remove the skin from the breasts, cut it into ¾-inch pieces, and cook it into crispy cracklings. You can do this step ahead and enjoy the extra cracklings with your aperitifs. (The fat rendered when cooking the skin is delicious in pâtés, or use it for sautéing potatoes.)

Then the duck breasts are sautéed at the last moment and served with an arugula salad sprinkled with the cracklings.

||||||||||||||||||||||||||||||||||||||||||||||||

FOR THE CRACKLINGS: Remove the skin of the duck breasts by pulling it off and slicing between the skin and the meat with a sharp knife. Cover and refrigerate the breasts. Cut the duck skin into ¾-inch pieces.

Put the pieces of skin in a saucepan with the salt and 3 cups water, bring to a boil, and cook, uncovered, for 40 to 45 minutes, or until all the water is evaporated and the pieces of skin are sizzling in the rendered fat. Then continue frying the skin in the fat until it is brown and crispy, about 10 minutes. Drain in a colander, reserving the fat for another use.

You need about 1 cup cracklings to serve with the duck; enjoy the rest with aperitifs.

Preheat the oven to 160 degrees.

FOR THE SALAD: Mix together the garlic, salt, pepper, vinegar, and both oils in a large bowl and set aside.

FOR THE DUCK: Heat the butter in a skillet until it is foaming. Sprinkle the duck breasts with the salt and pepper, add to the pan, and sauté over medium-high heat for 2½ to 3 minutes per side for rare meat. Transfer the duck to a plate and set in the oven to rest for 5 to 10 minutes.

Meanwhile, deglaze the pan with the wine and water, mixing for a few minutes to melt and incorporate the solidified juices. Remove from the heat.

TO ASSEMBLE: Reheat the cracklings in the microwave oven for about 45 seconds.

Toss the arugula with the dressing in the bowl and divide the salad among four plates. Place a duck breast on top of the salad on each plate and pour the deglazed juices on top. Sprinkle with the toasted nuts and cracklings and serve.

||||||||||||||||||||||||||||||||||||||||||||||||||

NOTE: *To toast the hazelnuts, scatter them on a baking sheet and toast in a 400-degree oven for 10 minutes. Rub off the skins after toasting.*

8 cups (loosely packed) arugula

¼ cup toasted hazelnuts (see Note)

Hamburger Royale

SERVES 4

One 2½-pound piece beef
   brisket, ground

4 ciabatta rolls (about 3 ounces
   each and 4 inches across),
   split

1 large garlic clove

4 slices (about 4 ounces)
   Comté, Beaufort, or
   Gruyère cheese

*I HAD A GREAT, JUICY, FLAVORFUL HAMBURGER
at my friend Jean-Claude's house, and he told me he had made
it with beef brisket. I tried it myself with great success. I buy
brisket from the thick, or fatty, end, which has more flavor
than the flat end. If you do not have a meat grinder (I have
one that attaches to my KitchenAid mixer), ask the butcher to
grind the meat for you. I sometimes buy a whole brisket and
grind some of it, keeping the rest to braise slowly.*

*I make hamburgers that weigh about 5 ounces each and cook
them on a grill or in a grill pan on top of the stove. Do not press
on the hamburgers as they cook, or you will lose the juices.*

The ciabatta rolls available at my market make great hamburger buns; I usually toast them and rub them with garlic. I also like to put cheese on my hamburgers—Comté, Beaufort, or Gruyère. I arrange the cheese on top of the finished burgers and then run them under the broiler to melt it. I make 8 patties and freeze half of them for another time; you can halve the beef quantity if you prefer.

||||||||||||||||||||||||||||||||||||||||||||||||||

Divide the ground meat into 8 portions of about 5 ounces each and form them into patties about ¾ inch thick. Wrap 4 of the patties and freeze them for future use.

At serving time, heat a grill until hot or preheat a grill pan for about 3 minutes. Preheat the broiler.

Toast the rolls on the grill or in a toaster oven and rub them with the garlic.

Arrange the hamburgers on the hot grill or in the grill pan and cook for 3 to 4 minutes on each side. Put 1 slice of cheese on each patty and run the patties under the hot broiler (about 2 inches from the heat source) for 1 minute.

Arrange the lettuce leaves on top of the bun bottoms, add the onions and tomatoes, and sprinkle with a little of the salt and pepper. Top with the burgers, sprinkle on the remaining salt and pepper, and finish with the tops of the buns. Enjoy as is or with ketchup, mustard, and/or mayonnaise.

About 6 leaves iceberg lettuce

4 thin slices mild onion, such as Vidalia or Maui

4 thick slices ripe tomato

½ teaspoon salt

½ teaspoon freshly ground black pepper

Ketchup, mustard, and/or mayonnaise, for serving (optional)

Beef Fillet Mini Steaks with Mushrooms and Shallots

SERVES 4

One 1¼-pound piece trimmed beef fillet

¾ teaspoon salt

¾ teaspoon freshly ground black pepper

3 tablespoons olive oil

1½ cups diced (½-inch) mushrooms

¼ cup chopped shallots

2 teaspoons chopped garlic

3 tablespoons chopped fresh parsley

3 tablespoons unsalted butter

1 tablespoon A.1. steak sauce

2 tablespoons water

1 lemon, cut into 4 wedges

FOR THIS VERY EASY RECIPE, I CUT A PIECE OF beef fillet into medallions, pound them into thin disks, and cook them briefly in a low oven right on the serving plates. Emerging warm, medium-rare, and tender as butter, the mini steaks are served with mushrooms, shallots, and garlic.

||||||||||||||||||||||||||||||||||||||||||||||||||

Cut the beef fillet into 4 medallions. Using a meat pounder, pound each slice into a disk about 7 inches across and ¼ inch thick. Place one disk on each of four ovenproof dinner plates and refrigerate until ready to cook.

At cooking time, preheat the oven to 250 degrees.

Sprinkle half the salt and half the pepper on the meat and place the plates in the warm oven for 12 minutes, for medium-rare.

Meanwhile, heat the oil in a large skillet. Add the mushrooms and sauté for 2 minutes. Add the shallots and cook for 30 seconds. Stir in the garlic, parsley, butter, A.1. sauce, water, and the remaining salt and pepper and heat through.

Remove the meat from the oven and turn each medallion upside down on the plate. (You will notice that the bottom is grayish and more cooked.) Sprinkle the mushroom garnish on top and serve with the lemon wedges.

Corned Beef and Cabbage

SERVES 4, WITH LEFTOVERS

I MAKE CORNED BEEF AND CABBAGE IN THE Irish tradition to celebrate St. Patrick's Day. I always buy a larger piece of corned beef than I need so that I can enjoy it in sandwiches for several days after serving the original dish. I especially like corned beef hash, which became a favorite of my brother, Roland, after he first came to see us from France. I buy the cut from the thick end of the brisket (called the point or front cut), which is more fatty and has a better flavor than the thin end.

I now cook the corned beef sous-vide style in its packaging bag, which keeps it moist and tender. I put the corned beef in a pot, add water to cover, place a small lid or plate on top of the bag to keep it under the water while it cooks, and bring the water to 180 degrees. I keep it as close to that temperature as possible for the 3 hours of cooking, although a margin of 10 degrees lower or higher is okay.

As well as hash and sandwiches, I often make a soup from the leftover broth and any remaining vegetables.

||||||||||||||||||||||||||||||||||||||||||||||||||

Place the packaged corned beef in a stockpot and add the water. Place a plate on top of the corned beef to keep it submerged and partially cover the pot with a lid. Attach a thermometer to the side of the pot, or use an instant-read thermometer, and bring the water to 180 degrees. Cook for 3 hours, keeping the water between 170 and 190 degrees. The bag may break during the cooking process, but it does not matter if it does.

Remove the bag from the water and remove the corned

One 3½-pound corned beef brisket, preferably from the thick end, still in the Cryovac bag

10 cups water

1 savoy cabbage (about 1½ pounds), cut into 8 wedges

4 celery stalks, cut into 4-inch pieces

3 large carrots (10 ounces), peeled and cut into 3-inch pieces

1 large leek, trimmed, leaving most of the green, cleaned, and cut into 3-inch pieces

3 potatoes (about 1½ pounds), peeled and quartered

Hot mustard, for serving

Cornichons (small sour gherkins), for serving

beef from the bag. The internal temperature of the meat should be between 160 and 170 degrees. Add any liquid from the corned beef to the stockpot. (If you are cooking the corned beef only for use in sandwiches, slice and enjoy the meat as needed.)

Add all the vegetables to the pot and bring to a boil. Cover and boil gently for about 20 minutes. Return the corned beef to the pot and cook for about 15 minutes to reheat.

Cut the corned beef into thin slices and arrange on plates. Divide the vegetables among the plates. Serve with a cup of broth on the side of each plate, along with hot mustard and cornichons.

Small Chuck Roast with Red Onion Sauce

SERVES 4

BEEF CHUCK, WHICH IS PART OF THE SHOULDER, is excellent not only when stewed or braised, as is common, but also when roasted. A small roast of about 1¾ pounds is enough for four people as part of a larger menu. In this recipe, it is sautéed briefly and then finished in the oven; it can also be grilled. Hoisin sauce lends sweetness, but it can be omitted if not on hand. A quick sauce of raw red onion, herbs, garlic, and oil is served with the roast.

|||||||||||||||||||||||||||||||||||||||||||||||||||||||

Preheat the oven to 170 degrees.

Rub the roast on both sides with the hoisin sauce, if using, and sprinkle it with the salt.

Heat the oil in a large ovenproof saucepan until very hot. Cook the roast over high heat for about 2½ minutes on each side for medium-rare. Transfer the roast to the oven and let it continue to cook and rest for at least 15 minutes (the roast can be left in the low oven for as long as 30 minutes).

MEANWHILE, FOR THE SAUCE: Mix all the ingredients together in a bowl.

Cut the roast on a diagonal into thin slices and serve with the red onion sauce.

|||||||||||||||||||||||||||||||||||||||||||||||||||||||

NOTE: *If the roast is thicker than 1¼ inches, even if it weighs the same amount, increase the cooking time; if it is thinner, shorten the cooking time.*

One 1¾-pound boneless beef chuck roast (about 1¼ inches thick, 9 inches long, and 5 inches wide)

1 tablespoon hoisin sauce (optional)

½ teaspoon salt

1 teaspoon peanut oil

SAUCE

¼ cup chopped red onion

¼ cup chopped fresh chives

1 tablespoon minced fresh sage

1 teaspoon chopped garlic

¼ teaspoon salt

¼ teaspoon freshly ground black pepper

2 teaspoons Dijon mustard

¼ cup extra-virgin olive oil

Spinach-Stuffed Pork Loin Chops

SERVES 4

STUFFING

1 tablespoon peanut oil

8 ounces baby spinach (about 9 cups)

½ teaspoon grated nutmeg

2 teaspoons chopped garlic

¼ teaspoon salt

½ teaspoon freshly ground black pepper

1½ cups grated Gruyère cheese (about 5 ounces)

STUFFED WITH SPINACH AND GRUYÈRE CHEESE, these boneless pork chops are sautéed and finished with a mixture of tomatoes, scallions, white wine, and black olives. It is a filling dish and, with just a salad, makes a perfect meal.

||||||||||||||||||||||||||||||||||||||||||||||||

FOR THE STUFFING: Heat the oil in a large skillet over high heat. Add the spinach, nutmeg, garlic, salt, and pepper and cook for about 3 minutes. Transfer to a plate and let cool. Mix the grated cheese into the cooled spinach.

FOR THE CHOPS: Place the chops on a work surface and, using a sharp paring knife, split them horizontally in half three quarters of the way through. Stuff with the spinach mixture and press the edges together. *(The chops can be stuffed ahead, covered, and refrigerated until cooking time.)*

At cooking time, preheat the oven to 140 degrees.

Heat the peanut oil and butter in a 12-inch skillet. Sprinkle the chops with half the salt and half the pepper, add to the pan, and sauté over high heat for about 3½ minutes. Turn them over, cover, and cook for 3½ minutes on the other side. Transfer to a plate and keep warm in the oven.

Add the scallions and garlic to the drippings in the skillet and cook for 30 seconds. Stir in the tomato, chicken stock, and white wine, bring to a boil, and boil over high heat for about 2 minutes. Add the remaining salt and pepper, stir in the olives, and mix well.

Arrange a stuffed pork chop on each of four hot plates. Coat with the sauce and top with the cilantro. Serve.

CHOPS

4 thick boneless pork loin
  chops (1¾ pounds total,
  about 1 inch thick)

1 tablespoon peanut oil

1 tablespoon unsalted butter

1 teaspoon salt

1 teaspoon freshly ground
  black pepper

½ cup sliced scallions

1 teaspoon chopped garlic

1 large ripe tomato
  (12 ounces), cut into
  ¾-inch dice (about 2 cups)

¼ cup homemade chicken
  stock or canned low-sodium
  chicken broth

¼ cup dry white wine

¼ cup diced kalamata olives

3 tablespoons chopped fresh
  cilantro

Pork Schnitzel with Crispy Rice Coating

SERVES 4

4 boneless pork loin steaks or chops (about 6 ounces each), trimmed of all fat and sinew (about 5 ounces each trimmed)

¾ teaspoon salt

¾ teaspoon freshly ground black pepper

1 egg, beaten well with a fork in a shallow bowl

3 rice cakes (about 1 ounce total), pounded or processed to a coarse powder (about 2½ cups), 1½ cups panko bread crumbs, or 1½ cups dried bread crumbs

2 tablespoons canola oil

1 tablespoon unsalted butter

3 tablespoons balsamic vinegar

½ cup homemade chicken stock or canned low-sodium chicken broth

⅓ cup Bloody Mary mix

2 tablespoons chopped fresh cilantro or chives

I MAKE THIS RECIPE WITH BONELESS PORK LOIN steaks or chops. I trim the exterior of any fat and sinew, then pound the meat into thin slices and bread them with a mixture of crushed rice cakes and Japanese-style panko bread crumbs (or regular bread crumbs) before sautéing them. I serve them with a sauce made with vinegar and Bloody Mary mix.

||||||||||||||||||||||||||||||||||||||||||||||

Using a meat pounder (or the side of a hammer), pound each of the pork steaks or chops so they are about 5½ by 4½ inches and ⅜ inch thick. Sprinkle the pork with the salt and pepper, then dip each piece into the beaten egg and coat well with the rice cake crumbs or bread crumbs. *(The meat can be prepared to this point a few hours ahead and refrigerated.)*

At cooking time, heat the oil and butter in one very large or two medium skillets, preferably nonstick. Add the coated pork and sauté for about 1½ minutes on each side. Transfer to a serving platter.

If using two skillets, combine the drippings in one skillet. Add the vinegar to the pan and cook for 30 to 45 seconds, until most of the liquid has evaporated. Add the chicken stock and Bloody Mary mix and cook for about 1½ minutes, until slightly thickened.

Pour the sauce over and around the steaks or chops and serve with the cilantro or chives sprinkled on top.

On Edge

THE KNIFE SKILLS I PERFECTED AS A TEENAGE APPREN-
tice who occasionally spent entire days doing little other than chopping have always stood me in good stead. I may even owe my television
career to my dexterity with a blade: An
early producer was so enchanted with
my rapid-fire cutting that what I looked
like, sounded like, and cooked may have
been secondary considerations in his selecting me for the show.

I love good knives. To me they are
extensions of my fingers. And I probably own about two hundred of them.
Frankly, I have no idea how many but I
could survive with just three, and so can
you. Everyone needs a chopping knife,
also called a chef's knife, with a blade
between 8 and 12 inches long, depending
on the size of your hand. You also need
a utility knife, about 6 inches long, with
a sturdy blade. Finally, you need a paring knife or two for peeling and other
small jobs.

The world is awash in knives for cooks. You can pick up cheap sets at discount stores or part with several hundred dollars for a single high-end knife. There are ceramic knives, Japanese knives, serrated knives. . . . The truth is, I like any knife as long as it's sharp. Sooner or later, any knife you buy has to be sharpened. Those ceramic models you see cutting through soft drink cans on late-night television ads are truly sharp when you first get them, but they become dull quickly and cannot be sharpened properly without being sent back to the factory. Heavy German knives such as Henckels are sharp when new, and their hard steel blades hold an edge for a long time. Unfortunately, it is difficult to sharpen them once they are dull.

To keep my knives sharp, I always use a steel. For me, and for most experienced chefs, using a steel is an unconscious action. I work with the steel and run the blade over it a few times, often without taking my eyes off the job or the person I'm talking to. Although it looks smooth to the naked eye, the cutting edge of a knife actually is made of tiny teeth. Chopping causes those teeth to get out of line. Running the blade on both sides over the steel realigns the teeth and keeps the knife sharp. Make sure you sharpen the whole blade and maintain the same angle as you do so, between 20 and 30 degrees. Constant steeling will keep your knives sharp for a year or more, but eventually they will need to visit a professional sharpener—or you'll have to spend a half hour or so working each knife across a whetstone to create new teeth. Alternatively, the electric sharpeners designed for home kitchens, such as those manufactured by Chef's Choice, can do a credible job of bringing new life to tired blades.

How do you tell if your knife is truly sharp? For me, the ultimate test is whether it will effortlessly go through a slightly overripe tomato. Sharp knives make your work not only easier, but safer. You are much more likely to cut yourself hacking away with a blunt instrument than you are effortlessly carving with a properly sharpened blade. A dull knife makes kitchen work tedious. Having to use one is guaranteed to put me a bad mood.

Smoked Ham Glazed with Maple Syrup

SERVES 8

1 bone-in cured smoked ham
from the shank end (about
6 pounds), with rind

⅓ cup pure maple syrup

⅓ cup ketchup

2 tablespoons hot chili sauce,
such as Sriracha

2 tablespoons balsamic
vinegar

*THIS HAM IS DELICIOUS SERVED HOT OR WARM,
as well as cold in sandwiches. It is a great dish to make ahead
for company. Although this type of ham comes "fully cooked
and ready to eat," it improves considerably when poached in
water, which removes some of the salt and makes the meat
moist, tender, and succulent. It is best if you poach the ham a
day ahead, then bake it before serving.*

||||||||||||||||||||||||||||||||||||||||||||||

Put the ham in a large pot, cover with hot water, and bring the water to 170 to 180 degrees (which will take about 40 minutes). Then cook, uncovered, for about 1½ hours, or until the internal temperature is about 140 degrees. Let the ham rest in the water until the water is lukewarm, then remove it from the water and refrigerate. *(This is best done the day before.)*

When ready to finish the dish, preheat the oven to 400 degrees.

Trim off the leathery skin from around and underneath the ham with a sharp knife, but leave the rind on. Put the trimmed ham in a roasting pan. Mix together the maple syrup, ketchup, chili sauce, and vinegar in a bowl and brush the ham generously with the sauce.

Bake for 45 minutes. Brush again with the sauce and continue cooking for 15 to 20 minutes longer. Brush the ham with any remaining sauce, slice, and serve.

Kale, Sausage, Rib, and Lima Bean Stew

SERVES 8 TO 10

PORK RIBS

1 slab baby back pork ribs
(about 3 pounds; about
10 ribs), cut into individual
ribs

¼ cup curing salt (optional;
see headnote)

¼ cup brown sugar (optional)

1½ pounds (about 5 cups)
small dried lima beans

10 cups water

1 teaspoon salt

1 pound curly kale, cut into
halves

1½ pounds hot Italian
sausage, cut into 2-inch
pieces

1½ pounds kielbasa, cut into
1½-inch pieces

1 leek, trimmed, leaving most
of the green, cleaned, and
cut into 2-inch pieces
(3 cups)

3 cups sliced (2-inch) onions

FOR THIS WINTER STEW, I CURE BABY BACK ribs for 24 hours in salt and brown sugar, a step that heightens their taste considerably, though you can skip it if you don't have time. (I use Morton Tender Quick curing salt, which can be purchased on the internet.) The type of sausages for the stew can be varied depending on your preference and market availability. I don't bother soaking the beans; I start them in cold water and cook them by themselves for 1 hour. Then I add the ribs, kale, sausages, and vegetables and cook them all together for another hour. I prefer dried baby lima beans here, although other kinds, such as Great Northern, will work as well. Like most stews, this one can be made ahead and reheated at serving time.

||||||||||||||||||||||||||||||||||||||||||||||||

TO CURE THE RIBS (OPTIONAL): Place the ribs in a heavy-duty plastic bag and sprinkle them with the curing salt and sugar. Close the bag tightly and shake it to distribute the salt and sugar. Refrigerate for 24 hours, turning the bag occasionally.

When ready to start cooking the stew, sort through the beans and discard any damaged beans or pebbles. Rinse the beans under cold running water and put them in a large pot. Add the water and salt, bring to a boil, cover, and boil gently for 1 hour.

After an hour of cooking, drain the ribs and rinse them under cold water. Add the ribs and kale to the pot with the beans, bring back to a boil (this will take about 10 minutes), and cook gently, covered, for 30 minutes.

Add the sausages, kielbasa, leek, onions, carrots, celery, garlic, and jalapeño to the pot and bring to a boil (which will take another 10 minutes). Boil gently, covered, for another 30 minutes, or until the beans are very soft and all the vegetables and meat are cooked through.

To serve, divide the ribs and sausages, along with the kale and beans, among the plates. Pass Tabasco sauce for guests to add as desired.

2 cups sliced (1-inch) peeled carrots

2 cups sliced (2-inch) celery

3 tablespoons coarsely chopped garlic

1 large jalapeño pepper, seeded and finely diced (3 tablespoons)

Tabasco sauce, for serving

The Other, Other White Meat

RABBIT MUST BE ONE OF THE MOST UNDERUSED AND unappreciated meats in this country, although young chefs are beginning to cook with it more nowadays.

I ate rabbit—both wild and farmed—growing up in France, and since coming to the United States, I have always had a reliable source. Today I buy my rabbit (and much of my meat) at an independent supermarket in New Haven, Connecticut, called Ferraro's. It has managed to stay competitive by adhering to the old-fashioned dictum of giving customers exactly what they want. Over the decades, those customers have come from increasingly diverse ethnic backgrounds, which has made Ferraro's a one-stop United Nations of food shopping. They would no more run out of rabbit, pigs' feet, kidneys, chicken feet, octopus, and chitterlings than they would chicken. The store is about a half hour from where I live, so whenever I'm there, I pick up a few rabbits. These are domestic rabbits, which are much superior to the cheaper Chinese specimens. Rabbit is also available at major supermarkets.

If a rabbit is young, 2 to 3 months old, and farmed, I might simply sauté or broil it, a process that takes no more than 30 minutes. Or, before putting it in the oven, I'll rub it with a little salt, pepper, and oil. About halfway through the cooking, I take it out and put French mustard and bread crumbs on top and then give it 10 to 15 minutes more. Or I will simply sauté it with mustard, adding a dab of cream at the end as a thickener. A large rabbit—or a wild one given to me by a friend who hunts—is a prime candidate for a slow-cooked stew, especially welcome on chilly fall and winter evenings.

No matter how you prepare it, rabbit really does taste like chicken (albeit exceptionally good chicken). It is tender, low in fat, and quick to cook. The only problem is that it does not occupy the place in Americans' cooking repertoire that it deserves, which means it's sometimes hard to find unless you are blessed with a store like Ferraro's. If you aren't, buy rabbits when you see them and keep a few on hand in the freezer. When you hanker for something a little bit different, you won't regret it.

Sauté of Rabbit with Mushrooms and Cream

SERVES 6

- 1 large rabbit (about 3½ pounds), preferably with liver, heart, and kidneys

- 2 tablespoons olive oil

- 4 ounces pancetta, cut into lardons (strips about 1 inch long and ½ inch thick)

- 2 cups coarsely chopped onions

- ¼ cup coarsely chopped garlic

- 3 tablespoons all-purpose flour

- 1 cup dry white wine

- 1 cup water

- 1 bouquet garni: 6 fresh thyme sprigs and 1 fresh sage sprig, tied together with kitchen twine

- ¾ teaspoon salt

- ¾ teaspoon freshly ground black pepper

NOWADAYS RABBITS ARE AVAILABLE IN MANY markets, and their lean white meat is excellent roasted or grilled or in a stew. This is my version of a stew my aunt used to make. It can be done ahead and refrigerated or even frozen (if freezing, don't add the cream until you reheat the stew), then reheated. If the liver and heart are included with your rabbit, add them to the stew at the end with the cream, so they aren't overcooked. A potato puree or a noodle dish is a great accompaniment to the rabbit.

||||||||||||||||||||||||||||||||||||||||||||||||

Using a cleaver or a large knife, cut the rabbit into 11 pieces: Separate the 2 back legs from the body and cut each leg in half. Remove the 2 front legs at the shoulders. Cut the "saddle," or back, into 3 pieces (the kidneys, if left intact, will be attached to the saddle). Cut the rib cage into 2 pieces.

Heat the oil in a saucepan or pot large enough (at least 12 inches in diameter) to accommodate all the rabbit pieces in one layer. Add the lardons and cook over high heat for 2 to 3 minutes. Add the rabbit pieces (reserving the liver and heart, if you have them) in one layer and brown, turning the pieces occasionally, for about 15 minutes, until browned on all sides. Transfer the rabbit pieces to a bowl.

Add the onions and garlic to the drippings in the pan and cook for about 2 minutes. Sprinkle the flour on top, mix well, and cook for about 1 minute. Add the wine and water, stir well, and bring to a boil. Add the rabbit pieces, along with the bouquet garni, salt, pepper, and mushrooms, and bring to a boil. Cover, reduce the heat to low, and cook gently for 1 hour. *(The stew can be made up to a day ahead to this point and refrigerated, then reheated at serving time.)*

Just before serving, add the liver and heart, if you have them, and the cream to the pan. Stir well and bring to a boil, then reduce the heat and simmer for 5 minutes.

Sprinkle the stew with the chives and serve.

4 cups diced (½-inch) mushrooms (about 10 ounces)

½ cup heavy cream

3 tablespoons minced fresh chives

Baked Rabbit with Mustard Crust

SERVES 4

1 small young rabbit (1¾ to
2 pounds)

2 tablespoons olive oil

½ teaspoon salt

½ teaspoon freshly ground
black pepper

CRUST

1 large slice firm white bread,
cut into 1-inch pieces

1 large garlic clove, crushed

2 teaspoons olive oil

3 tablespoons Dijon mustard

FOR THIS RECIPE, I LIKE A YOUNG, TENDER rabbit weighing no more than about 2 pounds. Flattened and panfried in a skillet for a few minutes on each side, the rabbit is then coated with a crust of mustard and bread crumbs and baked in the oven. This is an easy dish to make, requiring only a few ingredients, and it is best eaten with your fingers.

||||||||||||||||||||||||||||||||||||||||||||||

Preheat the oven to 425 degrees.

Put the rabbit open side down on a cutting board and, using your hands, press down on it to make it of a more equal thickness throughout.

Heat the oil in a 12-inch skillet. Sprinkle the rabbit with the salt and pepper and place it open side up in the hot oil. Cover and cook over high heat for about 4 minutes. Turn the rabbit over and cook it on the other side, covered, for another 4 minutes.

MEANWHILE, FOR THE CRUST: Put the bread cubes and garlic in a food processor and process to coarse crumbs. (You will have about 1 cup crumbs.) Transfer to a small bowl and toss with the oil to moisten the bread.

Remove the rabbit from the heat, uncover the pan, and brush the top and sides of the rabbit with the mustard. Spread the crumbs on top of the mustard. Bake for 20 minutes. Remove from the oven and let rest for 5 to 10 minutes.

Cut the rabbit into pieces and serve. Enjoy, preferably picking the rabbit pieces up in your fingers to eat them.

Punctuation Cuisine

FIVE OR SIX YEARS AGO, I MADE A TERRIBLE MISTAKE by taking my mother, then in her mid-nineties, out to dinner at a one-star restaurant in France. *Maman* had been surviving quite well on the simple food she still cooked herself in her tiny kitchen. The outing in a nice restaurant would be a change and a great treat, or so I thought. As I read her the menu items, she let out a delighted, "Oooooo," when I mentioned rabbit. "I haven't had rabbit in such a long time," she said. "I would love a nice rabbit."

Alarms should have sounded in my head. Elegant, esoteric preparations are often hallmarks of starred restaurants, and this establishment was no exception. My mother's face fell when her dinner arrived. The rabbit's back meat had been boned, rolled, and cut into one-inch-thick rounds about the size of silver dollars. The leg was smushed into something resembling confit and was deployed around an extraordinarily large plate in little dribs and drabs. Cubes of undercooked vegetables were also scattered across the expanse of porcelain. A brownish-red sauce had been added here and there in shapes that looked like awkwardly formed punctuation marks, everything from commas to dashes to question marks. When presented with the dish, *Maman* promptly informed the waiter that a mistake had been made. "Sorry," she said, "but I ordered the rabbit."

"*Maman*," I whispered in her ear. "That *is* the rabbit, believe me."

After casting a skeptical glance, she chewed through her meal listlessly.

Toward the end, the owner of the restaurant presented himself proudly at our table. "How was your dinner, *Madame*?" he said.

My mother, who has always said exactly what she thinks, said, "Your rabbit had no taste. No taste at all."

And she was right. I should have taken her to a simple bistro or retro brasserie where she would have recognized the dishes and the food—somewhere without "punctuation cuisine."

Like my mother, I have qualms about eating food I don't recognize. I have issues with molecular cooking, where the whole idea is to fool you. You bite into something that you expect to be salty and it's sweet, or vice versa. Something normally hot is ice-cold. Other times it is the obsession with creativity that turns me off. Roquefort on top of raspberries, sweet berries with fish: these things are not creative to me, just weird. This is not really dining, but rather the culinary equivalent of the fashions runway models wear. Striking. Beautiful. Often outrageous. But not in the least bit wearable for everyday life.

A good dish should taste of what it is. You should be able to be blindfolded and say, "This is chicken. There are mushrooms in it. And some white wine." But often these cooks keep adding to a dish, a small amount of this or that herb, a shake or two of that sauce, just to be different, and I have no idea what I'm eating. It's especially a problem with inexperienced chefs who are out to impress. If I'm asked if it's good, I'll say, "Well, it's very tender and moist, but I have no idea what it is."

Only occasionally do I enjoy tasting menus that offer a dozen or so small bites. I recognize that the food tastes excellent and that the chefs are nothing short of geniuses. Dining like that can be eye-opening. But to me, it is not quite satisfying. You go to a restaurant with small courses meted out in portions that could be plated on a tablespoon. You say, "Wow! That's good. But I wish I could have three or four tablespoons."

And as for wine, I get depressed if there are more than four different ones served at a meal. Instead of enjoying the wine with my food, sipping tiny glassful after tiny glassful becomes an intellectual analysis. That doesn't work for me. If I have six or seven incredible wines one after the other, I find that I can't really differentiate one from the other. Give me a glass of Champagne at the beginning, pass around decent bottles of red and white wine during the meal, and I'm a happy guy.

I get impatient when I am at a dinner where I have to comment on numerous small dishes and different wines. It turns a meal into a competition and it's like going to work. I want to relax and enjoy my meal, not analyze it. Frankly, the thought of these gastronomic endurance sessions makes me want to run out and grab a taco and a beer.

Rack of Lamb with Spice Crust

SERVES 4

1 large rack of lamb (about
    1½ pounds)

RUB

2 teaspoons 5-spice powder

2 teaspoons ground cumin

2 teaspoons Spanish paprika

1 teaspoon cayenne pepper

1 teaspoon garlic powder

1 teaspoon dry mustard

¾ teaspoon salt

1 teaspoon canola oil

A RACK OF LAMB ALWAYS MAKES AN ELEGANT dinner. It is expensive and a somewhat small cut, though, so it is best served as part of a menu that includes several other dishes, like a soup or fish course, potatoes and string beans, and a salad. As part of an extensive menu, a lamb rack will serve four, providing one double or two single chops per person.

After I trim the fat from the outside of the rack, I coat it with a spicy rub and refrigerate it until cooking time. The rack can be cooked in a skillet on top of the stove or on a grill, which is how I do it in this recipe. If you plan to serve the rack as it comes off the grill, place it in a 275-degree oven for about 15 minutes, for a medium-rare result. If the rack is grilled a couple of hours ahead and allowed to cool in the kitchen, place it in a 275-degree oven for 30 minutes to reheat and finish cooking.

|||||||||||||||||||||||||||||||||||||||||||||||||||

Trim the lamb rack of as much surface fat as you can. (The weight of the trimmed rack should be about 1¼ pounds.)

FOR THE RUB: Mix the 5-spice powder, cumin, paprika, cayenne, garlic powder, and dry mustard together. Coat the rack all over with the rub and refrigerate it until ready to cook, at least 30 minutes.

At cooking time, heat a grill until hot. Preheat the oven to 275 degrees.

Sprinkle the rack with the salt and rub the oil all over the meat. Place on the hot grill and cook for about 8 minutes, turning it occasionally with tongs, until it is blackened all over. Transfer it to a baking sheet.

Transfer the rack to the oven and cook for about 15 minutes for medium-rare. (Alternatively, if you choose to serve the meat later, set the rack aside at room temperature for up to a few hours, then cook in a 275-degree oven for 30 minutes before serving.) Let the lamb rest for 15 to 30 minutes.

Cut the rack between the ribs and serve on hot plates.

Sautéed Leg of Lamb Chinois

SERVES 4

One 1½-pound boneless leg
   of lamb (2 to 3 inches
   thick), completely cleaned
   of sinews and fat

MARINADE

1 tablespoon hoisin sauce

1 tablespoon soy sauce

1 tablespoon hot chili oil

1 tablespoon chopped garlic

2 teaspoons unsweetened
   cocoa powder

1 tablespoon peanut oil

¼ teaspoon salt

2 tablespoons water

FOR THIS RECIPE, LEG OF LAMB IS MARINATED in a mixture of hoisin sauce, Asian hot oil, and a little bitter cocoa powder. It is first sautéed, then finished in the oven.

||||||||||||||||||||||||||||||||||||||||||||||||||

Put the lamb in a gratin dish, add all the marinade ingredients, and turn to coat. Cover and refrigerate for at least an hour.

When ready to cook the meat, preheat the oven to 225 degrees.

Remove the meat from the marinade, reserving the marinade in the gratin dish. Heat the peanut oil in a heavy skillet. Sprinkle the meat with the salt and sauté it on all sides until it is nicely browned all over, 6 to 7 minutes total.

Return the meat to the marinade and deglaze the skillet with the water. Add the deglazing liquid to the lamb and place the dish in the oven for about 30 minutes.

Slice the lamb and serve with the natural juices.

Grilled Lamb Shashlik

SERVES 4

THIS IS MY INTERPRETATION OF A RECIPE WE used to prepare at the Plaza Athénée in Paris in the late 1950s, where the grilled skewered meat was called by its Russian name, shashlik. *After being cut into cubes, the meat is pounded, which tenderizes it, and marinated in a mixture of olive oil, onion, and thyme. Although the lamb pieces can be marinated for as little as a couple of hours, leaving them in the marinade for a few days makes them very flavorful and tender.*

Serve with rice, couscous, or potatoes.

||||||||||||||||||||||||||||||||||||||||||||||||||

1½ pounds boneless lamb leg, without fat or sinew, cut into 16 pieces (about 1½ ounces each)

1 large onion (10 ounces)

2 teaspoons fresh thyme leaves

1½ teaspoons freshly ground black pepper

⅓ cup extra-virgin olive oil

¾ teaspoon salt

½ lemon

Using a meat pounder, pound the meat into thin pieces, about ⅓ inch thick.

Cut the onion into quarters. Reserve the center for another use, and separate the remaining quarters into layers. You should have at least 24 onion pieces. Put the meat into a sealable plastic bag and add the onion, thyme, pepper, and oil. Mix well, then seal the bag and refrigerate until ready to cook. *(The meat can be refrigerated for several days.)*

At cooking time, heat a grill until hot. Preheat the oven to 150 degrees.

Thread the pieces of meat and pieces of onion alternately on metal skewers. Sprinkle with the salt and place on the hot grill, turning the meat pieces as necessary with a metal spatula or tongs so they lie flat on the grill. Grill for about 3 minutes on each side for medium-rare meat. Let rest on a baking sheet for a few minutes in the oven.

Sprinkle the *shashlik* with the juice of the lemon and serve.

Lamb Breast Navarin

SERVES 4

2 lamb breasts (about
    1½ pounds each)

2 teaspoons olive oil

1 cup coarsely chopped onion

1 tablespoon coarsely chopped
    garlic

2 teaspoons all-purpose flour

1 cup water

¾ cup dry white wine

8 fingerling potatoes
    (10 ounces), peeled and cut
    crosswise in half (about
    1½ cups)

3 carrots, peeled and cut
    into 2-inch sticks (about
    1½ cups)

1 teaspoon salt

¾ teaspoon freshly ground
    black pepper

1 bay leaf

1 fresh thyme sprig

½ cup frozen baby peas

1 tablespoon chopped fresh
    parsley

LAMB BREASTS WERE ALWAYS AVAILABLE AT MY market twenty-plus years ago, and then they disappeared. They are coming back now because of the proliferation of new restaurants with young chefs interested in low-priced cuts like these. I like to cook it in stews with the bones and cartilage left intact, which makes it a family meal, because then it is best eaten with the fingers. Properly cooked, the meat is very moist, flavorful, and tender, but the breast is also very fatty. I first trim the visible fat from the top and then cook the breast in a low oven with a weight on top to press out as much fat as I can. (This can be done a day ahead.) Then I cut the breast into pieces and sauté them in a Dutch oven, deglaze the pot with wine and water, and cook the lamb further with potatoes, carrots, onions, garlic, and herbs; I add peas at the end.

Preheat the oven to 275 degrees.

Using a sharp knife, remove as much fat as possible from the surface of the meat. Place the lamb on a baking sheet lined with aluminum foil and bake for 30 minutes. Then place another pan on top of the meat, set a 5- to 6-pound weight on it (a brick works well) to press out more fat, and cook for another hour. (I removed ⅔ cup fat from the 2 breasts this way.)

Cut each breast into 4 pieces. *(The lamb can be prepared to this point up to a day ahead and refrigerated.)*

When you are ready to finish the dish, heat the oil in a Dutch oven or sturdy cocotte. Add the onion and garlic, stir well, and cook for about 1 minute. Sprinkle with the flour and stir well. Add the water and wine, mix well, and bring to a boil. Add the potatoes, carrots, salt, pepper, bay leaf, and thyme and bring back to a boil.

Add the lamb and bring to a boil, then reduce the heat to low, cover, and cook gently for 1 hour.

Just before serving time, add the peas to the pot, bring to a boil, and cook for 2 to 3 minutes.

Serve the dish sprinkled with the parsley.

Spicy Lamb Ribs

SERVES 4

2 lamb breasts (about
1½ pounds each)

RUB

2 teaspoons salt

2 teaspoons brown sugar

1 teaspoon 5-spice powder

1 teaspoon ground cumin

1 teaspoon Spanish paprika

1 teaspoon garlic powder

½ teaspoon cayenne pepper

LAMB BREAST IS QUITE FATTY, SO IN THIS REC-ipe I cook it for a long time at a relatively low temperature to melt as much fat as possible. I make a dry rub with salt, sugar, and spices to flavor the breast. The meat can be rubbed just prior to cooking or up to 12 hours ahead; if done ahead, the meat gets cured and yields an even more flavorful result. This is a recipe best made for family and friends, since the meat should be eaten with your fingers.

|||||||||||||||||||||||||||||||||||||||||||||||||

Using a sharp knife, remove any visible fat from the surface of the meat. (I removed about 8 ounces of fat from the 2 breasts of lamb.)

FOR THE RUB: Mix all the ingredients together. Rub the spice mixture on both sides of the breasts. Cover and refrigerate until ready to cook. *(This can be done up to 12 hours ahead.)*

At cooking time, preheat the oven to 275 degrees.

Put the meat on a baking sheet lined with aluminum foil. Place in the oven and cook for about 4½ hours. The bones should pull out easily from the meat. Press on the breasts for a few seconds with a large spoon or a wide spatula to release more fat. (I removed ¾ cup of fat from the 2 breasts.)

Cut between the ribs and serve.

Wine Advice

SEVERAL YEARS AGO, SOMEONE GAVE ME TWO BOTTLES of 1959 Romanée Conti La Tâche, a rare red Burgundy worth close to $7,000 a bottle. They sat in my home awaiting a suitable occasion for breaking them out until I realized that such an occasion would never come about at our house. I ended up giving them to a friend who was a collector of fine wines and would appreciate adding them to his cellar.

Don't get me wrong—I love wine. Not a day goes by where we don't enjoy it. I can't imagine a lunch or dinner without a few glasses. And I can appreciate an exquisite bottling. But I'll have a glass, savor its depth and intricacy, say "Fantastic!" or "Great!" and then start wishing that there was something more ordinary on the table that I could drink in satisfying quantity. So I'm probably not a connoisseur of fine wine.

Blame genetics or my upbringing, but I lean toward wines that are young and fresh with the taste of berries, what the French call *vins de copain*, wines to drink "with a friend." I love the red wines of Beaujolais, because I grew up in the part of France where Gamay grapes, the grapes of Beaujolais wines, thrive. I also love the more robust wines made from the Côte du Rhône's Syrah, Grenache, and Carignan grapes, grown just to the south of where I lived. I'm always up for a red or white wine from Burgundy, to the north of Beaujolais. And recently there have been some marvelous and inexpensive wines coming from Languedoc and the far southwest of France. Because they can use whatever grapes they

choose, free from the strict limitations imposed by other Appellations Contrôlées, winemakers in Languedoc have created some fascinating blends. No wonder that marketing-savvy large American companies like Mondavi and Kendall-Jackson are buying vineyards there.

Personally, I find the jammy taste of many expensive California reds overpowering and their alcohol content of 15 or even 16 percent too high. Fortunately, many winemakers are producing lighter, inexpensive wines with different varietals nowadays, and this includes white wines, which used to be too oaky and are now more balanced and food friendly.

My taste in wine is also easy on the budget, which, given the quantity that we consume, is fortunate. I compare prices and shop in large liquor stores or wine suppliers, so I always find good deals and rarely spend more than $12 to $15 per bottle (up to $25 at most)—a bit more for Champagne.

Wine, to me, is no different from food. I want to drink something that I can enjoy without overanalyzing and overthinking. It's just one part of the dining experience. Ample quantities of it along with a satisfying meal, laughter, conversation, and the companionship of my favorite people add up to dining at its finest.

Veal Chops Dijonnaise

SERVES 4

4 veal rib chops (about
    7 ounces each)

1 teaspoon salt

1 teaspoon freshly ground
    black pepper

1½ tablespoons canola oil

2 cups sliced mushrooms

¼ cup dry white wine

¼ cup demi-glace (see
    headnote)

¼ cup heavy cream

1 tablespoon Dijon mustard

1 tablespoon chopped fresh
    tarragon

IN THIS CLASSIC RECIPE OF VEAL WITH MUSH-rooms, veal chops are sautéed and the pan juices deglazed with wine and demi-glace (an intensely flavorful reduction of veal, chicken, or beef stock), then finished with cream and mustard to make a luscious, smooth sauce. Good demi-glace is available at specialty stores, but if you are unable to obtain it, substitute chicken stock reduced by half.

|||||||||||||||||||||||||||||||||||||||||||||||||||

Preheat the oven to 140 degrees.

Sprinkle the chops with the salt and pepper. Heat the oil in a 12-inch nonstick skillet. When the oil is hot, add the chops and cook over medium-high heat for 1½ to 2 minutes on each side. Transfer to a plate and keep warm in the oven while you make the sauce with the pan drippings.

Add the mushrooms to the pan and cook for about 1 minute. Add the wine and demi-glace, bring to a boil, and boil for about 2 minutes. Stir in the cream and boil for about 30 seconds. Finally, mix in the mustard, but do not boil. Add any juices that have accumulated around the chops to the pan.

Arrange a chop on each of four very hot plates. Coat with the mushroom sauce, sprinkle with the tarragon, and serve.

Braised Veal Breast with Pearl Onions and Artichokes

SERVES 4

12 ounces pearl onions (about 20)

One 9-ounce box frozen artichoke hearts

2 tablespoons unsalted butter

1 bone-in veal breast (3 to 4 pounds)

1 teaspoon salt

¾ teaspoon freshly ground black pepper

1½ cups coarsely chopped onions

12 peeled garlic cloves

1 tablespoon all-purpose flour

½ cup homemade chicken stock or canned low-sodium chicken broth

½ cup dry white wine

1 fresh thyme sprig

2 bay leaves

2 tablespoons chopped fresh chives

WHILE THEY ARE NOT ALWAYS EASY TO FIND, veal breasts are inexpensive. There is a fair amount of meat around the bones and cartilage, and the taste is superb.

||||||||||||||||||||||||||||||||||||||||||||||||||

Cover the pearl onions with 1½ cups water in a saucepan and boil gently for 10 to 12 minutes, until tender. Drain.

Combine the onions with the frozen artichokes and set aside.

Preheat the oven to 275 degrees.

Heat the butter in a Dutch oven or enameled cast-iron cocotte until hot. Sprinkle the veal breast all over with the salt and pepper, place it in the hot butter, and brown over medium-high heat for a good 15 minutes, turning the veal to brown it on all sides. Transfer the meat to a plate.

Add the chopped onions and garlic to the drippings in the pot and cook for 1 minute, stirring. Sprinkle the flour on top and mix well. Add the stock, wine, thyme, and bay leaves, mix well, and bring to a boil.

Add the veal, cover, and bring to a boil. Transfer the pot to the oven and braise for about 3 hours. *(The recipe can be prepared ahead to this point and the veal set aside for up to 1 day. Bring to a simmer before proceeding.)*

At serving time, transfer the pot to the stovetop, add the boiled onions and artichokes, and boil gently for 10 to 15 minutes. Slice the veal and serve on hot plates, with the onions, artichokes, and a lot of the braising liquid, sprinkled with the chives.

Venison in Sweet-and-Sour Sauce

SERVES 4

1 strip lemon rind, removed
with a vegetable peeler

1 teaspoon dried oregano,
preferably Greek or
Mexican

1 teaspoon black peppercorns

4 venison loin steaks (about
4 ounces each and 1 inch
thick), totally cleaned of
fat and sinew

2 tablespoons peanut oil

¾ teaspoon salt

¼ cup chopped shallots

2 tablespoons red wine
vinegar

½ cup homemade chicken
or beef stock or canned
low-sodium broth

⅓ cup fruity dry red wine

2 tablespoons gooseberry
preserves

2 tablespoons unsalted butter

I HAVE SEVERAL FRIENDS WHO HUNT IN THE fall and winter, and I can count on them to provide me with venison, though it is also available now in specialty markets and can be ordered on the Internet. The loin and rack are the choicest pieces, and even though the meat is very lean, a 4-ounce loin steak per person is enough. For this dish, I flavor the meat with a rub and cook it in a sauce that is a reduction of vinegar and fruity red wine, to which sweet preserves are added. I use gooseberry, but most any berry preserves will work well.

||||||||||||||||||||||||||||||||||||||||||||||||

Cut the lemon rind into pieces and drop into a spice grinder, along with the oregano and peppercorns. Grind to a powder.

Put the steaks in a dish and sprinkle with the lemon rind mixture. Pour 1 tablespoon of the peanut oil over the steaks and refrigerate them, tightly covered with plastic wrap, for at least 2 hours, or overnight.

At cooking time, preheat the oven to 140 degrees.

Heat the remaining tablespoon of peanut oil in a heavy skillet large enough to hold the steaks in one layer. When the oil is hot, place the steaks in the pan, sprinkle them with half of the salt, and cook for about 1½ minutes on each side, for rare. Transfer the steaks to a platter and keep warm in the oven.

Add the shallots to the drippings in the skillet and sauté for 1 minute. Add the vinegar and cook for about 30 seconds,

until most of the liquid is gone. Add the stock and wine and boil for 3 to 4 minutes, until reduced by half. Add the preserves and the remainder of the salt and boil for 10 seconds. Remove from the heat, stir in the butter, and mix well with a whisk until smooth.

Place a steak on each of four warm plates, coat with the sauce, and serve immediately.

Cooking with Legends

WHEN I ARRIVED IN THE UNITED STATES FOR THE first time in 1959, the food revolution that has been sweeping the country for the past five decades was still a few years in the future, and the world of people who were seriously interested in food was both small and accessible. It was a time when future giants on the culinary landscape pursued their passion in obscurity. James Beard, perhaps the best known gastronomic personality of the era, had published magazine and newspaper articles and a few books, but these brought in just enough money to keep him housed, very well fed, and perpetually broke. Julia Child, the wife of a former diplomat, had worked for more than a decade on a massive manuscript on French cooking that a prominent U. S. publisher had rejected. Craig Claiborne had only recently taken the position of food editor at the *New York Times*, where he was starting to bring sophisticated restaurant criticism and reporting to a section that had previously been a housewife's guide to entertaining dinner guests. All of them were older than I was, but none had attained anything close to celebrity status, and they were all very generous to me and happy to befriend—and cook with—a young, classically trained French chef. And each of them brought a different approach to the kitchen.

■ ■ ■

IN THE EARLY DAYS, before I started teaching cooking classes for a living, I would offer the occasional lesson to small groups for extra cash.

With my apartment kitchen being small, and Jim Beard perpetually short of money, I rented the kitchen in his Greenwich Village brownstone for these sessions. Jim was a trencherman if there ever was one, and he could never resist the aroma of something good on the stove. Even though he was not "officially" supposed to be in the kitchen, his lumbering form would inevitably appear at the top of the spiral metal staircase leading down from the living quarters. He would descend, Buddha-like, and begin sniffing pots, swiping his finger through bubbling sauces, and tearing at the crisp edges of just-out-of-the oven chops and casseroles, offering good-natured suggestions, then head over to the wine cabinet, pop a cork, pour a glass, and settle into his favorite chair until the next tasty morsel lured him to his feet. Even though Jim enjoyed nibbling throughout the preparations, he was always ready to sit down for the real meal.

Jim loved being among company as much as he loved a good fatty mutton chop. He was a giant, jovial, generous man, with a laugh that rumbled forth from deep within his magnificent belly. His first loves were Dungeness crabs, oysters, salmon, and other foods from his native Pacific Northwest—shipments of which would regularly arrive at his door from admirers—but his appetites were nearly universal. For each windfall, he would send out an all-points bulletin to his food-loving friends to come over and help him prepare. The only times I ever saw him show irritation were when he encountered ingredients that were anything less than top quality.

Jim was not trained to be a chef, and he would object if you called him one. He was a gastronome, a lover of food and wine, and a serious

cook. His preference was for simple preparations: anything fresh and from the sea, a thick veal chop all to himself (woe to anyone who dared to ask him for a taste), smoky Virginia ham coated in apricot glaze, with an inch-deep layer of fat, which he gobbled down with unbridled gusto. And he loved big poultry, like turkey, capon, and goose.

■   ■   ■

I GOT TO KNOW Julia Child on paper before I met her in person. Helen McCully, then the editor of *House Beautiful* magazine, who had assumed the role of my career coach and surrogate mother, presented me with a cardboard box filled with manuscript pages. I sat down in her living room and read through it. I was awed and envious. This unknown woman from Cambridge, Massachusetts, had mastered, codified, and written down much of what I'd learned over many years spent in French kitchens. I couldn't wait to make her acquaintance.

Cooking with Julia was a blast. We joked with each other, teased each other, made light of each other's mistakes and foibles. I think that's why the television program we did together worked so well. The camera picked up how much we liked being in the kitchen together. Although her books are famous for their precise instructions and exacting detail, Julia was freewheeling when cooking. I don't remember a single occasion when we worked from a recipe at her house, or anywhere, even on television. We would start a show with nothing but a concept—let's make a stew—and proceed from there. At her house, the contents of the refrigerator often determined the menu. A bunch of scallions would find themselves in a savory dish for no other reason than that they were there.

In many ways, Julia's cooking was much more formally French than mine. Most of the time our culinary backgrounds overlapped so well that she could put down a spoon to answer the door or telephone and say, "Jacques, could you take over?" and I would proceed as if there had been no change in cooks. But on occasion, she would take me to task, saying, "That's not the way the French do it." I would reply, "I'm from Connecticut, and I'm doing it this way."

In life, as on television, Julia never took her cooking so seriously that she wouldn't have a glass of wine close at hand. But any nibbling and tasting done in the kitchen was strictly for testing purposes. I may have been stuffed by time we finished cooking at Jim's, but at Julia's, I was always hungry and ready to sit down at the table to enjoy a full formal meal together.

■   ■   ■

THE CRAIG CLAIBORNE who I met shortly after arriving in the United States was either always working or never working, depending on your perspective. He loved good food, reveled in the company of accomplished chefs, and had an insatiable curiosity about all things culinary. He had made a position for himself at the *New York Times* that demanded he spend all his waking hours indulging in his passions, sometimes to the consternation of the unfortunate clerks in the Gray Lady's accounting department who had to ride herd on his expense account.

Unlike Jim and Julia, Craig was a precise, detail-oriented, and structured cook. Because he was closer to my age than Jim and Julia were, I viewed him more as an older brother than a parent. But although he enjoyed a glass of wine or a highball while in the kitchen more than anyone, there was always a serious, business-like side to preparing a meal with him. When my friend and one-time boss Pierre Franey and I created dishes as we went along, based on the market's bounty, Craig would say, "Jacques, how many teaspoons of salt did you put in there?" "Did you time that?" "How did you know it was done?" Craig questioned everything I did, and then probed deeper if the answer failed to satisfy him. A pen and reporter's notepad occupied a prominent place on his counter, and he carefully jotted down every quantity, step, and length of time. He might go off to make a salad in one corner of the kitchen, but whenever anything interesting was happening, he was inevitably there, firing off questions, writing notes. We knew that everything that happened in Craig's kitchen would eventually make it into the pages of the paper.

Craig is the one who influenced my cooking and lifestyle the most, and I always felt happy and comfortable cooking around him. I was a frequent weekend guest at his summer home on Long Island. He hosted my wedding in 1966—where I cooked (they could not keep me away from the kitchen), preparing the feast along with well-known chefs Franey, Roger Fessaguet, Jean Vergnes, and René Verdon. My best friend Jean-Claude Szurdak made the cake.

At Craig's house, there was none of the rigidity and set schedules that French hosts imposed on their guests. We'd wake up when we wanted, pass the day as we wanted, and come together to go to the market, decide on the menu, and start to cook as the dinner hour approached. It was my first taste of American hospitality, and I loved it.

Organ Meats

||||||||||||||||||||||||||||||||||||||||||||||||||

Chicken Livers in Mushroom Port Sauce

SERVES 4

1 pound chicken livers
(about 12)

1 tablespoon olive oil

2 tablespoons unsalted butter

¾ teaspoon salt

¾ teaspoon freshly ground
pepper

2 cups diced (1-inch)
mushrooms (about
6 ounces)

⅓ cup coarsely chopped
shallots

⅓ cup coarsely chopped
scallions

1 tablespoon chopped garlic

⅓ cup dried cranberries

⅓ cup port

⅓ cup homemade chicken
stock or canned low-sodium
chicken broth

2 tablespoons ketchup

1 tablespoon chopped fresh
chives

CHEAP AND READILY AVAILABLE, CHICKEN LIVERS make a great hors d'oeuvre, mousse, pâté, or main course, which is the role they play here. The livers are sautéed in one layer in very hot oil and butter so they brown outside but remain pink inside. Dried cranberries, port, and ketchup add sweetness to the sauce. Serve with boiled rice.

|||||||||||||||||||||||||||||||||||||||||||

Cut each liver in half and remove and discard the connecting sinews. Pat dry with paper towels.

Heat the oil and butter in a 12-inch skillet over high heat until hot and foaming. Add the livers in one layer and sprinkle with the salt and pepper. Cook for 1 minute and then, using tongs, turn the livers over and cook for another minute. With the tongs, transfer the livers to a plate and set aside.

Add the mushrooms, shallots, scallions, and garlic to the drippings in the skillet and cook over high heat for about 3 minutes. Add the cranberries, port, and chicken stock, bring to a boil, and boil for about 1½ minutes. Add the ketchup and mix it in well. Add the livers to the skillet and bring the sauce back to a boil.

Serve the livers, sprinkled with the chives, on hot plates.

Chicken Feet in Hot Sauce

SERVES 4 AS A FIRST COURSE

OCCASIONALLY I FIND CHICKEN FEET AT JEWISH or Chinese or other ethnic markets. Very gelatinous, they make a great stock. As more and more chefs are cooking variety meats and realizing how tasty (and inexpensive) they can be, they will become more available in regular supermarkets. This recipe is for chicken feet prepared in a Chinese style. It is the type of dish you have to eat with your fingers, using plenty of napkins. Enjoy with good Chinese beer.

Put the chicken feet, water, and salt in a saucepan and bring to a boil over high heat. Cover, reduce the heat, and cook gently for 1 hour, or until the feet are soft and tender. Set the feet aside in the cooking liquid. *(This can be done up to a day ahead; refrigerate the feet in the cooking liquid.)*

When ready to serve, drain the feet, reserving the cooking liquid. Set aside ¼ cup of the broth for the hot sauce and freeze the remainder for use in a soup or stew.

FOR THE HOT SAUCE: Heat the oil in a medium saucepan. Add the garlic, ginger, and scallions and cook for 1 minute. Add the sesame oil, chili sauce, reserved stock, soy sauce, and dissolved starch and bring to a boil.

Add the feet to the sauce and heat until hot. Mix well and serve, sprinkled with the cilantro.

1 pound cleaned chicken feet, nails removed

4 cups water

½ teaspoon salt

HOT SAUCE

2 tablespoons canola or olive oil

1 tablespoon crushed and chopped garlic

1 tablespoon peeled, crushed, and chopped ginger

¼ cup sliced scallions

1 tablespoon toasted sesame oil

1 tablespoon Sriracha or other hot chili sauce

¼ cup reserved cooking liquid (from above)

3 tablespoons soy sauce

1 teaspoon potato starch or cornstarch, dissolved in 2 tablespoons water

¼ cup coarsely chopped fresh cilantro

Calves' Liver Lyonnaise Style

SERVES 4

CARAMELIZED ONIONS

3 tablespoons olive oil

2 onions (12 ounces total), thinly sliced (4 cups)

½ cup water

½ teaspoon sugar

¾ teaspoon salt

¾ teaspoon freshly ground black pepper

2 teaspoons fresh thyme leaves

⅓ cup red wine vinegar

LIVER

4 tablespoons unsalted butter

Eight ½-inch-thick slices calves' liver (about 1¼ pounds total)

¾ teaspoon salt

¾ teaspoon freshly ground black pepper

About 3 tablespoons all-purpose flour

3 tablespoons chopped fresh parsley

IN CLASSICAL FRENCH COOKING, "LYONNAISE-style" means liver served with onions. In this case, the onions are cooked until they caramelize, and then the pan is deglazed with a good red wine vinegar, sweet-and-sour style.

||||||||||||||||||||||||||||||||||||||||||||||||

FOR THE ONIONS: Combine the olive oil, onions, water, sugar, salt, and pepper in a large skillet and bring to a boil. Boil, uncovered, until all the water has evaporated, 5 to 6 minutes, then continue cooking, stirring occasionally, until the onions caramelize, about 6 minutes. Add the thyme and vinegar and cook and stir over high heat for about 30 seconds. Set aside.

FOR THE LIVER: Preheat the oven to 145 degrees.

Melt the butter in a very large ovenproof nonstick skillet or two smaller nonstick skillets that will hold the liver in one layer, then heat until hot over the highest heat. Meanwhile, dry the liver well with paper towels. Sprinkle it with the salt and pepper and dip it in the flour to coat it on both sides.

Add the liver to the hot butter and sauté for about 1 minute on each side. Sprinkle the liver with the parsley and place the skillet(s) in the oven for a few minutes to finish the cooking.

Meanwhile, reheat the onions and spread about half of them on four warm plates.

Arrange 2 slices of the liver on top of the onions on each plate and spoon the remaining onions on top of and around the liver. Pour any pan drippings over and serve immediately.

Veal Tongue and Lentil Stew

SERVES 6 TO 8

VEAL TONGUES ARE OCCASIONALLY AVAILABLE at my market, and I like to cook them in various ways. A classic method is to stew them with lentils. Tongue is moist, juicy, and tender and firm at the same time. This dish is best cooked ahead and reheated before serving.

||||||||||||||||||||||||||||||||||||||||||||||||||

Rinse the tongues under cool water. Place them in a saucepan with the water and 1 teaspoon of the salt and bring to a boil. Cover and boil gently for 30 minutes. Add the pancetta and boil for 30 minutes longer. Remove the tongues and pancetta from the pan, reserving the cooking liquid.

When the tongues are cool enough to handle, peel off the skin; it should come off easily. Cut each tongue into quarters. Cut the pancetta into lardons (strips about ¾ inch long and ½ inch thick).

Heat the oil in a large pot. Add the lardons and onions and cook over high heat for 5 to 6 minutes, stirring occasionally to brown.

Add the reserved cooking liquid and the tongue, then add the remaining 1½ teaspoons salt and the remainder of the ingredients except for the parsley and bring to a boil, stirring occasionally. Cover, reduce the heat, and boil gently for 45 minutes, until the lentils are tender and most of the liquid has been absorbed. *(The dish can be made a day or so ahead, refrigerated, and reheated before serving.)*

Serve the tongue sprinkled with the chopped parsley.

2 veal tongues (not cured; about 1 pound each)

5½ cups water

2½ teaspoons salt

About 6 ounces pancetta, in 1 piece

2 tablespoons olive oil

1½ cups diced (½-inch) onions

1 pound small dried lentils, preferably du Puy lentils from France, rinsed

2 cups diced (½-inch) peeled carrots

1½ cups diced (1-inch) tomatoes

1 tablespoon tomato paste

1 tablespoon finely chopped garlic

1 tablespoon finely chopped jalapeño pepper

2 bay leaves

½ teaspoon dried or fresh thyme leaves

¼ cup chopped fresh parsley

Beef Tongue with Ravigote Sauce

SERVES 6 TO 8

1 beef tongue (about
    3 pounds), preferably cured
    (see headnote and Note)

SAUCE

⅓ cup chopped onion

2 large hard-cooked eggs, cut
    into ¼-inch dice, using an
    egg slicer or a knife

1½ cups extra-virgin olive oil

RAVIGOTER *MEANS "TO INVIGORATE," "REVIVE,"
or "stimulate," and this classic sauce does precisely that.
Made with vinegar and olive oil, onion, garlic, herbs, capers,
and chopped hard-cooked eggs, it also goes well on poached
fish, or mix it into a bean salad.*

*Beef tongue can be boiled uncured, but it improves consid-
erably with curing, which gives it a deeper, more satisfying
taste. If you cannot find a salted and cured tongue, you can
cure it yourself. (See Note.)*

*Weighing about 3 pounds, a beef tongue needs about
3 hours of cooking; it should reach an internal temperature
of 170 to 180 degrees. After the tongue is cooked and cooled,*

the skin can be peeled off easily. The cured tongue can be cooked with lentils (see Veal Tongue and Lentil Stew, page 261).

||||||||||||||||||||||||||||||||||||||||||||||||||

Rinse the tongue under cold water. Place it in a saucepan, cover with cold water, and bring to a boil over high heat. Reduce the heat to very low, cover, and cook gently for 2½ hours, or until the tongue is tender when pierced with the point of a knife; the internal temperature should be 170 to 180 degrees. Remove the tongue from the broth and cool it until you can handle it.

Peel the skin off the tongue with a paring knife; it should come off easily. Place the peeled tongue in a bowl, covered with some of the cooking liquid, and set aside in a saucepan until serving time. Reserve 3 tablespoons of the cooking liquid for the sauce.

FOR THE SAUCE: Put the chopped onion in a sieve and rinse under lukewarm water to remove some of the sulfuric acid and make the onion milder. Drain well. Combine the onion and all the remaining sauce ingredients in a bowl.

At serving time, warm the tongue to lukewarm in the cooking liquid. Cut into ¾-inch-thick slices and serve with the sauce on top.

||||||||||||||||||||||||||||||||||||||||||||||||||

NOTE: *To cure the tongue, first cut it in half, which will make it easier to cure and cook. Place the tongue in a sealable plastic bag and add ½ cup Morton Tender Quick curing salt (available online), ½ cup (packed) light brown sugar, and 1 teaspoon hot pepper flakes to the bag. Mix well, close the bag tightly, and refrigerate for 6 days, turning the bag occasionally to redistribute the seasonings.*

2 tablespoons red wine vinegar

3 tablespoons reserved cooking liquid from the tongue

½ teaspoon salt

1 teaspoon freshly ground black pepper

2 teaspoons chopped garlic

2 teaspoons grated fresh or bottled horseradish

¼ cup drained capers

2 tablespoons chopped fresh chives

1 teaspoon chopped fresh tarragon

Tripe and Pigs' Feet Ragout

SERVES 6, WITH LEFTOVERS

4 pounds beef honeycomb tripe, cut into 2-inch pieces

2 pigs' feet (about 2 pounds), split in half

1½ cups homemade chicken stock or canned low-sodium chicken broth

1½ cups water

1½ teaspoons salt

1 teaspoon freshly ground black pepper

1 bouquet garni: about 6 fresh thyme sprigs, 3 bay leaves, and 2 fresh oregano branches, tied together with kitchen twine

2 cups sliced (1-inch) cleaned leeks

2 cups diced (1-inch) onions

1 cup diced (1-inch) peeled carrots

½ cup sliced (1-inch) scallion

¼ cup coarsely chopped garlic

One 14½-ounce can diced tomatoes

1 cup dry white wine

TRIPE IS INEXPENSIVE, DELICIOUS, AND UNDER-used in this country. There are many recipes for tripe in my repertoire, some with Puerto Rican and Mexican accents, along with French tastes and techniques, of course. I cook it in large batches and freeze some of it to enjoy later on cold winter days. The tripe found in most markets is the beef tripe called "honeycomb," which is the steer's stomach. I like to cook it with pigs' feet, which add flavor and give richness and texture to the dish. The tripe and pigs' feet are first cooked together for several hours, then the feet are boned and their meat returned to the pot of tripe, along with wine and vegetables, and cooked for another hour.

This ragout is always better made ahead and reheated. Serve with boiled or mashed potatoes, rice, beans, or pasta.

Put the tripe, pigs' feet, stock, water, salt, pepper, and bouquet garni in a stockpot and bring to a boil. Boil gently, covered, for 2½ hours. Remove the pigs' feet from the pot and let cool enough to handle. Keep the tripe at a gentle boil.

When the pigs' feet have cooled, pick out the bones and cut the meat into 1-inch pieces. Return the meat to the pot with the tripe, add the remaining ingredients, and bring to a boil. Cover and boil gently for 1 hour longer. The tripe will be tender to the knife and soft.

Serve. Freeze the leftovers for a later meal.

Cooking Inward

WHEN I FIRST CAME TO NEW YORK CITY, OBTAINING the organ meats that were a much-appreciated part of any Frenchman's diet required a lengthy sojourn up to an African American butcher shop in Harlem that specialized in offal, which is also prized in traditional black Southern kitchens. In both societies, what began as commonsense frugality became ingrained in the culinary culture.

In the early 1960s, for example, many American butchers threw out sweetbreads (thymus and pancreas glands); now they are more expensive than prime rib. I have a grand time shopping at a market not far from my home that caters to lovers of Southern food and offal, from pig snouts, ears, and feet to chicken feet, chitterlings, tripe, and brains. Cooking with these "lesser" parts is all the rage among contemporary chefs, and I believe that more home cooks will add them to their menus in the coming years.

I like to introduce friends to the world of offal with calves' liver sautéed in onion and vinegar. Many people have it in their heads that they don't like liver, or they may have distant memories of poorly prepared liver, and they are pleasantly surprised by mine.

Prepare offal according to my suggestions, and you will probably find you actually like it. And if you don't, well, you won't be out much money—most of these cuts cost a fraction of their more common counterparts.

Pork Neck and Bean Stew

SERVES 6

PORK NECK BONES ARE MEATY, AND WHEN braised, the meat is moist, tender, and tasty. This is a dish to eat with good friends and family, as you have to use your fingers and nibble on the bones to really enjoy them. This inexpensive stew gets even better when reheated. It also freezes well.

|||||||||||||||||||||||||||||||||||||||||||||||||||

Sort through the beans and discard any damaged beans or pebbles. Rinse the beans under cold running water and put them in a large pot. Add the neck bones, stock or bouillon cube and water, salt, and thyme and bring to a boil, which will take 12 to 15 minutes. Cover, reduce the heat to low, and boil gently for 1 hour. (Meanwhile, prepare the vegetables.)

When the neck bones and beans have cooked for an hour, add the remaining ingredients except the parsley and Tabasco sauce to the pot and bring to a boil. Cover and boil very gently for 1 hour longer. If the liquid reduces too much and the beans begin to look dry, add ½ cup water or so. The beans should be tender and moist, with some liquid remaining.

Serve in bowls, sprinkled with the parsley and thyme, if using. Pass Tabasco sauce for adding, if desired.

12 ounces (about 2 cups) dried Great Northern beans

3 pounds pork neck bones

4½ cups homemade chicken stock, or 1 chicken bouillon cube plus 4½ cups cold water

1½ teaspoons salt

3 fresh thyme sprigs

2 cups sliced (1-inch) cleaned leek (both green and white parts)

2 cups diced (about 1-inch) onions

2 cups diced (about 1-inch) tomatoes

1 cup diced (about 1-inch) carrots

½ cup diced (about 1-inch) celery

¼ cup chopped garlic

1 teaspoon freshly ground black pepper

2 tablespoons chopped fresh parsley and optional thyme sprig

Tabasco sauce, for serving

Pork Kidneys with Mushroom and Vermouth Sauce

SERVES 4

4 pork kidneys (about
    1¾ pounds total), partially
    frozen

SAUCE

2 tablespoons unsalted butter

⅓ cup chopped shallots

PORK KIDNEYS WERE NOT SERVED OFTEN WHEN I was growing up. My wife introduced me to them, and I prefer them to veal kidneys. Inexpensive and readily available at my market, they are good grilled, broiled with mustard, or sautéed and served with sauce.

Here the sauce is made with sautéed shallots and mushrooms, deglazed with red wine vinegar, white vermouth, stock, and V8 juice, and finished with shredded sage; the sage is good but can be omitted or replaced with another herb such

as savory or thyme. The sauce can be made ahead and the kidneys sautéed at the last moment. The trickiest part of the dish is cleaning the inside of each kidney of its tough white membrane. Rice, mashed potatoes, or pasta makes a nice accompaniment.

|||||||||||||||||||||||||||||||||||||||||||||||

P lace each kidney flat on a cutting board and, using a sharp knife, split it horizontally in half. Using the knife, remove the tough white membrane from the center of the kidneys. Cut each kidney half into 4 pieces. Set aside.

FOR THE SAUCE: Heat the butter in a large saucepan. Add the shallots and cook for 1 minute. Add the mushrooms and cook, stirring occasionally, for about 3 minutes. Sprinkle the flour on top and mix well, then add the stock, vermouth, V8 juice or Bloody Mary mix, and the vinegar and mix well. Bring to a boil and boil for 5 to 6 minutes to reduce the sauce to about 1½ cups and concentrate the flavor. Stir in the sage, if using, and set aside.

At cooking time, heat the olive oil in one very large or two smaller skillets over high heat until very hot. Pat the kidney pieces dry with paper towels and add them to the hot oil in one layer. Sprinkle with the salt and pepper and cook for 1 minute. Using tongs, turn the pieces over and cook them for 45 seconds to 1 minute longer. Add the sauce and heat almost to the boil. (Do not let boil, or the kidneys will be tough.)

Serve the kidneys on warm plates, sprinkled with the chives or sage.

2 cups diced (¾-inch) wild or cultivated mushrooms

1 teaspoon all-purpose flour

1 cup homemade chicken stock or canned low-sodium chicken broth

⅓ cup white vermouth

⅓ cup V8 juice or Bloody Mary mix

3 tablespoons red wine vinegar

1 tablespoon shredded fresh sage leaves (optional)

3 tablespoons olive oil

½ teaspoon salt

½ teaspoon freshly ground black pepper

2 tablespoons chopped fresh chives or sage

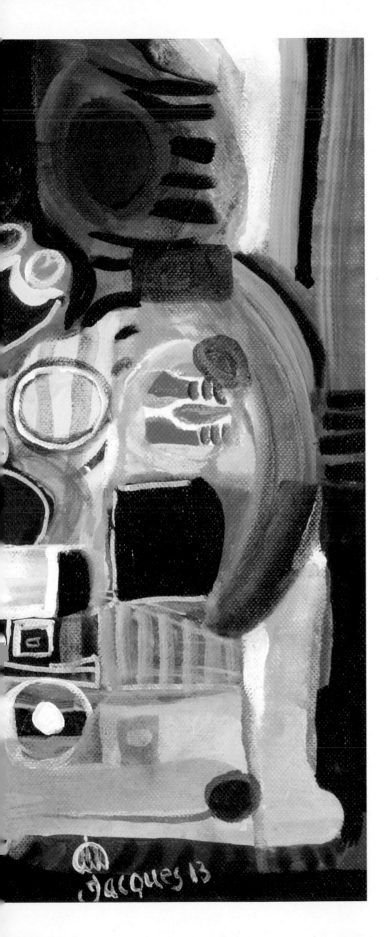

Rice and Pasta

||||||||||||||||||||||||||||||||||||||||||||||||||||||||

Rice Soubise

SERVES 4

1 tablespoon olive oil

1 tablespoon unsalted butter

2 cups coarsely chopped onions

⅓ cup coarsely chopped scallions

¾ cup coarsely chopped mushrooms

1 cup sushi rice

½ teaspoon salt

½ teaspoon freshly ground black pepper

3 cups homemade chicken stock or canned low-sodium chicken broth

FOR THIS SOUBISE, ONIONS, SCALLIONS, AND mushrooms are cooked in chicken stock with rice until soft and tender, then coarsely pureed. Soubise is a classic accompaniment for a veal roast or chicken, but it can be served with grilled meats, as well as fish. Although any rice will work, I like the soft texture that sushi rice acquires when cooked this way.

|||||||||||||||||||||||||||||||||||||||||||||||||||

Heat the oil and butter in a large saucepan over medium heat. When it is hot, add the onions, scallions, and mushrooms and cook for 1 to 2 minutes. Add the rice, salt, pepper, and stock, mix well, and bring to a boil. Cover, reduce the heat to very low, and cook for 20 minutes. The mixture should be soft and soupy.

Using a hand blender or a regular blender, pulse the mixture to a coarse puree. Serve.

Rice with Cumin and Green Olives

SERVES 4

LEEK GREENS ARE USUALLY DISCARDED OR added to stock, but I like to use them in this rice recipe. Green olives and cumin add a distinctive taste. The rice is excellent with Octopus Stew (page 187), as well as with any fish, meat, or poultry stew.

||||||||||||||||||||||||||||||||||||||||||||

Heat the butter in a medium saucepan over medium heat. Add the leek greens and onions and cook for about 5 minutes, stirring occasionally.

Add the rice, cumin, salt, and stock and bring to a boil. Stir in the olives, cover, reduce the heat to very low, and cook for 20 minutes, or until the rice is cooked through and tender. Fluff with a fork and serve.

3 tablespoons unsalted butter

1½ cups thinly sliced washed leek greens

1 cup diced (½-inch) onions

1½ cups (about 10 ounces) Carolina long-grain white rice

1 teaspoon ground cumin

¾ teaspoon salt (less if stock is salty)

3 cups homemade chicken stock or canned low-sodium chicken broth

½ cup pitted green olives, cut into ¾-inch pieces

Dirty Rice for Gloria

SERVES 6

3 ounces lean pancetta, cut into ½-inch pieces

2 tablespoons olive oil

1 cup finely chopped onion

3 chicken livers (about 4 ounces), sinews removed

1½ cups (about 10 ounces) Carolina long-grain white rice

3 cups homemade chicken stock or canned low-sodium chicken broth

1 teaspoon fresh thyme leaves

1 teaspoon Spanish paprika or piment d'Espelette

1 teaspoon salt

2 tablespoons coarsely chopped poblano pepper, or 2 teaspoons chopped serrano or jalapeño pepper

WHAT A NAME—DIRTY RICE! IT COMES FROM the chopped liver that is cooked with the rice. It just so happens that rice and liver stand at the top of my wife's list of favorite foods. I have made this Southern dish for her using duck livers, but it can also be made with chicken livers, as here. Sometimes I add gizzards as well. In this recipe, I chop some lean pancetta and sauté some onion with it before adding the liver, rice, and stock. Leftovers are great served with an egg on top.

||||||||||||||||||||||||||||||||||||||||||||||||

Put the pancetta in a food processor and process for a few seconds, until coarsely chopped.

Transfer the pancetta to a saucepan (set the processor bowl aside), add the oil, and cook for 2 to 3 minutes over medium heat. Add the chopped onion and cook for another 3 minutes.

Meanwhile, drop the livers into the processor bowl and process for 20 seconds, or until pureed.

Add the liver puree to the onions and mix well with a spoon for about 20 seconds. Add the rice and mix well, then add the stock, thyme, paprika or piment d'Espelette, salt, and chili pepper and mix well. Bring to a boil, reduce the heat to low, cover, and cook for 20 minutes, or until the rice is tender.

Serve.

A Peek into My Larder

I MAKE SURE TO ALWAYS HAVE CERTAIN ITEMS ON hand in my kitchen. Some are common, but others may seem surprising. Virtually all keep almost indefinitely. I heartily recommend you keep them in your kitchen too. You'll need them for some of the recipes in this book, but once you have them, you'll find yourself using them time and time again in your own preparations.

■ *Flour Tortillas:* I freeze these and use them whenever I want to serve a quick pizza for lunch. I simply place some tomato slices on top, add any cheese that lurks in the fridge, whatever herbs are handy, and a bit of hot sauce and place the mini pizzas in a hot oven for 10 minutes. Lunch *à la minute.*

■ *Canned Beans:* I always keep three or four types of canned beans in the pantry—navy, black, cannellini, and Great Northern—and their cousins, chickpeas. They are ready to be added to a soup, used as an accompaniment for meat, or made into a puree for hummus or an appetizer. Canned beans and sausage can give me a hearty stew in 10 or 15 minutes. The same holds true for chickpeas with some onion, garlic, and fresh tomato, with an egg plopped on top of the warm stew. And canned beans contain nothing more than beans, water, and salt, which is exactly what I would use if I started from scratch with dried beans. The only thing missing is a lot of my time.

- *Good Parmesan, Pecorino, and Gruyère Cheese:* I grate cheese over pasta dishes, add it to soups, and use it on top of my fast flour-tortilla pizzas. It seems to keep forever in the fridge. Even when it becomes dry and cracked with age, it still makes a great addition to a soup.

- *Assorted Olives:* I prefer to mix up an assortment at the market, or buy premixed olives. They keep almost forever in the fridge. They become a spur-of-the-moment appetizer when friends drop over for a drink. If I have a little more time and am feeling ambitious, I'll warm the olives and sprinkle some fresh herbs on top.

- *Anchovies, Sardines, Tuna, and Salmon:* Gloria loves anchovies, reason enough to make sure our pantry is never without them. They are the ultimate umami source. We eat them plain on toast, on hard-cooked eggs, in pasta, or on a salad. When tomatoes are in season, I slice them and top them with sliced red onion, anchovies, basil, and a sprinkling of olive oil for a first course. Try to get anchovies packed in olive oil from Portugal, Spain, or the South of France.

- *Salami (saucisson):* Always welcome with apéritifs.

- *Frozen Artichoke Hearts:* Artichokes in any form were once a rare treat at our house because they are expensive and require time to prepare, but then my daughter introduced me to frozen artichokes. They have the same flavor as fresh ones (unlike those in cans and jars, which are usually in some sort of acidic brine that gives them an off taste). They've become a lifesaver for me. I'll sauté them with onions and garlic as a starter, toss them into a stew, or use them as an accompaniment to chicken or veal dishes.

- *Frozen Baby Peas:* There is nothing like tiny fresh peas when I can get them from the farm next door in May and June. But later in the season, when the peas become larger and starchy, or when fresh peas are no longer in season, frozen baby peas are better—higher in sugar and lower in starch. If you want to do a puree, the skins of small peas will liquefy, creating a velvety dish. Or I'll cook them in the classic French way, with small boiling onions, Boston lettuce, chicken stock, and butter. I sprinkle frozen peas into stews for both taste and eye appeal.

- *Asian Sauces and Oils:* Sesame oil, oyster sauce, hot chili sauce, hoisin, and soy sauce need not be restricted to the cuisines of their homelands. They are great additions to a variety of dishes. I sauté ginger, garlic, and scallions and add chicken, chicken livers, shrimp, eggplant, or zucchini, then reach into my pantry and finish the dish with one of these sauces, depending on what direction I want the dish to go.

- *Peperoncini:* There's always a jar of these sweet, mildly hot pickled peppers in the fridge and they come in handy in a number of ways. I add them to scrambled eggs, put them in sandwiches, and use them to top pizzas. Sometimes I'll simply add a couple of tablespoons of the juice from the jar to a recipe that cries out for a little acidity and heat.

Fettuccine à la Playa

SERVES 4

1 pound fettuccine, preferably imported

Two 2-ounce cans anchovy fillets in oil

1 tablespoon chopped garlic

1 cup drained canned cannellini beans

¾ cup coarsely chopped spicy green olives

2 tablespoons chopped pickled peperoncini

¼ cup sliced sun-dried tomatoes in oil

¼ cup coarsely chopped fresh parsley

½ teaspoon salt

⅓ cup grated Pecorino Romano cheese, plus extra for serving, if desired

I FIRST PREPARED THIS SIMPLE RECIPE WHEN unexpected guests stayed for dinner at our vacation apartment in Mexico. Ever since, I've made sure to keep the ingredients for this dish in our pantry. The anchovies, garlic, spicy olives, and peperoncini add lots of flavor, along with some heat, and the beans and sun-dried tomatoes contribute body and texture.

||||||||||||||||||||||||||||||||||||||||||||||

Bring 4 quarts salted water to a boil in a large pot. Add the pasta, stir well, and cook the pasta for 10 to 11 minutes, until al dente (or to your taste).

Meanwhile, cut the anchovies into ½-inch pieces and combine them with their oil in a large glass bowl. Mix in the garlic, beans, olives, peperoncini, tomatoes, parsley, and salt. Heat in a microwave oven for 1½ to 2 minutes, until warm.

Scoop out 1 cup of the pasta cooking liquid and add it to the ingredients in the bowl. Add the cheese and mix well.

Drain the pasta and add it to the bowl. Mix well and serve immediately on warmed plates, with more cheese, if desired.

Fusilli in Spicy Garlic Tomato Sauce

SERVES 6

8 ounces pancetta

3 tablespoons olive oil

1/3 cup sliced garlic (about 8 cloves)

1 teaspoon hot pepper flakes, or to taste

One 20-ounce can plum tomatoes in puree (imported or domestic)

1/2 teaspoon salt

1/4 cup coarsely chopped fresh oregano

1 pound fusilli, penne, or cavatappi, preferably imported

1/3 cup minced fresh chives

1/3 cup grated Pecorino Romano cheese, plus extra for serving

USE ANY SHORT PASTA—FUSILLI, PENNE, CAVA-tappi ("corkscrews"), or even elbow macaroni—for this recipe. The sauce, which is flavored with pancetta, garlic, and a fair amount of red chili pepper flakes, is typically called arrabbiata *(which means "angry") in Italian restaurants. I use canned imported or domestic tomatoes for my sauces; for this one, I used peeled Roma (plum) tomatoes in tomato puree. A pound of pasta such as spaghetti or linguine will usually feed four people, while cooked fusilli, penne, elbow macaroni, and the like tend to yield a larger amount and will easily feed six.*

Cut the pancetta into 1-inch-long strips and then cut the strips into slivers about 1/4 inch thick. (You should have about 2 cups.)

Put the pancetta in a saucepan with 1/2 cup water and the olive oil, bring to a boil over low heat, and cook for about 8 minutes, or until all the water has evaporated and the pancetta is browning in the oil. (Cooking the pancetta in water first makes it more tender.) Add the garlic and pepper flakes and cook, uncovered, for a couple of minutes to lightly brown the garlic.

Meanwhile, put the tomatoes in a bowl and coarsely crush them with your hands.

Add the tomatoes to the garlic and pancetta mixture, along with the salt, bring to a boil, cover, and cook gently for 10 minutes. Add the oregano and mix well.

Meanwhile, bring 4 quarts salted water to a boil in a large pot. Add the pasta, stir well, and boil for about 13 minutes, until al dente (or to your liking).

Scoop out 1 cup of the pasta cooking liquid and drain the pasta. Add the pasta and enough of the cooking liquid to the sauce to thin it a little, then add the chives and grated cheese and mix well.

Serve in warm soup plates, with extra cheese.

Linguine with Cilantro and Chive Pesto

SERVES 4

WHILE VACATIONING WITH GLORIA AND HER mother, Julia, in Puerto Rico, where Julia was born, I spotted a small restaurant that looked inviting. A young woman who was the chef came out to talk to me, and we went there for dinner. She had cilantro pesto on her menu. Gloria and I loved it, and I have since made my version of the dish many times when cilantro and chives come up in my garden.

||||||||||||||||||||||||||||||||||||||||||||||||||||

FOR THE PESTO: Put the garlic, cilantro, chives, water, salt, and pepper in a blender (a blender makes a smoother pesto than a food processor) and blend for about 30 seconds, until pureed. (You may have to the push the mixture down into the blender a few times.) Add the nuts and all but 1 tablespoon of the oil and process until you have a beautiful green puree. (Makes about 2 cups.)

Transfer the pesto to a bowl and pour the remaining 1 tablespoon olive oil over the top; this coating will prevent discoloration. Refrigerate until ready to use. *(The pesto will keep for a couple of days.)*

At cooking time, bring 4 quarts salted water to a boil in a large pot. Add the linguine, stir well, and cook for about 10 minutes, until al dente (or to your taste).

Scoop out 1 cup of the pasta cooking liquid and drain the pasta. Return the pasta to the pot and add the reserved water, the pesto, and ¼ cup of the Parmesan cheese. Mix well.

Divide the pasta among four hot plates. Serve with the remaining ¼ cup cheese and, if desired, pepper flakes.

PESTO

4 garlic cloves, crushed

3 cups (lightly packed) fresh cilantro leaves

1¼ cups sliced (1-inch) fresh chives

⅔ cup water

1¼ teaspoons salt

1¼ teaspoons freshly ground black pepper

½ cup hazelnuts, toasted in a 350-degree oven for 10 to 12 minutes, skin left on, or pecans

½ cup extra-virgin olive oil

1 pound linguine, preferably imported

½ cup grated Parmesan cheese

Hot pepper flakes, for serving (optional)

Spaghetti with Tomatoes and Herbs

SERVES 4

2 cups coarsely chopped
onions

3 tablespoons coarsely
chopped garlic

1 tablespoon fresh thyme
leaves

1/3 cup extra-virgin olive oil,
plus extra for serving

2 pounds very ripe tomatoes,
cut into 1-inch pieces
(6 cups)

2 tablespoons tomato paste

1½ teaspoons salt

1 teaspoon freshly ground
black pepper

1 cup chopped mixed fresh
herbs, such as ½ cup chives
and ¼ cup each tarragon
and basil

1 pound spaghetti, preferably
imported

1/3 cup grated Parmesan
cheese, plus extra for
serving

Minced fresh chives (optional)

*FOR A SIMPLE DISH OF PASTA AND TOMATO
sauce, it makes an amazing difference when the tomatoes are
ripe from the garden. Of course, when my tomatoes are ripe,
thyme, basil, chives, and tarragon are plentiful in my garden
too, so they end up flavoring the pasta.*

*I like lots of onion and garlic in my sauce, and I like the
finished dish moist. Once the pasta is cooked, I add some of
the pasta water to the sauce to loosen it further. Then I let
the sauced pasta stand for a few minutes to marry the flavors
before I serve it.*

|||||||||||||||||||||||||||||||||||||||||||||||||

Put the onions, garlic, thyme, and olive oil in a large
saucepan and cook, uncovered, over high heat for about
3 minutes. Add the tomatoes, tomato paste, salt, and pepper
and cook, covered, over medium-high heat for 10 minutes.
Uncover and cook over medium heat for another 7 to 8 minutes, then stir in the herbs.

Meanwhile, bring 4 quarts salted water to a boil in a large
pot. Add the pasta, stir well, and boil for about 8 minutes,
until al dente (or to your liking).

Scoop out ¾ cup of the pasta cooking water, add it to the
tomato sauce, and mix well. Drain the pasta and add it to
the sauce, along with the cheese. Mix well and let sit for 5 minutes to merge the flavors.

Serve the spaghetti on warm plates, with plenty of sauce
and a drizzle of olive oil on top, sprinkle with chives, if using,
and pass extra cheese at the table.

Spaghetti à la Bolognese

SERVES 8

SAUCE

3 tablespoons olive oil

2 cups diced (½-inch) onions

¾ cup diced (½-inch) carrots

¾ cup diced (½-inch) celery

3 tablespoons chopped
crushed garlic

12 ounces bulk Italian sausage

12 ounces ground beef

2 cups homemade chicken
stock or canned low-sodium
chicken broth

One 28-ounce can plum
tomatoes in puree

1 cup dry white wine

3 tablespoons tomato paste

1 teaspoon fresh thyme leaves

3 tablespoons shredded fresh
sage leaves

1 small serrano pepper, seeded
and chopped, or to taste

¼ teaspoon salt

BOLOGNESE SAUCE IS ONE OF THOSE RECIPES that transcends its particular cuisine: I remember preparing it at the Plaza-Athénée in Paris in the 1950s. Recipes for different versions abound. My wife, who loves spaghetti Bolognese, makes hers with beef, pork, and veal. The most common version is made with beef only, but in this recipe, I use half Italian sausage and half ground beef.

It is sometimes difficult to combine the meat with the other ingredients without lumps forming. To prevent this, I put the meat in a bowl, add some chicken stock, and crush the meat into the stock with my fingers. As the meat gets wet, it becomes a smooth mixture without lumps. Then I add it to the pot with the remainder of the ingredients and proceed with the cooking. If you are serving a smaller group, just freeze the extra sauce for another time.

I like to cook the spaghetti and season it apart from the Bolognese sauce, then serve it with the sauce on top.

||||||||||||||||||||||||||||||||||||||||||||||||||

FOR THE SAUCE: Heat the olive oil in a large saucepan. Add the onions, carrots, celery, and garlic and cook for 5 minutes.

Meanwhile, put the sausage and ground beef in a bowl, add 1 cup of the stock, and crush the meat with your hands to separate it. Put the tomatoes in another bowl and coarsely crush them with your hands.

Add the meat and stock mixture to the saucepan, along with the tomatoes and the rest of the ingredients, including the remaining cup of stock. Bring to a boil, cover, reduce the heat to low, and cook gently for 1½ hours. (Makes 9 cups sauce.)

FOR THE PASTA: When ready to cook the pasta, bring 6 quarts salted water to a boil in a large pot. Add the pasta to the water, stir well, and cook for about 9 minutes, until al dente (or to your liking).

Scoop out 1½ cups of the pasta cooking liquid and drain the pasta. Return the pasta to the pot, add the reserved cooking water, the oil, salt, and pepper, and mix well.

Divide the pasta among eight warm plates and pour a good cup of the Bolognese sauce on top of each serving. Sprinkle with the Parmesan cheese and chives and serve immediately.

PASTA

1½ pounds spaghetti, preferably imported

5 tablespoons olive oil

1½ teaspoons salt

1½ teaspoons freshly ground black pepper

1 cup grated Parmesan cheese

¼ cup minced fresh chives

Gloria's Linguine with Clam Sauce

SERVES 4

6 tablespoons olive oil

2 cups coarsely chopped
onions

2 tablespoons coarsely
chopped garlic

2 teaspoons dried oregano,
preferably Mexican

18 top neck or cherrystone
clams, cleaned and opened
(see the headnote on
page 134), clams and clam
juice reserved separately

1 cup dry white wine

1 teaspoon hot pepper flakes,
or to taste

1 teaspoon salt

1 pound linguine, preferably
imported

½ cup chopped mixed fresh
parsley and chives

½ teaspoon freshly ground
black pepper

½ cup grated Parmesan
cheese (optional)

ONE OF GLORIA'S SPECIALTIES IS HER LINGUINE with clam sauce, and I have included this recipe with her seal of approval. I like to use medium-size top neck or cherrystone clams (about 6 clams per pound).

The sauce, made with onions, garlic, oregano, pepper flakes, wine, and the juice from the clams, can be prepared ahead and the clams added at the last moment, when ready to serve.

||||||||||||||||||||||||||||||||||||||||||||||||

Heat 3 tablespoons of the oil in a medium saucepan. Add the onions, garlic, and oregano and sauté for about 5 minutes. Add 1½ cups of the reserved clam juice, the wine, pepper flakes, and ¾ teaspoon of the salt and bring to a boil. Boil gently for 5 minutes, then set the sauce aside. *(This can be done an hour ahead.)*

At cooking time, bring 4 quarts salted water to a boil in a large pot. Add the pasta, stir well, and cook for 10 minutes, or until al dente (or to your liking).

Meanwhile, bring the sauce back to a boil. Add the clams, parsley mixture, and pepper.

Scoop out ¾ cup of the pasta cooking liquid and drain the pasta. Return the pasta to the pot, add the reserved cooking liquid, the remaining 3 tablespoons oil, and the remaining ¼ teaspoon salt, and mix well.

Serve the linguine in warm soup bowls, with a good ladle of clam sauce on top of each serving. Garnish with the grated Parmesan cheese, if you like.

Pasta and Shrimp with Pressed Caviar Shavings

SERVES 4

2 tablespoons olive oil

½ cup chopped shallots

2 cups sliced (½-inch) mushrooms

½ cup dry white wine

1 cup light cream

1 teaspoon salt

1 teaspoon freshly ground black pepper

12 ounces fusilli, preferably imported

12 ounces large shrimp (about 25), shelled and halved crosswise

3 tablespoons minced fresh chives

Grated Parmesan cheese, for serving (optional)

About 2 ounces pressed caviar (see headnote), frozen

CAVIAR IS ALWAYS A GOOD COMPLEMENT TO shellfish. I use pressed caviar, or payusnaya, *in this recipe. Available in cans from specialty stores or online sources, it is made with sturgeon roe that is salted and pressed. It is smooth, intense in taste, complex, and full-flavored. Because of its texture, it can be sliced, molded, spread, or frozen and shaved, as it is here; it can also be used in sauces. Freezing makes it easier to cut shavings of the caviar: Remove it from the can, wrap it in plastic, and freeze. But if you can't get pressed caviar, the dish will still be good without it.*

The creamy mushroom sauce can be prepared ahead and reheated at the last moment with the shrimp and chives while the pasta cooks. Although grated Parmesan cheese is not conventionally served with shellfish and pasta, I like to use it in this recipe, but it is optional.

||||||||||||||||||||||||||||||||||||||||||||||

Put the oil, shallots, and mushrooms in a large saucepan and cook over high heat, stirring occasionally, for 5 minutes. Add the wine, bring to a boil, and boil for 1 minute. Add the cream, salt, and pepper, bring back to a boil, and boil for a few seconds. Remove from the heat. *(The sauce can be prepared up to 1 hour ahead.)*

At serving time, bring 3 quarts salted water to a boil in a large pot. Add the fusilli, stir well, and cook for 13 to 15 minutes, until al dente (or to your liking).

Meanwhile, bring the cream sauce to a boil. Add the shrimp and chives, bring back to a boil, and simmer for 1 minute.

Drain the pasta and return it to the pot, along with the shrimp sauce. Mix well. Add Parmesan cheese, if desired, and mix well.

Transfer the pasta to very hot plates. Using a vegetable peeler, shave the caviar over the pasta, adding at least 4 to 5 shavings per person; it will soften when it touches the hot pasta. Serve immediately.

Spinach and Ricotta Lasagna

SERVES 10

TOMATO SAUCE

3 tablespoons olive oil

1½ cups coarsely chopped
onions

1½ tablespoons coarsely
chopped garlic

One 28-ounce can diced
tomatoes

1½ cups water

¾ teaspoon salt

¾ teaspoon freshly ground
black pepper

SPINACH

One 1-pound bag baby spinach

⅛ teaspoon freshly grated
nutmeg

1 tablespoon olive oil

½ teaspoon salt

½ teaspoon freshly ground
black pepper

USING LASAGNA THAT DOESN'T NEED TO BE boiled takes the tedium out of preparing this dish. The addition of Gruyère cheese is not conventional, but it gives the gratin a rich, different taste; it can be replaced with grated mozzarella.

There are three different subrecipes that come together to make my lasagna: tomato sauce, ricotta filling, and spinach. Each of these recipes can also stand on its own. The tomato sauce is very thin, as it should be, to accommodate the final cooking of the lasagna noodles in the dish. The ricotta mixture could also be cooked in individual molds and served on its own. And the spinach is great as an accompaniment to any meat or poultry dish.

||||||||||||||||||||||||||||||||||||||||||||||||

FOR THE SAUCE: Heat the oil in a large saucepan. Add the onions and cook over high heat, stirring occasionally, for about 3 minutes. Add the rest of the ingredients, bring to a boil, and boil gently, uncovered, for 5 minutes. Set aside.

FOR THE SPINACH: Poke a few holes in the bag of spinach with the point of a knife and cook in a microwave oven for 4 minutes. The spinach should be wilted and soft. Transfer to a bowl and mix in the nutmeg, olive oil, salt, and pepper. Set aside.

FOR THE RICOTTA FILLING: Mix all the ingredients well with a whisk in a bowl until smooth. Set aside.

TO ASSEMBLE AND BAKE THE DISH: Preheat the oven to 375 degrees.

Pour about 1½ cups of the tomato sauce into the bottom of a 9-by-13-inch baking dish (about 2 inches deep). Arrange 4 sheets of the lasagna crosswise on top, overlapping them slightly. Spread half the ricotta mixture on top of the lasagna and top with another 4 sheets. Spread the spinach mixture on top and cover with 4 more sheets. Spread the remaining ricotta mixture on top and cover with the last 4 lasagna sheets. Pour the remaining tomato sauce on top and around the edges of the dish. (It may seem like a lot of tomato sauce, but it is needed.) Finally, sprinkle both grated cheeses all over the top.

Cover the dish with aluminum foil and place it on a baking sheet. Bake for 45 minutes. At this point, the pasta should be cooked and tender. Remove the foil and cook for another 15 minutes to brown the top. Let rest for 10 minutes.

Using a wide hamburger spatula, cut the lasagna into sections and serve.

RICOTTA FILLING

1 pound ricotta cheese

3 large eggs

¼ cup minced scallions

¼ cup minced fresh parsley

½ teaspoon salt

½ teaspoon freshly ground black pepper

One 9-ounce box preboiled (no-cook) lasagna noodles (16 sheets, about 7 by 3½ inches)

1 cup grated Gruyère or Emmenthaler cheese (about 3 ounces)

¼ cup grated Parmesan cheese

Jacques 72

Vegetables

Artichoke Hearts and Peas

SERVES 4 TO 6

3 tablespoons olive oil

¼ cup chopped onion

1 tablespoon chopped garlic

2 teaspoons all-purpose flour

¾ cup homemade chicken stock, canned low-sodium chicken broth, or water

2 teaspoons chopped fresh savory or thyme

One 9-ounce package frozen artichoke hearts

One 10-ounce package frozen baby peas

¾ teaspoon salt

½ teaspoon freshly ground black pepper

I LOVE FROZEN BABY PEAS, WHICH ARE THE smallest, sweetest peas. Frozen artichokes are another favorite. I always keep both on hand, so I can put this dish together whenever I have to feed unexpected guests.

||||||||||||||||||||||||||||||||||||||||

Heat the oil in a large saucepan. Add the onion and garlic and sauté for 1 minute. Sprinkle on the flour, mix well, and cook for 30 seconds. Add the stock or water and savory and bring to a boil, stirring occasionally.

Add the artichokes and peas (frozen or defrosted), salt, and pepper, mix well, and bring to a boil (this will take longer if the vegetables were frozen when added). Cover, reduce the heat to low, and cook for 2 to 3 minutes. Serve.

Artichoke and Tomato Gratin

SERVES 4

FROZEN ARTICHOKE HEARTS AND GRAPE TOMA-toes tossed with bread cubes, scallions, and Parmesan cheese make a simple, savory gratin.

||||||||||||||||||||||||||||||||||||||||||||||||||

Preheat the oven to 400 degrees.

Put all the ingredients in a bowl and toss together until well mixed. Transfer to a 6-cup gratin dish.

Bake the gratin for about 30 minutes, until nicely crusted on top. Serve.

One 9-ounce package frozen artichoke hearts

2 cups grape tomatoes

2 cups 1-inch pieces baguette

3 tablespoons olive oil

⅓ cup sliced scallions

½ teaspoon salt

½ teaspoon freshly ground black pepper

¼ cup grated Parmesan cheese

Asparagus Topped with Bread Crumbs and Egg

SERVES 4

1¼ pounds large asparagus spears with tight heads (about 20)

¾ teaspoon salt

2 slices white bread, cut into ¼-inch pieces (about 1¼ cups)

2 tablespoons unsalted butter

1 tablespoon canola oil

3 tablespoons minced scallions

½ teaspoon freshly ground black pepper

1 tablespoon olive oil

1 large hard-cooked egg, chopped with an egg slicer or a sharp knife

Minced fresh chives (optional)

I ALWAYS BUY LARGE ASPARAGUS WITH TIGHT heads and firm stalks. I peel the lower third of each stalk so the entire spear is tender. We love asparagus steamed and served cold with a mustard vinaigrette or warm with hollandaise sauce or melted butter, as well as in gratins with a white sauce and cheese crust. In this recipe, I serve it just warm, topped with crunchy bread crumbs, chopped egg, and scallions. The fried bread crumbs are also great on top of salads, soups, or pasta.

||||||||||||||||||||||||||||||||||||||||||||||||||||

Peel the lower third of each asparagus spear and cut the spears into 2-inch pieces. (You should have about 4 cups.)

Pour 1 cup water into a large skillet, add ¼ teaspoon of the salt, and bring the water to a boil. Add the asparagus, cover, and bring back to a boil (this should take about 2 minutes). Cook for another 2 minutes. Transfer to a plate to drain and let the asparagus cool.

Process the bread to crumbs in a food processor. (You should have about 1 cup.)

Melt the butter with the canola oil in a small skillet. Add the bread crumbs and stir with a spoon so the bread is moistened with the butter and oil; the mixture will be soft. Keep cooking and stirring the bread for about 2 minutes. Add the scallions and cook, stirring and sautéing, until the mixture gets drier. Then cook for about 2 minutes longer, still stirring,

until the crumbs are nicely browned and dry. Transfer the crumbs to a plate.

At serving time, sprinkle the asparagus with the remaining ½ teaspoon salt, the pepper, and olive oil. Heat for about 1½ minutes in a microwave oven, until the asparagus is warm.

Divide the asparagus among four plates, sprinkle on the bread crumbs, chopped egg, and chives, if using, and serve immediately.

Asparagus with Black Olives and Mustard Dressing

SERVES 4

16 large firm asparagus spears
(about 1 pound)

1 cup diced (½-inch) country
bread or baguette

1 tablespoon canola oil

2 large hard-cooked eggs,
diced

¼ cup diced (¼-inch)
oil-cured black olives

MUSTARD DRESSING

1 tablespoon Dijon mustard

1 tablespoon water

¼ teaspoon salt

¼ teaspoon freshly ground
black pepper

¼ cup walnut oil

OLIVES, CROUTONS, AND CHOPPED EGGS MAKE a great garnish for this asparagus with a mustard sauce. I cut the bottoms of the asparagus spears into small pieces and add them to the dressing for another texture. This dish is best served at room temperature, not cold.

Preheat the oven to 400 degrees.

Peel the bottom third of each asparagus spear. Pour 2 cups water into a saucepan or skillet large enough to hold the asparagus in one or two layers. Add the asparagus, cover, bring to a boil, and boil for about 3 minutes. Drain.

Cut about 2½ inches from the bottom of each asparagus spear and cut these lengths into ½-inch pieces. Set the asparagus aside.

Toss the bread cubes with the canola oil and spread on a baking sheet. Bake for 9 to 10 minutes, until nicely browned. Set aside.

FOR THE DRESSING: Mix all the ingredients together in a bowl.

At serving time, toss the chopped asparagus stems, eggs, and olives with the mustard dressing. Arrange 4 asparagus spears on each of four plates to form a square. Fill the centers with the olive garnish and top with the croutons.

Green Beans with Mustard and Cream Dressing

SERVES 4

MOST COOKS UNDERCOOK STRING BEANS NOW-adays, but the true taste comes out only if they are cooked through. Small, thin haricots verts are very good here, but larger string beans are also fine if they are deep green in color and firm and snap when broken. The cream and mustard dressing is a standard at our house. If it is made an hour or before serving, it will thicken considerably; add 1 or 2 tablespoons of water to the dressing at serving time to thin it to a creamy consistency.

||||||||||||||||||||||||||||||||||||||||||||||||||

Pour 6 cups water into a large saucepan, add the salt, and bring to a boil. Meanwhile, trim the ends from the beans.

Add the beans to the boiling salted water and bring back to a boil. (This will take about 2 minutes.) Cook the beans for 4 to 5 minutes, until they are tender but still firm. Drain.

FOR THE DRESSING: Combine all the ingredients in a bowl large enough to hold the beans. Add the lukewarm beans to the dressing, thinning it first with 1 or 2 tablespoons water if needed, and mix well.

Divide the beans among four plates and surround each serving with 4 half slices of tomato to make a border. Sprinkle with the parsley and serve.

½ teaspoon salt

1 pound haricots verts or
    green beans

DRESSING

2 tablespoons Dijon mustard

¼ cup heavy cream

½ teaspoon salt

½ teaspoon freshly ground
    black pepper

2 tablespoons finely chopped
    shallots

1 large tomato (about
    8 ounces), cut into 8 slices,
    each slice halved

2 tablespoons coarsely
    chopped fresh parsley

Carrots with Chives

SERVES 4

5 or 6 large carrots (about 1 pound), peeled

1 tablespoon unsalted butter

1 tablespoon peanut or canola oil

½ teaspoon salt

½ teaspoon sugar

¼ cup water

¼ cup chopped shallots

½ teaspoon freshly ground black pepper

2 tablespoons minced fresh chives

THINLY SLICED CARROTS COOK IN JUST A FEW minutes. They can be sliced ahead but are best sautéed at the last moment. By the time the liquid evaporates, the carrots will have glazed in the butter, oil, and sugar.

||||||||||||||||||||||||||||||||||||||||||

Using a mandoline or a knife, slice the carrots into ⅛-inch slices. (You should have about 3½ cups.)

Combine the carrots, butter, and oil in a skillet. Sprinkle the carrots with the salt and sugar, add the water, and cook, covered, for about 3 minutes over high heat. Add the shallots and pepper and cook, covered, for about 2 minutes.

Add the chives and cook for about 1 minute, uncovered, until the pan is dry, tossing the carrots occasionally. Serve.

Cauliflower Sauté à Cru

SERVES 4

THE CONVENTIONAL WAY TO COOK CAULI-
*flower is to first separate the head into florets, which are then
boiled before they are sautéed or used in a gratin. Here the
whole cauliflower head is quartered, then sliced and sautéed
in olive oil. No precooking is required, and the cauliflower has
a clean, fresh taste. There will be some cauliflower "crumbs"
when you slice it; they should be sautéed along with the slices.
Hazelnut oil gives the dish a wonderful nutty taste. If it is
unavailable, use peanut oil.*

|||||||||||||||||||||||||||||||||||||||||||||||

Cut the cauliflower through the stem into quarters. Cut
each quarter into ½-inch slices. You will have about
16 slices, plus crumbs.

Divide the oils between two large (12-inch) skillets, preferably nonstick, and heat the oil. (If you have only one large
skillet, cook the cauliflower in two batches, using half the
oil for each batch.) Add the cauliflower slices in one layer
(with the crumbs) and cook over high heat for about 5 minutes, until browned on the bottom. Turn the cauliflower and
cook for another 4 minutes, or until lightly browned on the
second side.

Add the salt, pepper, garlic, and chives, stir to combine, and
cook for another minute. Serve.

1 cauliflower (1½ to
 2 pounds), cleaned of
 any green leaves

3 tablespoons extra-virgin
 olive oil

1 tablespoon hazelnut oil

½ teaspoon salt

½ teaspoon freshly ground
 black pepper

2 teaspoons chopped garlic
 (about 3 cloves)

¼ cup minced fresh chives

Celery Gratin

SERVES 4

1 bunch celery (about
    1 pound), as white as
    possible

½ cup homemade chicken
    stock or canned low-sodium
    chicken broth

¼ teaspoon salt

¼ teaspoon freshly ground
    black pepper

1½ tablespoons olive oil

1 tablespoon unsalted butter

⅓ cup grated Gruyère cheese

2 tablespoons grated
    Parmesan cheese

ALTHOUGH CELERY IS NOT OFTEN SERVED AS A cooked vegetable, celery hearts make a wonderful gratin. It is a good accompaniment for a roast of veal or roasted chicken.

Preheat the oven to 400 degrees.

Using a vegetable peeler, peel the outside of the celery stalks, especially where they are green, tough, or fibrous. Split each large stalk lengthwise in half. Cut the celery into 2-inch pieces. (You should have about 4 cups.)

Bring 2½ cups water to a boil in a skillet. Add the celery, bring back to a boil, and boil, covered, for 4 to 5 minutes, until the celery is slightly tender.

Drain the celery and transfer to a 4- to 5-cup gratin dish. Add the chicken stock, salt, pepper, olive oil, and butter and mix well. Sprinkle with the Gruyère and Parmesan cheeses.

Bake the celery for 30 to 35 minutes, until tender and lightly browned on top. Serve.

Swiss Chard Gratin

SERVES 4

SWISS CHARD WAS COMMON IN FRANCE WHEN I was a child. My mother usually prepared it as a gratin. However, the chard leaves were very large and she only used the ribs, peeling them beforehand. With the small chard I buy at my farmers' markets, there is no need to peel the ribs, and the tender greens can be cooked as well.

||||||||||||||||||||||||||||||||||||||||||||||||||

Preheat the oven to 400 degrees.

Bring 4 cups water to a boil in a large saucepan. Add the Swiss chard and push the chard down into the water as it comes back to a boil. Boil, uncovered, for 3 to 4 minutes, until the chard is tender. Drain in a colander and rinse under cold water. Drain well.

Transfer the chard to a 6-cup gratin dish. Mix in half the salt and pepper and ¾ cup of the cheese.

Melt the butter in a saucepan. Add the flour, mix well with a whisk, and cook for about 30 seconds. Add the milk and the rest of the salt and pepper and bring to a boil, mixing with the whisk until the mixture thickens and boils. Pour in the cream and mix to incorporate. Remove from the heat.

Combine the bread crumbs with the remaining ¼ cup cheese and the paprika in a bowl, mixing well.

Pour the white sauce over the chard and mix it in. Sprinkle the bread crumb mixture over the top.

Put the dish on a baking sheet and bake for about 30 minutes, until well browned and crusty on top. Serve.

1 pound Swiss chard, washed and cut into 2- to 3-inch pieces

1 teaspoon salt

1 teaspoon freshly ground black pepper

1 cup grated Gruyère cheese (about 3 ounces)

1½ tablespoons unsalted butter

2 tablespoons all-purpose flour

1½ cups milk

¼ cup heavy cream

2 tablespoons panko (Japanese-style dried bread crumbs) or regular dried bread crumbs

½ teaspoon paprika

Chickpeas and Spinach

SERVES 4

¾ cup diced (½-inch) onion

3 tablespoons peanut or
canola oil

1 pound baby spinach

One 16-ounce can chickpeas,
drained

¾ teaspoon salt

½ teaspoon freshly ground
black pepper

A GOOD SOURCE OF PROTEIN, FIBER, AND CAL-cium, chickpeas give this spinach dish an appealingly chunky and satisfying consistency.

||||||||||||||||||||||||||||||||||||||||||||||||||||

Sauté the onion in the oil in a large skillet for 1 to 2 minutes. Add the spinach, cover, and cook for 1 minute. Remove the lid and move the spinach around with tongs so it wilts throughout.

Add the chickpeas, salt, and pepper and cook, uncovered, over high heat until the spinach is soft and most of the moisture that comes out of it has evaporated. Serve.

Corn and Shallots with Sun-Dried Tomatoes

SERVES 4

LIKE MOST PEOPLE, WE USUALLY EAT LOCAL fresh sweet corn on the cob, just steamed for a few seconds over boiling water. But when the urge for a change hits during corn season, I remove the kernels for use in fritters and soup, or simply sauté them, as here.

||||||||||||||||||||||||||||||||||||||||||||||||

Using a sharp knife or a mandoline, slice the kernels off the ears of corn. (You should have about 3 cups kernels.)

Heat the oil and butter in a large skillet until very hot. Add the shallots and sauté for 30 seconds, then add the corn kernels and cook over high heat, tossing, for about 2½ minutes. Add the salt, pepper, tomatoes, and cilantro and cook for about 30 seconds longer.

Mix well and serve.

4 ears sweet corn, as young and fresh as possible, husked

1 tablespoon peanut oil

1 tablespoon unsalted butter

¼ cup chopped shallots

¼ teaspoon salt

½ teaspoon freshly ground black pepper

¼ cup diced (½-inch) sun-dried tomatoes in oil

¼ teaspoon coarsely chopped fresh cilantro

Corn Soufflé

SERVES 4

2 large or 3 smaller ears sweet
corn, as young and fresh as
possible, husked

½ cup diced Gruyère cheese

½ cup half-and-half

3 large eggs

2 tablespoons diced poblano
or jalapeño pepper, or to
taste

½ teaspoon salt

½ teaspoon freshly ground
black pepper

2 tablespoons chopped fresh
chives

1 tablespoon unsalted butter,
for the soufflé molds

FOR THIS SOUFFLÉ, CORN KERNELS ARE PUREED in a blender with Gruyère, eggs, half-and-half, a chili pepper, and chives, then cooked in individual ramekins or a gratin dish. It makes a great first course for dinner or accompaniment for grilled meat or fish.

The soufflé can be assembled a few hours ahead and baked when needed. It will come out of the oven puffy and should be eaten as soon as possible, since it tends to deflate.

|||||||||||||||||||||||||||||||||||||||||||||||||||

Preheat the oven to 400 degrees.

Using a sharp knife or mandoline, cut the corn kernels off the cobs. (You should have 2½ to 3 cups corn kernels.)

Put the corn, Gruyère, half-and-half, eggs, chili pepper, salt, and pepper in a blender (a blender makes a smoother mixture than a food processor) and blend for about 1 minute, until smooth. Add the chives and pulse to mix them in.

Butter four ¾- to 1-cup soufflé molds or a 4-cup gratin dish. Fill with the corn mixture and place on a baking sheet. *(The soufflé can be refrigerated for several hours before baking.)*

Bake the soufflé for about 25 minutes, until puffy, golden, and set. Serve right away.

Edamame Ragout

SERVES 4

1 pound frozen shelled edamame (soybeans)

3 cups shredded Boston lettuce

1 tablespoon finely chopped garlic

½ cup minced scallions

2 tablespoons unsalted butter

2 tablespoons olive oil

½ teaspoon salt

½ teaspoon freshly ground black pepper

⅔ cup homemade chicken stock or canned low-sodium chicken broth

IN THE LAST FEW YEARS, EDAMAME (SOYBEANS) have become readily available as a snack, dried and crunchy; fresh in the pod; preserved in sea salt; and—my preference—shelled and frozen. The ones I buy at my market are young, and the skin of the beans is very tender. I use them as I would fresh fava beans, but, unlike favas, there is no need to peel them. They are less expensive than favas and easier to cook. This recipe, similar to the classic dish of peas prepared French style with lettuce and onion, is a great accompaniment to grilled poultry.

||||||||||||||||||||||||||||||||||||||||||||||||||

Combine all the ingredients in a large saucepan and bring to a boil. Cover and continue boiling for about 4 minutes, then uncover and boil over high heat for about 2 more minutes to reduce the liquid and finish cooking the edamame.

Serve.

Eggplant with Cheese Crust

SERVES 4

SLICES OF EGGPLANT ARE TOPPED WITH PAR-mesan cheese and baked for this easy accompaniment to grilled fish, meat, or poultry. Any leftovers can be coarsely chopped and tossed with pasta or rice.

||||||||||||||||||||||||||||||||||||||||||||||||||||

Preheat the oven to 400 degrees.

Slice the eggplant into 16 slices of about equal thickness. Mix the salt and pepper together and sprinkle on the slices.

Line a baking sheet with a nonstick baking mat and spread the oil evenly over the mat. Arrange the eggplant slices side by side on the oiled mat, then turn them over so they are lightly oiled on both sides. Sprinkle the cheese evenly on top.

Bake for 30 minutes. Cool to lukewarm.

At serving time, sprinkle the chives on top of the eggplant and drizzle with a little extra-virgin olive oil.

1 large eggplant (about 1 pound)

½ teaspoon salt

½ teaspoon freshly ground black pepper

2 tablespoons olive oil

⅓ cup grated Parmesan cheese

2 tablespoons chopped fresh chives

Extra-virgin olive oil, for sprinkling on top

Fried Eggplant Fans

SERVES 4

2 Japanese or Chinese
   eggplants (about 6 ounces
   each, 8 to 10 inches long
   and 2 inches thick)

BATTER

2 large egg yolks

½ cup all-purpose flour

¾ cup ice-cold water

About ½ cup canola oil,
   for frying

Salt

FOR THIS RECIPE, I USE THE LONG, THIN, DEEP red or bright purple eggplant variously called Japanese, Chinese, or Asian eggplant. They are firm with small seeds. Each eggplant is split lengthwise in half and then the halves are cut into thin slices still attached at one end; when spread out and fried, they look like beautiful crisp brown fans. The fans are good as a garnish for grilled meat or poultry, as an appetizer, or on a salad. They are best eaten right out of the skillet, but you can keep them for 10 or 15 minutes if you arrange them in one layer on a wire rack, so they don't get soggy underneath, and put them in a warm oven.

The batter should be very cold to produce the crispest coating.

||||||||||||||||||||||||||||||||||||||||||||||||||||

Cut each eggplant lengthwise in half on a diagonal on a cutting board, so one end of each half eggplant is thicker than the other end. To make the fans, turn a half eggplant cut side down with the thick end toward you and cut lengthwise into thin slices (about ¼ inch thick), cutting from the thin end to the thick end and leaving the slices attached at the thin end. You should get 7 or 8 slices. Press on the slices to spread them out to create a fan about 6 inches wide at the wide end. Repeat with the remaining eggplant halves.

FOR THE BATTER: Mix the egg yolks, flour, and ¼ cup of the ice water with a whisk in a bowl to make a thick, smooth

batter. Add the remaining ½ cup ice water and mix it in. *(If making the batter ahead, refrigerate.)*

At cooking time, heat the oil in two large nonstick skillets (or fry in two batches, using half the oil for each one). Dip each fan into the batter so it is well coated on both sides, place 2 of them, in one layer, in the hot oil in each skillet, and press lightly to make the fans spread out. Cook over high heat for about 4 minutes on the first side, then turn over and cook for 3 to 4 minutes on the other side, until cooked through, crisp, and well browned on both sides.

Using a spatula, transfer the eggplant to a wire rack. Sprinkle with salt and serve. Or keep warm on the rack in a 145-degree oven for a few minutes, until ready to serve.

Eggplant-Tomato Gratin

SERVES 4

2 eggplants, preferably long,
    narrow Chinese eggplants
    (about 14 ounces total)

¼ cup olive oil

1 teaspoon salt

2 ripe tomatoes (about
    1 pound)

1 cup diced (½-inch) day-old
    baguette

¾ cup diced (½-inch)
    Gruyère cheese (about
    3 ounces)

3 fresh thyme sprigs

⅓ cup minced fresh chives

½ teaspoon freshly ground
    black pepper

WHEN MY GARDEN IS PRODUCING IN FULL summer, I love to make vegetable gratins. I top this one with bread crumbs from a day-old baguette and Gruyère cheese. Mixed with a little olive oil, it makes a crusty, chunky topping.

||||||||||||||||||||||||||||||||||||||||||||||

Preheat the oven to 400 degrees.

Trim off both ends of the eggplants. Cut them crosswise in half, then cut each half lengthwise in half, so you have 8 pieces.

Line a baking sheet with aluminum foil. Pour 2 tablespoons of the oil on the foil and put the eggplant slices cut side down in the oil. Turn the slices cut side up and sprinkle with ½ teaspoon of the salt.

Bake the eggplant for about 20 minutes, until tender. Remove from the oven.

Meanwhile, cut the tomatoes into ½-inch slices.

Process the diced bread and cheese in a food processor for about 30 seconds, until very coarsely chopped.

Arrange the baked eggplant pieces in a 4-cup gratin dish, alternating them with the tomato slices. Sprinkle with the thyme, chives, the remaining ½ teaspoon salt, and the pepper. Toss the bread and cheese mixture with the remaining 2 tablespoons oil and spread on top of the vegetables. *(The gratin can be prepared to this point hours ahead.)*

Bake the gratin for 30 minutes, or until crusty and brown. Serve.

A Green Thumb in the Kitchen

ALTHOUGH MY GARDEN NOW IS MUCH SMALLER THAN it used to be, it still brings a huge amount of pleasure to our lives. Advancing years and competing priorities have cut back on the amount of land I cultivate, but I will maintain a plot until I am no longer physically able to, and I recommend that every cook do the same, even if yours is no more than a few potted herbs in a sunny corner of your deck or balcony.

The main crop I harvest from the raised bed I tend is excitement. It begins only a few weeks after the ground has thawed and the first tiny arugula plants miraculously put forth leaves that will enliven weary winter salads and omelets. I haven't planted arugula for ages, but my plants dutifully seed themselves and the patch expands every year with no input from me other than a bit of fertilizer and a sprinkle from the hose. The arugula is followed by chives, thyme, parsley, sage, tarragon, and oregano, as well as some difficult-to-find herbs such as chervil and savory. Nothing compares to cooking with herbs that are minutes from the garden.

A few basil plants keep me supplied all summer, and when frost threatens, I pull the plants up and hang them in the garage to dry. I also cut the oregano, sage, and thyme plants at ground level and dry them as

well. I use the dried "wood" from these plants to smoke salmon, bass, or even poultry.

I save space in the garden for a few cornichons and hot peppers, which Gloria adores. We grow shallots that we then store over the winter in the basement. And we always allot space for lettuce and other salad fixings. Our local farmers' market is awash with great tomatoes in the summer, but I plant a few special, hard-to-get varieties to supplement the local abundance. Summer would not be summer without them.

Eggplant Chinois

SERVES 4

1 tablespoon dark soy sauce

1 tablespoon oyster sauce

1 tablespoon hoisin sauce

2 teaspoons hot chili sauce, such as Sriracha

⅓ cup water

4 small, narrow (about 1½ inches in diameter) Chinese or Japanese eggplants (about 1 pound)

2 tablespoons canola oil

1 tablespoon chopped garlic

1 tablespoon chopped peeled ginger

⅓ cup sliced (½-inch) scallions

¼ cup coarsely chopped fresh cilantro

THIS IS MY INTERPRETATION OF AN EGGPLANT dish that we always order at one of our favorite Chinese restaurants. The beauty of many Chinese dishes is the use of bottled sauces, which I always have on hand in my refrigerator or pantry. The eggplants are cut into chunks, sautéed in oil, and finished with garlic, ginger, and several of these sauces. This is a nice dish to serve with a roast.

Mix the soy sauce, oyster sauce, hoisin sauce, hot chili sauce, and water together in a small bowl. Set aside.

Slice the eggplant crosswise 1¼ inches thick, then slice the disks into wedges. (You should have about 4 cups.)

Heat the oil in a large skillet. Add the eggplant and sauté over high heat, covered, for about 7 minutes, turning the pieces in the hot oil occasionally. Remove the lid, add the garlic, ginger, and scallions, and sauté, uncovered, for about 1 minute, tossing the mixture a few times.

Add the soy sauce mixture to the skillet, cover, and cook for about 1 minute. Uncover and cook for 1 minute longer, then add the cilantro, toss, and serve.

Endive Gratin

SERVES 4

4 large endives (about
   1 pound)

½ cup water

¼ teaspoon salt

¼ teaspoon sugar

2 tablespoons fresh lemon
   juice

WHITE SAUCE

2 tablespoons unsalted butter

1 tablespoon all-purpose flour

1 cup milk

¼ teaspoon salt

¼ teaspoon freshly ground
   black pepper

¼ cup diced mozzarella

1 tablespoon grated Parmesan
   cheese

FIRST COOKED IN A MINIMAL AMOUNT OF WATER (which can be done as early as the day before), the endives are then coated with a white sauce, mozzarella, and Parmesan cheese and finished under the broiler.

||||||||||||||||||||||||||||||||||||||||||||||

Clean the endives of any damaged leaves. Remove and discard the browned ends of each and wash under cool water. Put the endives in a large saucepan, add the water, salt, sugar, and lemon juice, and bring to a boil. Cover, reduce the heat, and cook for about 25 minutes, until the endives are tender and most of the water has evaporated. Transfer the endives to a gratin dish, in one layer, and press on them with a spoon to flatten them.

FOR THE SAUCE: Melt the butter in a small saucepan. Stir in the flour and mix well. Add the milk, salt, and pepper and bring to a boil, stirring with a whisk until the sauce is smooth and bubbling. Cook for about 10 seconds longer.

Spread the sauce evenly over the endives. Scatter the mozzarella on top and sprinkle on the Parmesan cheese. *(The gratin can be prepared to this point a couple of hours ahead and refrigerated.)*

At serving time, preheat the broiler. Place the gratin under the hot broiler so it is about 10 inches from the heat source. Cook for 5 to 7 minutes, until the gratin is warmed through and nicely browned.

Serve.

Lima Bean Ragout

SERVES 8

1 pound small dried lima
    beans

1 chicken bouillon cube

6 cups water

1½ teaspoons salt

2 cups diced (1-inch) leeks,
    including greens

2 cups diced (1-inch) onions

1 cup diced (1-inch) peeled
    carrot

1 cup diced (1-inch) celery

1 cup diced (1-inch) fennel
    stalks and fronds

½ cup salsa, homemade
    (Pico de Gallo, page 152)
    or store-bought

WHEN MY MOTHER VISITED FROM FRANCE many years ago, I cooked lima beans for her. She had never eaten them before and she loved them, so I made them in one form or another for her every time she visited afterward. This stew uses small dried limas, and it takes about 2 hours to cook from the dry state—I do not presoak the beans and I always start them in cold water. The cooked beans freeze well and are a bonus when I need something to accompany poultry or meat. Here the red salsa (I often use store-bought) is a fresh addition to the beans, lending color and piquancy.

||||||||||||||||||||||||||||||||||||||||||||||

Sort through the beans and discard any pebbles or damaged beans. Rinse the beans in a strainer under cold water and put them in a saucepan. Add the bouillon cube, water, and salt and bring to a boil, then reduce the heat to low, cover, and cook for 1 hour.

Add the rest of the ingredients and bring to a boil. Reduce the heat to low and cook, covered, for another hour.

Serve.

Peas with Basil

SERVES 4

THERE IS NOTHING BETTER THAN FRESH PEAS just out of the pod in late spring, and they are always worth a special trip to a local farm or farmers' market when they're in season. (Frozen baby peas make a fine substitute at other times of year.) Basil is plentiful in my summer garden, and this dish is a delicious variation on the old favorite of peas and mint.

||||||||||||||||||||||||||||||||||||||||||||||||||

Combine the peas, butter, sugar, salt, pepper, and water in a saucepan, bring to a boil, and boil over high heat for about 5 minutes, stirring occasionally, until most of the water has evaporated and the peas are tender.

Add the basil, mix well, and serve.

1 pound (a good 3 cups) shelled small fresh peas (about 6 pounds peas in the pod) or one 1-pound bag baby peas, thawed

2½ tablespoons unsalted butter

¾ teaspoon sugar

¾ teaspoon salt

½ teaspoon freshly ground black pepper

⅓ cup water

⅓ cup shredded fresh basil leaves

Peas and Fennel with Lardons

SERVES 4

THE COMBINATION OF FENNEL, WITH ITS
*slightly licorice flavor, and salt pork complements the sweet-
ness of the peas. This is an ideal accompaniment to grilled
meats.*

||||||||||||||||||||||||||||||||||||||||||||||||||

Cut the pork or pancetta into ¾-inch pieces and put them
in a large saucepan. Add the water and bring to a boil
over high heat. Cover, reduce the heat to low, and boil gently
for 10 minutes. There should about 1¼ cups of liquid left in
the pan.

Add the onions, fennel, and garlic and bring to a boil.
Reduce the heat and boil gently for about 8 minutes.

Add the peas, salt, sugar, pepper, oil, and butter and bring
to a boil. Boil, uncovered, for about 3 minutes to cook the
peas and reduce the liquid. Serve.

4 ounces lean cured pork or
pancetta

2 cups water

2 cups coarsely chopped
onions

2 cups diced (1-inch) fennel
(about 8 ounces)

1 tablespoon coarsely chopped
garlic

8 ounces (a good 1½ cups)
shelled small fresh peas
(about 3 pounds peas in the
pod) or frozen baby peas

½ teaspoon salt

¼ teaspoon sugar

½ teaspoon freshly ground
black pepper

1 tablespoon olive oil

1 tablespoon unsalted butter

Quick Pickled Red Onions and Radishes

SERVES 8 TO 10

2 cups warm water

½ cup kosher salt, or ⅓ cup
table salt

½ cup sugar

½ cup cider vinegar

2 teaspoons Tabasco sauce,
or to taste

2 medium red onions (about
1 pound), sliced (about
4 cups)

3 cups sliced radishes

*MY FRIENDS LOVE THIS PICKLE. I USE IT ON
hamburgers, grilled meat, or cold meats and in sandwiches.
The onions and radishes can be sliced by hand or in a food
processor fitted with the slicing disk. You can also make this
recipe with just onions.*

Pour the warm water into a medium bowl and mix in the
salt, sugar, vinegar, and Tabasco. Add the sliced onions
and radishes and mix well. Set aside for at least 3 hours.

Transfer the vegetables and brine to a jar, refrigerate, and
use as needed. The pickle will keep for at least 3 months.

Poblano Relish

SERVES 4 TO 6

4 nice, plump poblano peppers
(about 1 pound)

¼ cup olive oil

½ teaspoon salt

THIS RELISH IS A STANDARD AT OUR HOUSE, and we use it in sandwiches, egg dishes, stews, and salads and on grilled meat or fish—any time we want to add some zest or bite to a dish. Sometimes when Gloria is making the relish, she peels extra peppers (which is the tedious part of the recipe), cuts them into strips, and puts them in plastic bags in batches to freeze. When we need more, she just defrosts a batch overnight and seasons the peppers with the oil and salt. Stored in a jar in the refrigerator, the relish will keep for a couple of weeks.

Poblano peppers can range from quite hot to just slightly spicy.

||||||||||||||||||||||||||||||||||||||||||||||||

Heat the broiler. Arrange the peppers on a rack set over the broiler tray. Place the tray under the hot broiler so the peppers are about 1 inch from the heat source and roast for 12 to 14 minutes, turning them often with tongs, so they get charred on all sides. Immediately transfer them to a sealable plastic bag and let them steam for about 10 minutes (the steam helps release the skin).

Holding the peppers under cool running water, pull or scrape off the skin. Cut the peppers lengthwise in half and remove and discard the seeds and ribs.

Dry the peppers with paper towels and cut them into ¼-inch-wide strips. Mix with the oil and salt in a bowl or jar, cover, and refrigerate until ready to serve.

Potatoes Rachael Ray

SERVES 4

SEVERAL YEARS AGO I MADE A POTATO DISH called pommes fondantes *("melting potatoes") for a magazine article. I peeled and trimmed potatoes, cutting them into football shapes, and cooked them in a skillet in one layer with chicken stock and butter until the potatoes were done and the stock was practically gone. Then, using a large spoon, I pressed on the potatoes to crack them open without crushing them and cooked them for a few minutes longer. They absorbed the rest of the cooking liquid, browning beautifully in the butter.*

Not long ago, I was invited to appear on the Rachael Ray Show*, and, in my honor, she made those potatoes, incorporating a few changes of her own. She used small Yukon Gold potatoes and did not peel them. Since this made the dish easier to prepare and the result was just as good, I adjusted my own recipe accordingly.*

|||||||||||||||||||||||||||||||||||||||||||||||||||||||

1¼ pounds baby yellow potatoes, such as Yukon Gold (about 20)

1½ cups homemade chicken stock or canned low-sodium chicken broth

2 tablespoons olive oil

¼ teaspoon salt (less if stock is salted)

2 tablespoons unsalted butter

2 tablespoon minced fresh chives

Remove and discard any eyes from the potatoes. Wash the potatoes and arrange them in one layer in a large skillet, preferably nonstick. Add the stock, oil, and salt and bring to a boil. Cover and cook gently for about 15 minutes, or until the potatoes are tender; there should be a little liquid left.

Using a metal measuring cup, press gently on each potato to crack it open, but do not mash the potatoes. Add the butter and cook the potatoes, uncovered, over medium heat, turning once, for about 3 minutes on each side, until all the liquid is gone and the potatoes are golden brown on both sides. Sprinkle with the chives and serve.

Fried Potatoes

SERVES 4 TO 6

1½ pounds Yukon Gold
   potatoes (about 8)

¾ teaspoon salt

About 1 cup canola oil

ONE OF THE TASTIEST WAYS TO MAKE POTA-toes is to boil them with the skin on until they are tender and then peel them, thickly slice, and fry them in oil. The outside gets crunchy and brown while the inside remains moist and creamy. The potatoes can be boiled ahead and then fried just before serving. I do not do much deep-frying at my house, pre-ferring to use a minimal amount of oil in a skillet to achieve my goal. For this recipe, which uses 1½ pounds potatoes, I fry the potato slices in two batches in 1 cup oil; at the end of cooking, I have about ¾ cup oil left, which means that I've used only ¼ cup oil, or 1 tablespoon per person.

||||||||||||||||||||||||||||||||||||||||||||||||||||

Put the potatoes in a saucepan, cover with water, add ½ teaspoon of the salt, and bring to a boil. Boil for about 40 minutes, until tender. Drain and let cool enough to handle.

Peel the potatoes and cut into ½-inch slices.

At serving time, pour the oil into a skillet; it should be at least ½ inch deep. Heat the oil to between 375 and 400 de-grees. Place half the potatoes in the hot oil and cook, stirring occasionally, for about 6 minutes, or until nicely browned on both sides but still creamy inside. With a slotted spoon, trans-fer the potatoes to a platter. Repeat with the second batch of potato slices.

Sprinkle the remaining ¼ teaspoon salt on top of the pota-toes and serve.

Small Potatoes in Olive Oil

SERVES 4

ONE EVENING WE WERE EATING FRESHLY grilled sardines in Albufeira, in the south of Portugal, when the waiter brought us a plate of delightful boiled potatoes doused with olive oil. I adapted the recipe by adding olives for saltiness and color and cracking the potatoes open so they absorb some of the olive oil and coarse salt.

||||||||||||||||||||||||||||||||||||||||||||||||||||||||||

Put the potatoes in a saucepan and cover with water. Add the salt and bring the water to a boil, then reduce the heat to low and boil the potatoes gently for 25 to 30 minutes, until very tender.

Drain the potatoes and put in one layer in a serving dish. Using a fork or the flat bottom of a measuring cup, press down gently on the potatoes to crack them open a little. Sprinkle with the oil, coarse salt, olives, and chives. Serve.

1½ pounds small potatoes, such as Yukon Gold or Red Bliss (about 16), scrubbed

½ teaspoon salt

¼ cup extra-virgin olive oil (best possible)

1 teaspoon fleur de sel or other coarse salt

12 kalamata olives, pitted and cut into ½-inch pieces

1½ tablespoons minced fresh chives

Broiled Maple Sweet Potatoes

SERVES 4

2 large sweet potatoes
(2 pounds)

4 tablespoons unsalted butter,
melted

4 teaspoons pure maple syrup

½ teaspoon salt

1 teaspoon freshly ground
black pepper

FOR THIS DISH, I COOK THE SWEET POTATOES in a microwave oven while I heat up the broiler. Then I halve the potatoes, rub them with butter, top with maple syrup, and finish them under the broiler.

||||||||||||||||||||||||||||||||||||||||||||||||

Heat the broiler. While it is heating, microwave the potatoes for 8 minutes. They should be cooked through.

Split the potatoes lengthwise in half and score the flesh of each half with a knife, cutting a crisscross pattern about ½ inch deep. Brush the cut sides with half the butter and top with the maple syrup, salt, and pepper.

Arrange the potato halves cut side up on an aluminum-foil-lined baking sheet and broil about 7 inches from the heat source for 4 minutes. Turn the potatoes over and broil for another 3 to 4 minutes.

Arrange the tomatoes cut side up on a plate, brush with the remaining butter, and serve.

Sautéed Radicchio

SERVES 4

MY FAMILY LIKES BITTER VEGETABLES, AND this recipe is perfect as a palate cleanser after a rich dish. For a milder flavor, substitute romaine lettuce or napa cabbage for the radicchio or use half radicchio, half romaine for a nice, colorful combination.

||||||||||||||||||||||||||||||||||||||||||||||

Heat the oil in a large skillet. When hot, add the radicchio, salt, and pepper and stir well. Cover and cook for about 3 minutes, stirring a few times, until the radicchio softens.

Add the scallions and garlic and cook, uncovered, stirring a few times, for about 1 minute. Serve.

3 tablespoons olive oil

1 large head radicchio (about 1 pound), cut into 8 wedges

½ teaspoon salt

½ teaspoon freshly ground black pepper

⅓ cup minced scallions

1 tablespoon chopped garlic

Stew of Radishes

SERVES 4

1 pound radishes (2 to
   3 bunches), trimmed of
   root ends and stems and
   washed

1 tablespoon almond or
   walnut oil

1 tablespoon unsalted butter

½ teaspoon salt

2 tablespoons water

*RADISHES ARE NOT USUALLY SERVED AS A
cooked vegetable, but they make a crunchy, flavorful accompaniment to fish, poultry, and meat dishes. As they cook, the
hotness in the radishes disappears and they become almost
transparent. Almond or walnut oil adds a wonderful flavor,
but if unavailable, it can be replaced by another nut oil, such
as hazelnut or peanut.*

||||||||||||||||||||||||||||||||||||||||||||||||

Cut the radishes into ¼-inch slices.
   Combine the radishes with the remaining ingredients in
a very large skillet, cover, bring to a boil, and cook for about
1½ minutes. Remove the lid and cook over high heat for another 2 to 3 minutes, until all the moisture has evaporated
and the radish slices are tender but still firm. Serve.

Velvet Spinach

SERVES 4

THIS PUREE, OR "VELVET," IS BEST MADE WITH tender baby spinach, but any fresh spinach will work. A little butter, salt, and pepper are the only enhancements in this preparation, which concentrates the beautiful green color and the pure taste of the fresh spinach.

1 pound baby spinach

3 tablespoons unsalted butter

¾ teaspoon salt

¾ teaspoon freshly ground
   black pepper

||||||||||||||||||||||||||||||||||||||||||||||||||

Bring 3 cups water to a boil in a medium saucepan. Add the spinach and push it down into the water to wilt it. Bring the water back to a boil and boil the spinach, uncovered, for about 1 minute.

Drain the spinach in a colander, reserving a little of the cooking water, and transfer to a blender. Add the butter, salt, and pepper and blend until the spinach is finely pureed. If the mixture is too thick to process properly, add 1 or 2 tablespoons of the reserved cooking water and process until smooth. Serve.

Stuffed Tomatoes

SERVES 6

6 large not-too-ripe tomatoes
  (about 10 ounces each;
  3½ pounds total)

1¼ teaspoons salt

2 tablespoons olive oil

2 tablespoons potato starch,
  dissolved in 2 tablespoons
  water

5 ounces baby bella or cremini
  mushrooms, washed, cubed,
  and coarsely chopped in
  a food processor (about
  2 cups)

2 small firm zucchini
  (8 ounces total), cubed
  and coarsely chopped in
  the food processor (about
  2 cups)

½ cup chopped onion

1 tablespoon chopped garlic

½ cup chopped fresh parsley
  or minced chives, plus
  2 tablespoons for garnish

2 teaspoons chopped jalapeño
  pepper

ANY GOOD HOME COOK IN FRANCE HAS HER own special recipe for stuffed tomatoes. My mother, aunt, cousins, and niece all made their versions when the season yielded large and inexpensive tomatoes. For mine, I combine mushrooms and zucchini with meat, onions, garlic, and hot pepper to a make a flavorful and moist stuffing. I use a mixture of hot Italian pork sausage and ground beef.

I cut a good ¾-inch slice from the stem end of each tomato and then hollow out the tomatoes. These top slices and the insides of the tomatoes are pureed in a food processor to become the sauce. If you have extra tomato puree, it can be used for soup, pasta, or even drinks.

||||||||||||||||||||||||||||||||||||||||||||||||||

Preheat the oven to 400 degrees.

Remove the stems of the tomatoes, if any, and reserve for decoration. Cut a thick slice (about ¾ inch) from the stem end of each tomato. Using a sharp spoon (a metal measuring spoon is good), hollow out each tomato to make a receptacle, leaving a ½- to ¾-inch-thick shell.

Process the slices and insides of the tomatoes in a food processor. (You should have about 3 cups; if you have more, keep the excess for a soup or sauce.) Transfer to a bowl, add ½ teaspoon of the salt, the olive oil, and potato starch, and mix well with a whisk.

Transfer the mixture to a saucepan, bring to a boil, and cook, stirring occasionally. The sauce will thicken as it comes to a boil. Strain through a food mill or sieve. Set aside.

Combine the mushrooms, zucchini, onion, garlic, parsley, jalapeño pepper, the remaining ¾ teaspoon salt, the pepper, ground beef, and sausage in a bowl and mix well with your hands. Arrange the tomato receptacles side by side, hollow side up, in a large gratin dish and fill with the stuffing mix (about 1 cup per tomato). Place the stems, if you have them, on top for decoration. Pour the sauce around and over the tomatoes.

Bake the tomatoes for 1 hour. Serve with some of the sauce and a sprinkling of the remaining 2 tablespoons parsley or chives.

½ teaspoon freshly ground black pepper

8 ounces ground beef

8 ounces hot Italian sausage patties, bulk Italian sausage, or links, casings removed

Sliced Tomato Gratin

SERVES 4

2 pounds large ripe tomatoes

3 tablespoons olive oil

2 cups diced (½-inch) baguette or country bread

⅔ cup sliced shallots

⅓ cup sliced garlic

1½ teaspoons fresh thyme leaves

½ teaspoon salt

½ teaspoon freshly ground black pepper

THICK SLICES OF RIPE TOMATO ARE BAKED with a topping of diced bread and seasonings in this gratin. Success depends on using the highest-quality ingredients.

||||||||||||||||||||||||||||||||||||||||||||||||||||

Preheat the oven to 425 degrees.

Cut the tomatoes into ½-inch slices and arrange the slices in a 6- to 8-cup gratin dish. Sprinkle with 2 tablespoons of the oil.

Combine the bread, shallots, garlic, thyme, and the remaining 1 tablespoon oil in a bowl and mix well. Sprinkle the salt and pepper on the tomatoes and top with the bread mixture.

Bake for about 25 minutes, until the tomatoes are browned on top and cooked. Serve.

Tomato Tatin

SERVES 4

THE CLASSIC TARTE TATIN IS MADE WITH AP-
*ples that are caramelized in a skillet with butter and sugar,
then covered with a sheet of dough and baked. The finished
tart is unmolded and served with the dough underneath. I use
this same idea with tomatoes, caramelizing them and then
baking them in small molds with a thick slice of baguette on
top of each one until the bread is lightly browned. The result
is pure tomato essence, delicate and straightforward. Plum
(Roma) tomatoes are ideal for this dish.*

||||||||||||||||||||||||||||||||||||||||||||||

1½ pounds plum tomatoes
(about 8), cut lengthwise
into quarters

3 tablespoons olive oil

½ teaspoon salt

½ teaspoon freshly ground
black pepper

Four 1-inch-thick slices
baguette, about 3 inches in
diameter (the diameter of
the soufflé molds)

1 tablespoon chopped fresh
chives

Preheat the oven to 400 degrees.
Press on the tomato wedges to remove most of the seeds
and juice (reserve the juice for stock, if desired).

Heat the olive oil in a large nonstick skillet. When it is hot,
add the tomatoes, salt, and pepper and cook, covered, over
high heat for about 12 minutes, until all the liquid evaporates
and the tomato wedges start caramelizing.

Divide the tomatoes among four ½-cup soufflé molds or
small Pyrex custard cups. Cover each with a baguette slice.
(The dish can be prepared a couple of hours ahead to this point.)

Bake the tomato Tatins for 12 to 15 minutes, until the filling
is very hot and the bread is lightly browned. Remove from the
oven and let rest for 5 minutes.

Unmold the Tatins by turning each one upside down, with
the bread as a base, onto a small plate. Sprinkle with the
chives and serve.

Caramelized Tomatoes Provençal

SERVES 4

8 firm plum tomatoes (about
  2 pounds)

4 tablespoons olive oil

½ teaspoon salt

½ teaspoon freshly ground
  black pepper

1¼ cups diced (¼-inch) stale
  baguette

¼ cup coarsely chopped fresh
  parsley

1 tablespoon coarsely chopped
  garlic

2 tablespoons grated Gruyère
  or Emmenthaler cheese

THERE ARE MANY VERSIONS OF TOMATOES Provençal, in which tomatoes are baked with parsley, garlic, and olive oil. I use plum (Roma) tomatoes, which stay quite firm and meaty even when fully ripe. I get the pan quite hot before I add the oiled tomato halves. The tomatoes caramelize, but they can often stick to the pan: The secret is to leave them off the heat for 5 to 10 minutes after browning so they soften, release some of their liquid, and release from the pan.

|||||||||||||||||||||||||||||||||||||||||||||||||

Preheat the oven to 400 degrees.

Cut the tomatoes lengthwise in half. Spread 2 tablespoons of the olive oil in a gratin dish that can accommodate all the tomatoes and place them cut side down in the oil.

Heat a heavy saucepan (not nonstick) over high heat for at least 5 minutes, until it is very hot. Add the oiled tomato halves, cut side down, in one layer and cook for about 5 minutes to caramelize the cut sides of the tomatoes. Turn the heat off and let the tomatoes stand for 5 to 10 minutes. They will release some juices and so will not stick to the pan anymore.

Return the tomato halves to the gratin dish, arranging them browned side up. Sprinkle with the salt and pepper. Mix the bread pieces with the parsley, garlic, cheese, and the remaining 2 tablespoons oil. Spread on top of the tomato halves. *(This can be done hours ahead.)*

Shortly before serving time, place the tomatoes in the center of the oven and cook for 20 to 25 minutes, until hot, bubbling, and browned on top. Serve.

Turnip Puree with Garlic

SERVES 6

THIS PUREE IS ESPECIALLY GOOD MADE WITH *fresh young white turnips; it can taste assertive when the turnips are older. Turnips are often cooked with potatoes for a puree to give the puree texture and a milder taste; by themselves, turnips tend to be watery. Here I first cook the turnips with a fair amount of garlic in salted water, then emulsify the whole mixture with a hand blender into a puree, thicken it with potato flakes, and flavor it with butter. This is great with grilled meat or poultry.*

||||||||||||||||||||||||||||||||||||||||||||||||||||||||

About 1½ pounds white turnips (6 to 8), peeled and quartered (about 1¼ pounds after peeling)

5 garlic cloves

3 cups water

½ teaspoon salt

1 cup potato flakes

4 tablespoons unsalted butter, cut into pieces

¼ teaspoon freshly ground black pepper

Put the turnips in a saucepan, along with the garlic, water, and salt. Bring to a boil, reduce the heat, cover, and boil gently for about 30 minutes, until the turnips and garlic are soft.

Using a hand blender, emulsify the turnips and garlic into a smooth puree (or puree in a regular blender and return to the saucepan). Add the potato flakes and mix with a whisk until incorporated. Bring to a boil, then add the butter, piece by piece, and the pepper and mix well. Serve.

Pureed Zucchini Gratin

SERVES 4

1 pound zucchini, cut into
   1-inch pieces

¾ cup half-and-half

2 tablespoons all-purpose
   flour

2 large eggs

½ teaspoon salt

½ teaspoon freshly ground
   black pepper

½ cup grated Gruyère cheese

1 teaspoon unsalted butter,
   softened, for the gratin dish

1 tablespoon grated Parmesan
   cheese

MY MOTHER USED TO MAKE A GRATIN SIMILAR to this at her restaurants. I microwave the zucchini first to cook it partially, then puree it and combine it with eggs, half-and-half, and cheese before browning it in the oven. The gratin mixture can be made ahead, but don't transfer it to the buttered gratin dish until just before baking, or the zucchini water may bleed and separate.

||||||||||||||||||||||||||||||||||||||||||||

Preheat the oven to 400 degrees.

Drop the zucchini pieces into a glass bowl and heat them in a microwave oven for 5 to 6 minutes.

Transfer the zucchini to a food processor and process for 15 to 20 seconds, until smooth. Add the half-and-half, flour, eggs, salt, and pepper and process for about 30 seconds. Add the cheese and process for a few seconds.

Butter a 3- to- 4-cup gratin dish with the butter and pour the zucchini mixture into it. Sprinkle the Parmesan cheese on top. Bake for about 30 minutes, until the gratin is set and brown on top. Serve.

On Baby Vegetables

IN THE VEGETABLE KINGDOM, SMALL IS OFTEN NOT beautiful, at least from the standpoint of taste. In fact, it seldom is, with the exception of summer squash and peas. Yet chefs often serve vegetables of ever-diminishing age and size. If this trend continues, we'll soon be dining on unborn baby vegetables that will be both tasteless and outrageously expensive.

The reason for the lack of taste is that these microveggies are harvested before they reach any level of maturity. A baby carrot is okay, but a carrot that is allowed to reach the peak of maturity is going to be sweeter and full of flavor—provided it hasn't become too old. String beans should reach the stage in life where they *are* string beans, or at least haricots verts. No one wants to eat old, fibrous salad greens, but properly mature Boston lettuce is far more tasty than paper-thin silver-dollar-size leaves.

Occasionally baby greens or vegetables can add some color and interest to a dish, and that's fine. But normal-size vegetables are just as good or better, for a fraction of the price.

Baby Zucchini with Chives

SERVES 4

1 pound baby zucchini (about 2 dozen)

1½ tablespoons canola oil

¼ teaspoon salt

¼ teaspoon freshly ground black pepper

1 tablespoon unsalted butter

3 tablespoons chopped fresh chives

I DO NOT OFTEN USE BABY VEGETABLES; THEY are usually expensive and somewhat tasteless. I make an exception for baby zucchini, which are available at my market during the summer for a good price and are crunchy and tasty.

||||||||||||||||||||||||||||||||||||||||||||||||

Wash the zucchini and trim both ends.

Heat the oil in a 12-inch nonstick skillet. Add the zucchini in one or two layers and sauté, covered, over high heat until lightly browned, about 4 minutes. Uncover, add the salt, pepper, butter, and chives, and cook, tossing the zucchini in the pan a few times, for about 1 minute. The zucchini should be cooked but still slightly crunchy. Serve right away.

Fruit Desserts and Preserves

Apple Galette

SERVES 4 TO 6

⅓ cup sugar

1 pound prepared regular or whole wheat pizza dough

3 large Golden Delicious apples (about 1½ pounds)

4 tablespoons unsalted butter, cut into ½-inch pieces

⅓ cup apricot preserves

I LIKE APPLE TARTS, APPLE GALETTES, OR APPLE pies in any form. I recently found a new way of making the crust for apple galette using pizza dough that I buy at my market.

||||||||||||||||||||||||||||||||||||||||||||||

Sprinkle 2 tablespoons of the sugar on a baking sheet lined with nonstick aluminum foil. Place the pizza dough on top and press it out with your hands as thin as possible. Let rest and proof at room temperature for 15 to 20 minutes.

Preheat the oven to 400 degrees.

Press the dough out further into a roundish 12-inch shape. (It will be less elastic and easier to stretch after it has rested.)

Peel and core the apples and cut each one into 8 wedges. Starting about ½ inch from the outer edges of the round of dough, arrange the apple wedges in concentric circles on top, pushing them gently into the dough. Dot with the butter and sprinkle evenly with the remaining sugar.

Bake the galette for 45 minutes, or until nicely browned and crusty. Slide a spatula underneath the galette while it is still hot to make certain it hasn't stuck to the sheet, and then let cool on the sheet. Spread the apricot preserves on top.

Cut the galette into wedges and serve at room temperature.

Apples in Lemon Sauce

SERVES 4

2 large Golden Delicious apples (about 1 pound total)

1½ tablespoons fresh lemon juice

3 tablespoons apricot or other preserves

¼ cup water

2 tablespoons unsalted butter

1½ tablespoons sugar

¼ cup dried cranberries

¼ cup crème fraîche or sour cream

THESE BAKED APPLE HALVES, FLAVORED WITH lemon juice and fruit preserves and sprinkled with dried cranberries, are a great dessert served warm or at room temperature.

|||||||||||||||||||||||||||||||||||||||||||||||

Preheat the oven to 400 degrees.

Halve the apples lengthwise and core them. Peel about half the skin from each apple piece, leaving the remainder to give chewiness to the finished dish. Arrange the apples cut side up in a small gratin dish.

Mix the lemon juice, preserves, and water together in a small bowl and spoon the mixture over the apples. Divide the butter among the apple hollows and sprinkle the apples with the sugar. Sprinkle the cranberries around and on top of the apples.

Bake the apples for 40 to 45 minutes, until tender and lightly browned. Cool slightly, and serve warm with the crème fraîche or sour cream.

How Sweet It Is

HEALTH-CONSCIOUS EXPERTS TELL US THAT REFINED sugar is virtually a poison and that butter lubricates a slippery slope to heart disease. But I want to assure you that none of those assertions account for the large number of fruit desserts in this book. They are here for a simple reason: I like them. I always have.

In her restaurants, my mother favored fruit desserts. She'd make a tart of apples, rhubarb, or pears, depending on the season. Frequently her meals would end with a fruit salad or crepes filled with fruit at the height of ripeness. I like simple preparations made with berries of all types, and I love baked apples. When I'm feeling energetic (provided that great pears are available), I will peel a pear, top it with sugar, and bake it in a hot oven for fifteen or twenty minutes, depending on the ripeness of the fruit, until the sugar caramelizes. Then I pour cream over the pears and caramel and let the mixture come to a boil, until it becomes an unctuous sauce.

But all the sugar and cream and kitchen tricks in the world will not compensate for unripe fruit. Unless what's available at your market is fresh, sweet, and fragrant, forget what you had in mind and substitute another fruit that is at its prime.

Although my recipes give specific cooking times and precise quantities of sugar, these are by necessity merely guidelines. What you do to fruit entirely depends on what it is like before you begin to cook.

Smell your fruit, have a taste of it, and judge its texture, then adjust your cooking technique and the amount of sugar accordingly. And keep an eye on your dish while it cooks, because times can vary wildly. How long does it take to cook a pear? The answer is until it is soft—and depending on the pear's variety and degree of ripeness, that can happen in a few minutes or require an hour.

Always keep in mind that the best ending to a meal might be the simplest. Gloria loves blueberries picked from the bush and seasoned with a bit of honey and lemon juice. When the berries are good, I can't think of a recipe that can top that.

Bananas in Caramel

SERVES 4

THIS DESSERT IS SIMPLE, FAST, AND DELICIOUS, but you will need a small kitchen torch to caramelize the sugar. It is best made no more than half an hour before serving, so the caramel will still be crunchy.

||||||||||||||||||||||||||||||||||||||||||||||||||||

4 bananas (6 to 7 ounces each)

1/4 cup sugar

1/2 cup sour cream

4 fresh mint sprigs

1/2 lemon

Cookies (optional)

Peel the bananas and cut each one lengthwise into 3 long slices. Arrange the slices about 1 inch apart on a baking sheet lined with nonstick aluminum foil.

Sprinkle each slice of banana with 1 teaspoon of the sugar. Holding a blowtorch so the flame is 1 to 2 inches from the slices, cook the sugar until it becomes a nice blond caramel color, 1 to 1½ minutes for each slice.

When all the slices are caramelized, arrange 3 slices (1 sliced banana) on each plate. Divide the sour cream among the plates, spooning it around the bananas. Top each dessert with a sprig of mint and a few drops of lemon juice and serve, with cookies, if desired.

Banana Gratin

SERVES 4

2 ripe bananas (6 to 7 ounces each)

2 tablespoons pure maple syrup

2 tablespoons dried cranberries

2 tablespoons unsalted butter, melted

2 slices white bread (about 2 ounces), cut into ¼-inch pieces

1 cup plain whole-milk yogurt

IN JUST A FEW MINUTES, BANANAS CAN BE transformed into a delicious dessert gratin. I like to serve this dish with old-style whole-milk yogurt that has a layer of cream on top. I bake the gratins in individual gratin dishes, but you can use any small ovenproof dishes you have.

||||||||||||||||||||||||||||||||||||||||||||||||||

Preheat the oven to 400 degrees.

Peel the bananas and slice them into a bowl. Combine with the rest of the ingredients except the yogurt. Divide among four small gratin dishes, about 4 inches across and 1 inch deep.

Bake the gratins for 15 minutes. Serve warm or at room temperature, topped with the yogurt.

Cherries with Sweet Wine and Brioche

SERVES 4

I LOVE TO MAKE THIS RECIPE WHEN I HAVE fresh cherries, especially the sour ones that I gather from my own tree. You can make the brioche or buy it. The Sauternes, a sweet dessert wine from the Bordeaux region of France, is added to the dessert at the table for show as well as for taste. If unavailable, replace with another sweet wine like Madeira or port.

|||||||||||||||||||||||||||||||||||||||||||||||||||||

Mix the cherries with the sugar in a bowl, cover, and re-frigerate. *(This can be done a couple of hours ahead.)* Whip the cream to a soft peak. Refrigerate.

At serving time, arrange a brioche half in each of four champagne coupes or martini glasses. Cover with the cherries and their juices. Top with the cream and mint sprigs and serve.

At the table, pour about ⅓ cup of the Sauternes into each dessert glass, taking care to pour it around the whipped cream, not over it. Serve the extra Sauternes in wineglasses as an accompaniment to the dessert.

2 cups sour cherries (sweet can be substituted), pitted

¼ cup sugar (2 tablespoons sugar if using sweet cherries)

½ cup heavy cream

2 brioche rolls (about 2 ounces each), split in half

4 fresh mint sprigs

One 375-ml bottle sweet Sauternes, chilled

Cherry Crumble

SERVES 4 TO 6

GLORIA LOVES CHERRY PIE AND THE CLASSIC French clafoutis, and so do I, but when time is short, I'm happy with this simple cherry crumble. Serve it warm with ice cream, crème fraîche, or sour cream. I often buy frozen pitted cherries for this dessert.

||||||||||||||||||||||||||||||||||||||||||||||

Preheat the oven to 400 degrees.

Combine the cherries and sugar in a bowl and mix well, then transfer to a 4- to 5-cup gratin dish.

FOR THE DOUGH: Mix the ingredients by hand or in a food processor just until the mixture comes together. Crumble the dough over the cherries.

Bake the crumble for 45 minutes. Serve warm, topping each portion with a heaping spoonful of ice cream, crème fraîche, or sour cream.

1 pound dark sweet cherries, pitted, or frozen pitted sweet cherries

2 tablespoons sugar

DOUGH

¾ cup all-purpose flour

1 teaspoon baking powder

6 tablespoons unsalted butter, softened

Ice cream, crème fraîche, or sour cream, for serving

Rice Pudding with Dried Cherries and Blueberry Sauce

SERVES 4

RICE PUDDING

2 cups cooked white rice

3½ cups milk

½ cup dried cherries or dried cranberries

⅓ cup pure maple syrup

2 teaspoons grated lime rind

1 teaspoon pure vanilla extract

¼ cup sugar

½ cup sour cream

SAUCE

1 pint (about 12 ounces) small blueberries, preferably wild berries

⅓ cup sugar

Thinly sliced lime rind (optional)

I ALWAYS BRING HOME THE LEFTOVER RICE when I go to a Chinese restaurant, and if I don't use it in a soup or stir-fry, I make rice pudding with it. This is the type of soft and creamy rice pudding my mother and aunts used to make. I usually serve the pudding with a blueberry sauce.

To make the pudding, I add milk to my cooked rice, bring it to a boil on top of the stove, and then cook it in a 350-degree oven. It may seem as if there is a lot of milk for the amount of rice, but it is necessary to get the creamy consistency I like. If you don't have leftover rice, bring ¾ cup Carolina rice and 1½ cups water to a boil, reduce the heat to low, cover, and cook for 25 minutes.

||||||||||||||||||||||||||||||||||||||||||||

FOR THE RICE PUDDING: Preheat the oven to 350 degrees. Put the rice and milk in an ovenproof saucepan, mix well, and bring to a boil. Cover, place in the oven, and bake for 30 minutes; the rice should be very creamy.

Remove the rice from the oven and stir in the dried fruit, maple syrup, lime rind, vanilla, sugar, and sour cream. Let cool.

FOR THE SAUCE: Combine the blueberries and sugar in a saucepan and bring to a boil, stirring occasionally. The blueberries will break down. Boil for 1 to 2 minutes longer. Cool and refrigerate until needed.

Serve the rice pudding with the blueberry sauce on the side or on top and garnish with the lime rind, if desired.

Grapefruit Granité with Mango and Mojito Cocktail

SERVES 4

GRANITÉ

2 to 3 pink grapefruits (about 1 pound each)

2 tablespoons honey

2 tablespoons grenadine syrup

2 tablespoons Mexican *jarabe* or other simple syrup or sugar

2 ripe mangoes (8 to 10 ounces each)

MOJITO COCKTAIL

½ cup (loosely packed) fresh mint leaves

1 tablespoon sugar

3 tablespoons fresh lime juice

2 tablespoons simple syrup (see above) or sugar

¼ cup white rum

4 fresh mint sprigs, for garnish

THE GRANITÉ FOR THIS DESSERT CAN BE PRE-pared up to several days ahead, but if frozen hard, it should be transferred from the freezer to the refrigerator a couple of hours before serving time so it will be soft enough to be scooped. The flavor of honey accents the grapefruit granité.

The mint sauce for the mojito cocktail should be prepared at the last moment; if it is made too far ahead, the mint will turn brown. (If you must make it ahead, strain to remove the mint before serving.) I like to crush the mint leaves in a mol-cajete, or mortar, with a pestle, but they can also be crushed in a small glass bowl with a sturdy wooden spoon or in the food processor.

|||||||||||||||||||||||||||||||||||||||||||||||||||

FOR THE GRANITÉ: Halve the grapefruits and squeeze to obtain as much juice as possible from them. (You should have about 2¼ cups juice.) Pour the juice into a bowl, stir in the honey, and mix in the grenadine and simple syrup or sugar. Place in the freezer until frozen.

Shortly before serving, peel the mangoes. Cut away the flesh from each of them parallel to the seed, to get 2 halves from each fruit. Cut the mangoes into smaller pieces, if desired. Set aside.

FOR THE MOJITO COCKTAIL: Using a mortar and pestle, a wooden spoon and a bowl, or a food processor, finely crush the mint leaves with the sugar. Add the lime juice, syrup or additional sugar, and rum and mix well.

At serving time, divide the cocktail among four soup plates. Arrange half a mango hollow side up (or pieces of mango) on each plate and add a good scoop of grapefruit granité. Top each serving with a sprig of mint and serve.

Lemon Mousseline

SERVES 4

2 teaspoons grated lemon rind, plus (optional) strips of lemon peel for decoration

¼ cup fresh lemon juice

Half a 14-ounce can sweetened condensed milk (about ¾ cup)

1 tablespoon Grand Marnier

1 cup heavy cream

4 sugar cookies

MADE WITH SWEETENED CONDENSED MILK, this rich and creamy lemon mousseline can be prepared in a few minutes, and it can be made up to a day ahead. I sometimes drop a cookie into the bottom of each of four individual soufflé molds and spoon the mousseline on top. The cookies make it easier to unmold the dessert and provide a nice topping for it. But I don't always unmold the mousseline: Sometimes, as here, I serve it directly from a crystal bowl, forming it into quenelles with two spoons or scooping it out with an ice cream scoop and setting it on top of cookies. You can double this recipe for a large party of 8 to 10 people.

Combine the lemon rind and juice with the condensed milk in a bowl and mix well. The mixture will thicken. Stir in the Grand Marnier.

Whip the cream to a soft peak. (Don't overwhip; cream tends to taste more like butter than sweet cream when it is whipped until stiff.) Fold the whipped cream into the lemon mixture and spoon it into a serving bowl. Smooth the top and cover with plastic wrap. Refrigerate for at least 1 hour, or for up to 1 day.

At serving time, place a cookie on each of four serving plates. Using an ice cream scoop, scoop the mousseline onto the cookies. Decorate the top of each dessert with strips of lemon peel, if desired.

Melon and Blueberry Medley

SERVES 4

THE SECRET OF A GREAT MELON RECIPE IS TO get a ripe, sweet, juicy fruit, and that is not always easy. The stem end of the fruit should be fragrant and the other end a bit soft when pressed. Cavaillon and Charantais melons, two of my favorite varieties, are sometimes available at my market. Use whatever type your market offers, provided the melon is ripe.

||||||||||||||||||||||||||||||||||||||||||||||||||||||

Peel the melon as you would an apple, removing any green flesh. Cut the melon crosswise in half and remove the seeds with a spoon. Cut 2 slices, or rings, about ¾ inch thick from each melon half. (Save the rest of the melon for another use.)

Combine the blueberries, maple syrup, and lemon juice in a bowl.

At serving time, place a ring of melon on each of four plates. Fill the hollow centers with the blueberries and juice. Garnish each dessert with a sprig of sage. Serve.

1 ripe melon, such as Cavaillon, Charantais, or cantaloupe (2¼ to 2½ pounds)

1 cup blueberries

⅓ cup pure maple syrup

3 tablespoons fresh lemon juice

4 fresh sage sprigs

White Peaches with Cointreau

SERVES 4

WHITE PEACHES ARE AVAILABLE FOR ONLY A matter of weeks in the summer. When the peaches are well ripened, the skin pulls off easily or can be removed with a small paring knife. If the peaches are not quite ripe and are very firm, remove the skin with a vegetable peeler. Cointreau or Grand Marnier enlivens this dessert, but if you prefer, you can make it without a liqueur.

||||||||||||||||||||||||||||||||||||||||||||||||

4 ripe white peaches (about 1¼ pounds)

2 tablespoons fresh lemon juice

2 tablespoons sugar

2 tablespoons Cointreau or Grand Marnier (optional)

4 slices pound cake (about 3 ounces total)

2 tablespoons shredded fresh basil leaves

Cut the peaches into wedges and drop them into a bowl. Add the lemon juice, sugar, and Cointreau or Grand Marnier, if using, and mix well. Cover and refrigerate until chilled.

At serving time, arrange the slices of pound cake on individual plates, or push them into shallow glasses. Spoon the peaches and their juice over the cake and top with the shredded basil. Serve.

Peaches Marty

SERVES 4

2 large ripe (but not overripe) yellow peaches (about 1½ pounds)

2 tablespoons unsalted butter, softened

¼ cup (packed) light brown sugar

⅓ cup water

6 tablespoons mascarpone cheese (optional)

2 tablespoons shredded fresh basil leaves

4 sugar cookies (optional)

WHEN YELLOW PEACHES ARE RIPE IN THE SUMmer, I make this recipe I have enjoyed at the home of my friend Marty. She places brown sugar and butter in the hollows of halved peaches and bakes them, serving them with mascarpone and basil. I serve only half a peach per person, as this is rich; for a lighter dessert, you can omit the mascarpone.

Preheat the oven to 400 degrees.

Cut the peaches in half and remove the pits. Place the peaches hollow side up in a small gratin dish that holds them snugly.

Mix the butter and sugar into a paste and divide the mixture among the peach hollows. Pour the water around the peaches.

Bake the peaches for 45 minutes, or until tender and lightly browned. Serve warm, with any juices accumulated around them; if desired, divide the mascarpone among the peaches, spooning it into the hollows. Sprinkle the basil on top and serve, with the cookies, if desired.

Pears with Honey and Cranberries

SERVES 4

¼ cup fresh lemon juice

¼ cup honey

⅓ cup dried cranberries

3 ripe pears, such as Bartlett
(about 1¼ pounds)

⅓ cup unskinned whole
hazelnuts

Cookies (optional)

WHENEVER I PLAN TO USE PEARS—EITHER cooked or raw—in a dessert, I buy them ahead to make sure they are fully ripe when needed. For this very simple recipe, sliced ripe pears are served in a lemon juice and honey mixture. Cranberries and roasted nuts add texture and contrast.

||||||||||||||||||||||||||||||||||||||||||||||||

Preheat the oven to 375 degrees.

Mix the lemon juice and honey in a bowl with a whisk until smooth. Mix in the cranberries.

Peel the pears, quarter them, and remove the cores and stems. Toss them in the lemon-honey mixture. Cover tightly with plastic wrap and refrigerate until serving time, tossing the pears in the liquid occasionally to ensure that they stay white.

Meanwhile, scatter the nuts on a baking sheet and roast for about 10 minutes. Let cool to lukewarm, then rub the nuts between paper towels to remove the skins. (Do not worry if some of the skin doesn't come off.)

Using a heavy skillet as a pounder, crush the nuts into chunks. Set aside.

Serve the pears with some of the sauce and the cranberries and the nuts sprinkled on top, with cookies, if you like.

Caramelized Pear Custard

SERVES 4

WHEN FALL COMES, I ALWAYS FEEL LIKE COOK-ing pears or apples—in a puree or tart, baked whole, or sautéed with maple syrup.

For this recipe, I first caramelize pear wedges (I love the flavor of Bartletts, but any pears will work) in a skillet with butter and sugar, then transfer them to a gratin dish and bake them in a custard mixture. The custard is served at room temperature with a sprinkling of confectioners' sugar on top.

|||||||||||||||||||||||||||||||||||||||||||||||||||||||

Preheat the oven to 400 degrees.

Peel and halve the pears, core them, and cut each half into 3 wedges. Put them in a skillet with the granulated sugar and butter and cook, uncovered, over high heat for 6 to 8 minutes, turning them once, until lightly caramelized. Transfer to a 4- to 5-cup gratin dish.

Mix together the half-and-half, vanilla, rum (if using), beaten egg, and maple syrup in a bowl. Pour the custard over the pears.

Place the gratin dish on a baking sheet and bake for 15 to 25 minutes, until the custard is just set.

Serve at room temperature, with a sprinkling of the confectioners' sugar on top.

2 ripe hard pears, such as Bartlett or Comice (about 1 pound)

3 tablespoons granulated sugar

2 tablespoons unsalted butter

¾ cup half-and-half

1 teaspoon pure vanilla extract

1 tablespoon dark rum (optional)

1 large egg, beaten with a fork

2 tablespoons pure maple syrup

1 tablespoon confectioners' sugar

Prunes in Red Wine

SERVES 4

1 pound large pitted prunes

2 cups fruity red wine

⅓ cup honey

8 strips lemon peel, removed
with a vegetable peeler
(from 1 lemon)

Juice of 1 lemon (¼ cup)

24 walnut halves

4 small slices pound cake
(about 3 ounces)

Port, for serving (optional)

½ cup sour cream

4 fresh tarragon or mint sprigs

ONE OF THE GREATEST DESSERTS I EVER HAD was at La Pyramide, a 3-star restaurant south of Lyon. It was made with the large pruneaux d'Agen, *prunes from Southwest France, which were poached in red port, cooled, and served in a brioche with crème fraîche. This easy variation brings back fond memories of the original. For extra flavor, add port to the prunes at serving time.*

||||||||||||||||||||||||||||||||||||||||||||||||||

Combine the prunes, wine, honey, lemon peel and juice, and walnuts in a saucepan and bring to a boil, then reduce the heat to very low, cover, and simmer for 20 minutes. Let the prunes cool in the liquid.

At serving time, place a slice of pound cake in each of four champagne coupes or glass dessert dishes and cover with the prunes and sauce. Sprinkle with a bit of port, if desired. Top with the sour cream and sprigs of tarragon or mint. Serve.

FRUIT DESSERTS AND PRESERVES ■ 375

Locust-Flower Fritters

SERVES 6 (MAKES 12 TO 15 FRITTERS)

4 cups (unsprayed) acacia flowers, stems removed

¼ cup Grand Marnier

¼ cup granulated sugar

1½ cups all-purpose flour

One 12-ounce can beer

1 teaspoon pure vanilla extract

2 large egg whites

About 1½ cups canola oil, for cooking the fritters

Confectioners' sugar, for dusting the fritters

MY AUNT HÉLÈNE USED TO MAKE THESE BEIG-nets, or fritters, in late spring, and I still enjoy this treat from my youth a few times each summer when the two large locust trees next to our garden bloom. Cook the fritters as close to serving time as possible, and keep them on a wire rack so they don't get soggy underneath.

||||||||||||||||||||||||||||||||||||||||||||||||

Mix the flowers, Grand Marnier, and granulated sugar together in a bowl. Cover and refrigerate for 1 hour.

When ready to cook the fritters, combine the flour, about two thirds of the beer, and the vanilla in a bowl and mix well with a whisk until smooth, then add the remainder of the beer to the batter and mix well.

Beat the egg whites in a bowl until they form peaks but are not too firm. Using the whisk, combine them with the beer batter. Fold in the acacia flower mixture.

Pour ⅓ cup oil into a large saucepan. Heat the oil to 350 degrees. Using a large spoon or a small measuring cup, add about ⅓ cup of the batter to the hot oil. Repeat to make a total of 4 or 5 fritters. Cook the fritters for about 4 minutes on the first side, then turn with a slotted spatula or tongs and cook for about 4 minutes on the other side, until crisp and nicely browned on all sides. Lift the fritters from the oil and place them on a wire rack. Repeat with the remaining batter.

Dust the fritters with confectioners' sugar before serving.

||||||||||||||||||||||||||||||||||||||||||||||||||

NOTES: *You can make savory fritters with squash or zucchini flowers. Omit the liqueur, sugar, and vanilla in the batter and sprinkle the finished beignets with salt.*

The fritters are best cooked right before serving. If you have to cook them ahead, recrisp them in a 425-degree oven for 5 to 6 minutes, or until crisp and hot. Dust with confectioners' sugar just before serving.

My Best Friend

DURING THE TWO YEARS I WORKED AS PERSONAL CHEF to the president of France, my duties grew increasingly more difficult and complex. I soon realized that the job was simply becoming too big for one cook, and I came to the conclusion that I needed help, especially in the dessert department. Chefs for French government officials—even the president—were often drawn from the ranks of the military at that time. I had been drafted into the Navy to serve mandatory service for eighteen months. Most men in the armed services were sent to fight the war in Algeria. My older brother, Roland, was drafted into the Air Force and, since two drafted brothers could not by law be sent into combat situations at the same time, I was dispatched to Navy headquarters in Paris to cook for the admiralty mess and, eventually, the president. So, when my request for a pastry chef was granted, I was relieved.

Relieved, that is, until I saw the guy they sent over. He was a gawky kid, skinny almost to the point of starvation and wearing a brand-new khaki uniform that had been designed for a much huskier soldier. I thought that the military bureaucracy had made a mistake.

"*Attention!*" I barked, thinking that he'd see it as a little joke. I did not rank high enough to issue such a command.

The poor guy nearly jumped out of the too-big uniform. He gave a nervous salute and stammered something about not being very experienced and not knowing why he'd been sent to the presidential residence. I teased him for a few minutes, circling around and grumbling, then asked him, "Do you want a glass of red or white?" He almost collapsed with relief. He became my best friend ever.

My new associate, Jean-Claude Szurdak, was a couple of years my junior but had already completed two full apprenticeships, one in pastry, one in cooking—jobs requiring skill that is rarely found in one person. We made a great team, cooking and learning together and complementing each other. We have since made thousands of meals together in France and the United States and are still cooking together more than half a century later.

An interviewer called us "the original odd couple" after he observed us preparing a lobster soufflé and a rack of lamb together for a charity dinner in Phoenix. "Those two guys work together, yet they never say a word," he said to another journalist. "One does one thing, the other will pick up where he left off and continue. One stops, the other starts." It's true. We don't have to talk. We know what the other is doing. We know what the other wants. We can take over from each other seamlessly. It's fun. We talk the same food language. We understand cooking in the same way. Our palates are similar. Yet on a personal level, we *are* the odd couple. Jean-Claude is unassuming and far more cautious and more reserved than I am. I have often pushed him into doing things he might not have done on his own—the most important being his decision to join me in the United States in 1960 for what we thought would be a two- or three-year lark before we returned home to begin our "real" careers.

In the states, Jean-Claude pursued his passion for pastry, eventually opening several shops in New York City and catering for the likes of Ronald Reagan, Henry Kissinger, and Jimmy Carter. He made pastries for Air France back in the era when airlines prided themselves on the quality of food they served, especially on overseas flights.

In the kitchen, ours is a partnership of equals. For obvious reasons, I have learned a great deal about making pastries and confections from him. (He also taught me about gardening.) Whenever we are working on a dish, each of us contributes ways to make it quicker, simpler, or better. He concocted one of the best shrimp recipes out there by boiling them in a broth of onions and herbs, putting the shrimp in a plastic bag, adding some of the cooking broth along with some sugar and

hot peppers, and leaving the bag in the fridge for forty-eight hours. The shrimp absorb all that liquid and become moist and piquant. I would never have thought of the method, but I was quite happy to add it to my culinary bag of tricks. We love to find new ingredients like pork tongue and kidneys and figure out how to create something delicious with them. There are traces of Jean-Claude in every cookbook I have written, including this one.

Jean-Claude retired in the mid-1990s to a plot in the Catskill Mountains a couple of hours from where I live. We see each other often, both socially and professionally, through the classes we team-teach. He owns forty acres of land with a lake. He has raised cattle, pigs, and sheep, which we slaughtered together, and he still shoots a deer every fall that I help skin and prepare. No one makes better jams and preserves than Jean-Claude. His vegetable garden is legendary, and he is an expert trout fisherman, a sport at which I am sadly inept, despite my wholehearted efforts.

Maybe we owe our long friendship to there being absolutely no jealousy between us. He is happy for my success, and I am happy to see him living life to the fullest on a patch of land that is as close to heaven as a retired French chef is likely to get while still on this earth.

Rhubarb-Honey Coupe with Creamy Yogurt Sauce

SERVES 4

I COOK THE RED RHUBARB THAT I GET FROM my garden in late spring in pies, in relishes, with strawberries, and, sometimes, very plainly, as in this recipe, which I serve with a creamy yogurt sauce. I flavor the rhubarb with crème de cassis liqueur, but if it is unavailable, you can substitute ¼ cup red wine plus 1 tablespoon sugar. Mint is delicious with rhubarb.

|||||||||||||||||||||||||||||||||||||||||||||||||||

Trim and wash the rhubarb, then cut it into 2-inch segments. Combine with the honey and crème de cassis in a saucepan and bring to a strong boil, stirring to mix the ingredients well. Cover, reduce the heat to low, and cook for about 3 minutes, watching it closely, until the rhubarb is soft but not falling apart. Let cool, then refrigerate.

FOR THE SAUCE: Mix together all the ingredients in a bowl. Refrigerate.

At serving time, spoon 2 to 3 tablespoons of the sauce into each of four Champagne coupes or wineglasses. Add about ½ cup of the rhubarb to each and top with a sprig of mint.

1 pound rhubarb

½ cup honey

¼ cup crème de cassis

SAUCE

½ cup sour cream

½ cup plain yogurt

1 tablespoon sugar

4 fresh mint sprigs

Tartine of Confiture

SERVES 4

4 to 6 thin slices white country bread or whole-grain bread

About ¼ cup whipped cream cheese, or 4 tablespoons unsalted butter, softened

About 1 cup best-quality apricot, cherry, or strawberry (see page 385) preserves

WHEN I WAS A KID, ONE OF MY FAVORITE DESserts was fruit jam or my mother's homemade preserves spread on crusty French bread. That taste has stayed with me, and since Gloria and I rarely make desserts unless we have guests, when I feel a need for a little sweet after dinner, I eat a little tartine of confiture, or bread and jam. My favorite preserves are the apricot jam that my friend Jean-Claude makes and the cherry or strawberry preserves that we make ourselves or buy. I like my confiture with chunks of fruit in it. I toast thin slices of white country or whole-grain bread, spread them with butter or soft cream cheese—my American touch—and then thickly coat them with the preserves. Simple but so good!

||||||||||||||||||||||||||||||||||||||||||

Toast the bread slices lightly. Spread them with the cream cheese or butter and the preserves. Cut each slice in half and enjoy.

Strawberry Confiture

MAKES SEVERAL JARS

I MAKE JAM IN THE SUMMER WHEN THE FRUIT is really ripe. My favorites are strawberry and apricot, and I cook the fruits in a low oven for about 24 hours. This produces a jam where the fruit stays whole and is almost candied in heavy syrup. It is great over ice cream as well as with toast.

3 pounds small very ripe strawberries

3 cups sugar

||||||||||||||||||||||||||||||||||||||||||||||||||||

Preheat the oven to 170 degrees.

Wash and hull the berries. While they are still wet, put them in a roasting pan, preferably stainless steel, sprinkle the sugar on top, and mix it in well. (The sugar will not be dissolved.)

Place the pan in the oven and cook for about 24 hours, until the berries are almost candied and the liquid is syrupy; shake the pan a couple of times during baking so the mixture doesn't get too dry on top.

Ladle the fruit and syrup into clean jars. (I usually run Mason jars through the cycles of my dishwasher before filling them.) Refrigerate.

Rose Hip Jelly

MAKES ABOUT THREE ½-PINT JARS

1 pound rose hips

One 1.75-ounce package
    Sure-Jell

1½ cups sugar

¼ cup fresh lemon juice

I WALK THE BEACH WITH MY DOG AT THE END of the summer and pick the wild rose hips that are plentiful along the sand dunes. One can make good rose hip jelly when the rose hips, which are the fruit of the rose plant, are deep, dark red and soft on top and the flesh is sweet. Be sure to use gloves to pick them; the thorns on the stems are vicious and the seeds inside are an irritant to the skin.

Many recipes recommend removing the skin from the flesh, which is a tedious and time-consuming process. I leave the rose hips whole, including the prickly green ends. Then, when they have cooked long enough to be soft, I push them through a food mill and finish the jelly. I sterilize the jars and lids in a 200-degree oven for 15 minutes, which is the easiest way to do it, before filling them with the jelly. The jelly is very mild, with a good fragrance.

Wash the rose hips under cold water and drain. Put them in a saucepan with 2 cups water, bring to a boil, cover, reduce the heat, and cook for 1 hour, or until the hips are tender.

Push a dozen rose hips or so at a time through a food mill fitted with a fine screen into a bowl; remove and discard the seeds each time before straining more hips. You should have a good 2 cups puree; if not, add water.

Preheat the oven to 200 degrees.

Pour the puree into a clean saucepan, add the Sure-Jell, sugar, and lemon juice, and mix well with a whisk. Bring to a

boil over high heat, stirring occasionally, and boil for a couple of minutes.

Meanwhile, place three ½-pint jars and lids on a baking sheet and sterilize in the oven for 15 minutes.

Fill the jars with the jelly and screw the lids on tightly. Refrigerate.

Candied Rose Petals and Mint Leaves

MAKES ABOUT 12 EACH ROSE PETALS AND MINT LEAVES

1 large egg white

1 cup sugar

About 12 wild rose petals

About 12 fresh mint leaves

WHEN I WALK ON THE BEACH IN LATE SPRING and early summer, it's a treat to smell the amazing fragrance from the wild roses that line the beach and sand dunes. I always make a few candied petals when my granddaughter, Shorey, comes to visit. The petals of other rose varieties can be used as well (although they may not have as much flavor), but be sure to use only petals that have not been sprayed with insecticides.

I do the same with mint leaves, which are great as a garnish for desserts. Use your imagination and candy some herbs, like basil, or petals from other edible flowers, like pansies or violets.

Beat the egg white with a fork to loosen it and pour it onto a plate. Spread the sugar on another plate. One at a time, dip the rose petals in the egg white so they are covered on both sides, rub off excess egg white, and place the petals in the sugar. Press the petals into the sugar to coat them and form a crust on both sides, then place on a wire rack. Do the same with the mint leaves.

Let the petals and leaves dry for at least a few hours.

Store in a plastic container with a tight-fitting lid; the petals and leaves will remain stiff for weeks. Use to decorate desserts or as a treat on their own.

Beach Plums in Alcohol

MAKES TWO ½-PINT JARS

Enough beach plums to fill two 8-ounce jars

½ cup grain alcohol

⅓ cup light corn syrup

¼ cup good tap or bottled water

I ALWAYS HAVE A FEW JARS OF ALCOHOL- preserved cherries, apricots, or plums in my cellar. For this recipe, I use the tiny astringent and tart beach plums (Prunus maritima) that are plentiful at the beach in late summer. Called prunelles *in French, they grew wild when I was a kid, and when we tasted them, they were so harsh and sour that our tongues would stick to the roofs of our mouths.*

It is important not to pull out the stems of the beach plums. If you do, the alcohol will seep into the resulting hole in the fruit and make it mushy. Some people make preserved fruits with brandy or vodka. I like to use grain alcohol, which is 190 proof, and dilute it with good water and corn syrup.

The beach plums should be either deep purple or gold in color; when they are just reddish in color, they are not ripe enough to preserve. Fruit in alcohol is usually served in cognac glasses as a digestive after dinner.

I also dry fresh juniper berries in the microwave oven for a couple of minutes to use in stews or sauerkraut.

Trim the stems of the plums to ¼ inch (do not remove them). Wash the plums and dry. Pack into two 8-ounce jars.

Using a whisk, mix together the alcohol, syrup, and water in a bowl. Fill the jars with the mixture and tighten the lids.

Place in a cool place, like a cellar, or refrigerate. After 1 month, enjoy anytime.

Wine-Sherbet Finale

SERVES 4

1 pint raspberry sherbet

1 cup raspberries

1 cup blueberries

1 cup fruity dry red wine, such
as Merlot

1 tablespoon honey

Pound cake or cookies
(optional)

REAL FRUIT SHERBET IS MADE OF FRUIT PUREE and sugar, with no egg, milk, or cream; it is called sorbet *in French and* sorbetto *in Italian. Containers of store-bought sherbet or ice cream at the market start to soften on the outside before I can get them home. I unmold them and cut them into portions, which I wrap individually in plastic bags for storage in the freezer, so I can retrieve them one at a time when needed.*

For this dish, I transfer the portions from the freezer to the refrigerator to soften a little while we eat the main course. Then I top them with berries and wine at the last moment.

Remove the frozen sherbet from its container and cut it into 4 individual portions. Drop each portion on a square of plastic wrap and form into a ball, and return to the freezer.

Forty-five minutes to 1 hour before serving, transfer the sherbet portions to the refrigerator.

At serving time, unwrap the portions and place each in a stemmed wineglass or glass dessert dish. Spoon the berries over and around the sherbet. Mix the honey with the wine and divide among the glasses. Serve, if desired, with pound cake or cookies.

Hibiscus Flower Cocktail

MAKES 4 CUPS TEA, ENOUGH FOR 8 COCKTAILS

I MADE THIS COCKTAIL OFTEN IN MEXICO during our vacations there. The first time I bought jamaica, or hibiscus, flowers at the local market, I did not know what they were, but they looked and smelled wonderful. I soon learned from local friends how to transform them into an aromatic and refreshing bright red tea. Then I graduated to a cocktail by adding lime juice and tequila. If you can't get dried hibiscus flowers, use 3 Red Zinger tea bags.

||||||||||||||||||||||||||||||||||||||||||||||||||

FOR THE TEA: Bring the water to a boil in a saucepan. Add the dried flowers, bring back to a boil, and boil for 1 minute. Cover and let steep for 15 minutes.

Strain the tea and cool.

FOR EACH COCKTAIL: Combine all the ingredients in a large glass, mix well, and serve.

FOR THE TEA

4 cups water

1 cup dried hibiscus (jamaica) flowers (see headnote)

FOR EACH COCKTAIL

½ cup Hibiscus Tea (above)

2 tablespoons Mexican *jarabe* or other simple syrup, grenadine, or sugar

1 tablespoon fresh lime juice

1½ to 2 ounces tequila

A dash or more of habanero hot sauce

Plenty of ice

Cakes, Cookies, Custards, and Chocolate

||||||||||||||||||||||||||||||||||||||||||||||||||

Instant Orange Cake

SERVES 4

3 seedless oranges (about
10 ounces each)

½ cup mascarpone cheese

1 tablespoon sugar

1 pound cake (12 ounces),
brown edges trimmed off all
around, cut lengthwise into
¾-inch slices

2 tablespoons Grand Marnier

½ cup orange marmalade

A few fresh mint sprigs, for
decoration

I MADE THIS DESSERT ONE EVENING WHEN friends came by for drinks and didn't leave. I found a pound cake in the freezer and a couple of oranges and some leftover mascarpone in the refrigerator, although crème fraîche or sour cream would have done as well. Often these impromptu dishes work out the best.

‖‖‖

Using a sharp knife, peel the oranges, removing the skin and pith so the flesh is exposed. Cut between the membranes of the orange and remove the segments (you will have about 25). Then squeeze the membranes over a small bowl to extract all the juice (about ⅓ cup) and reserve it.

Mix the mascarpone cheese with the sugar.

Arrange the slices of pound cake side by side in the bottom of a gratin dish, pie plate, or glass platter (about 9 inches across and 1 inch deep) nice enough to go to the dining room.

Mix half the reserved orange juice with the Grand Marnier and sprinkle it on the cake slices. Spread the mascarpone on top and arrange the orange segments on top of the mascarpone. Combine the remaining juice with the orange marmalade and coat the orange segments with it. Decorate with the mint.

Serve, using a large spoon to lift up the cake.

Faux Savarins

4 SERVINGS

SAVARINS ARE MADE WITH A YEAST DOUGH and are sometimes studded with raisins. They are soaked in rum syrup and served with fruit and cream. For this dessert, I use store-bought madeleines, the small shell-like sponge cakes, but brioche rolls or slices of yellow cake from the supermarket will work just as well.

||||||||||||||||||||||||||||||||||||||||||||||||||

FOR THE SYRUP: Mix the rum, sugar, and water together in a small bowl.

Arrange the madeleines side by side on a tray and pour the syrup over them. Let soak, turning occasionally, until most of the syrup is absorbed.

Combine the fruit and preserves in a bowl. Place 2 madeleines in each of four small bowls or on four dessert plates. Cover with the fruit and top with the sour cream. Serve immediately.

RUM SYRUP

2 tablespoons dark rum

2 tablespoons sugar

3 tablespoons lukewarm water

8 madeleines (about 1 ounce each)

1¼ cups diced (½-inch) fruit (bananas, blueberries, etc.)

3 tablespoons apricot preserves

½ cup sour cream

Chocolate Pistachio Biscotti

MAKES ABOUT 10 BISCOTTI

1 cup all-purpose flour

¼ cup unsweetened cocoa
   powder

⅓ cup sugar

1 teaspoon baking powder

Pinch of salt (¹⁄₁₆ teaspoon)

1 large egg

2 tablespoons unsalted butter,
   softened

⅓ cup shelled pistachio nuts

2 tablespoons milk

EVERYBODY LOVES BISCOTTI: THEY ARE GOOD dipped in coffee for breakfast and as a companion for ice cream after an elegant dinner. The dough is baked twice, hence the name biscotti *("twice-cooked"), first in a log and then in slices. These biscotti are flavored with bitter cocoa powder and pistachio nuts. The dough is made in a few minutes in a food processor.*

The biscotti freeze well.

|||||||||||||||||||||||||||||||||||||||||||||||||

Preheat the oven to 350 degrees.

Process the flour, cocoa powder, sugar, baking powder, and salt in a food processor for 5 seconds. Add the egg, butter, pistachios, and milk and process for another 6 to 8 seconds, until the dough starts coming together.

Line a baking sheet with aluminum foil. Transfer the dough to the sheet (don't worry if it is still somewhat loose). Put a piece of plastic wrap on top of the dough and press it together into a log about 6 inches long, 3 inches wide, and 1 inch high. Remove the plastic.

Bake the log for 25 minutes. Remove from the oven and let cool for 10 minutes.

Transfer the log to a cutting board and, using a serrated knife, cut it crosswise into ½-inch slices (10 to 12); do this gently, as the biscotti tend to crumble.

Arrange the slices flat on the lined baking sheet and bake for 30 to 40 minutes. Cool for at least 30 minutes.

Pain de Quatre Heures (Chocolate and Hazelnut "Sandwich")

SERVES 4 ·

WHEN I WAS A CHILD, THE CLASSIC AFTER-school snack was a piece of crunchy ficelle, a thin, crusty baguette, and a chunk of dark chocolate. It was called le quatre heures, or the "four o'clock." It is still the typical snack for French children after school. Using store-bought pizza dough, I duplicated this taste of my youth by making a large "sandwich," with chocolate, butter, and hazelnuts.

||||||||||||||||||||||||||||||||||||||||||||||||||

Line a jelly-roll pan with aluminum foil. Using your hands, spread the dough out into a rectangle about 11 by 13 inches on the pan. Scatter the nuts and chocolate over half the dough (lengthwise). Using the foil, lift and fold the plain half of the dough over the chocolate-nut side to make a "sandwich." Press lightly on the dough to secure the filling. Cut 3 or 4 slits in the top surface. Brush with the softened butter and sprinkle with the sugar.

Place a second jelly-roll pan or large baking pan upside down over the sandwich as a lid. Let the dough rise for 30 minutes.

Meanwhile, preheat the oven to 425 degrees.

Bake the sandwich for about 25 minutes, until crusty and brown. Cool to room temperature, then cut into slices and enjoy.

1 pound prepared pizza dough

About 25 whole hazelnuts, unskinned

⅓ cup chopped (½-inch pieces) bittersweet chocolate

1½ tablespoons unsalted butter, softened

2½ tablespoons sugar

Cooking with Shorey

SHORTLY AFTER HER THIRD BIRTHDAY, I TOOK MY granddaughter, Shorey, out for breakfast. She ordered blueberries. I asked her if she liked blueberries, and she replied, "Oh, yes, Papy. And you know they have lots of antioxidants in them."

If Shorey is precocious when it comes to matters of food, it was unavoidable. Her father is a chef. Her great-grandmother and grandfather were chefs. Her mother, my daughter, Claudine, knows her wine and cooks for the family every day, using the best ingredients she can find at her market. Shorey was born with a naturally sensitive palate, and her parents frequently ask her to analyze food and even wine. She will sniff a glass and say, "I smell raspberries" or "I smell chocolate."

If she says she doesn't like something, her parents tell her to taste a bit anyway. If she still does not like it, they say, "Fine, don't eat it." As a result of that policy and her curious palate, there are very few things Shorey refuses to eat, and she loves many foods that kids typically push to the sides of their plates. She enjoys Brussels sprouts, spinach, artichokes, olives, mushrooms, sweetbreads, oysters, and clams. Yet she avoids some foods that most children like, like scrambled eggs. She doesn't like my headcheese. But I know that will change with time.

In my opinion, the biggest food mistake parents make with kids is giving them something other than what is on the family's menu for a meal. Falling on your knees and praising a child who does eat spinach,

a food they claim they don't like, is nearly as bad. They will think that they deserve an award if they eat it. The best policy is to put the meal on the table and eat without questioning it.

A surefire way to encourage kids to add new foods to their diets is to let them be part of the cooking—the younger the better. When Claudine was two, I began holding her up so she could help stir a skillet or saucepan. She would tell Gloria that she had "made dinner," and she was eager to taste the fruits of her labors. Shorey was introduced to cooking the same way. When she was seven years old, she started to come into the kitchen as soon as she arrived at our house, upturn a box that she used as a stool, and ask if there was anything she could do. I'd have her peel a carrot or do some other basic task, and I always allowed her to taste as I cooked, asking her opinion: "Do you think that could use more salt?"

She doesn't pull her punches when something fails to meet her expectations. Reading through a menu journal that we keep after one of her visits, I noticed that she had written, "All the food was terrific, except Papy's headcheese."

Shorey has "costarred" with me in several television broadcasts, and I hope there are more to come. Like most kids, she loves being on television, but she acts naturally. More important, we have a great time together.

She is very thoughtful, giving, and complimentary, and she will even call me out of the blue to say that she's just seen me on television and thought I did a good job. She has a good manner at the table, and she does not interrupt adults. She has an even disposition and always smiles. Her grades are excellent, and she speaks pretty good French. She's a great little girl. We are very lucky.

Sorry, but boasting a bit is every proud grandfather's prerogative.

Croque Bébé

SERVES 4

THIS RECIPE IS MY PLAY ON THE CLASSIC CROQUE *monsieur, the French sandwich consisting of Gruyère cheese and ham between slices of white bread that is buttered on the outside and sautéed in a skillet or baked in the oven. In honor of my granddaughter, I created a* croque bébé *("baby"), with a filling of chocolate and peanut butter.*

||||||||||||||||||||||||||||||||||||||||||||||||

Preheat the oven to 375 degrees.

Melt the chocolate in a microwave oven or in a double boiler over hot water.

Spread 4 slices of the bread with the peanut butter and the remaining 4 slices with the melted chocolate. Sandwich the slices together. Butter the outsides of the sandwiches with the softened butter and sprinkle them on both sides with the sugar.

Arrange the sandwiches on a baking sheet and bake for about 10 minutes, turning the sandwiches after 5 minutes so they are nicely browned on both sides. Let cool for 5 minutes.

Trim off the crusts and cut each sandwich into 4 little triangles or squares. Serve.

½ cup semisweet chocolate morsels (about 3 ounces)

8 slices Pepperidge Farm thin white bread

6 tablespoons peanut butter

About 1½ tablespoons unsalted butter, softened

About 1½ tablespoons sugar

Sabayon with Madeira and Grapes

SERVES 4

4 large egg yolks

⅓ cup dry Madeira

2 tablespoons honey

1 tablespoon sugar

1 cup seedless grapes

Mint sprig (optional)

Cookies (optional)

SABAYON IS A QUICK AND EASY DESSERT MADE with egg yolks, but it is best prepared at the last minute and served warm, in stemmed glasses with berries or other fruit. It is cooked on top of the stove in a bowl set over hot water and it requires constant beating to prevent the eggs from scrambling. The water should be hot but not boiling and the eggs should be cooked enough to thicken the mixture and no longer taste raw. If it is undercooked, the sabayon tends to liquefy in the bottom of the glasses when served.

||||||||||||||||||||||||||||||||||||||||||||||

Put the egg yolks, Madeira, honey, and sugar in a stainless steel bowl and whisk until well mixed. Place the bowl on top of a saucepan of hot but not boiling water (170 to 180 degrees) and beat vigorously over low heat for 8 to 10 minutes, until the mixture is thick, creamy, and smooth.

Divide the grapes among four stemmed glasses and pour the sabayon over the grapes. Garnish with the mint, if using. Serve, if you like, with cookies.

Coffee Panna Cotta

SERVES 4

2 teaspoons plain gelatin
(from 1 envelope)

¼ cup water

5 tablespoons sugar

½ cup hot espresso

1½ cups half-and-half

Cookies (optional)

MY PANNA COTTA IS VERY DELICATE, SO IT IS best eaten from the molds, like crème brûlée or junket. If you prefer to unmold it, add an extra ½ teaspoon gelatin to make it firmer. Using a microwave oven to melt the gelatin makes this dessert a cinch.

|||||||||||||||||||||||||||||||||||||||||||||||||||

Moisten the gelatin with the water in a small bowl. Heat in a microwave oven for 30 seconds to dissolve.

Mix the sugar with the espresso in a medium bowl until dissolved. Add the gelatin mixture and stir well with a rubber spatula, as the gelatin mixture tends to stick to the bottom of the bowl. Mix in the half-and-half.

Pour into four espresso cups. Refrigerate. The panna cotta will take 1 to 2 hours to set.

At serving time, set the molds on small plates and serve with cookies, if desired.

Custard with Shortbread

SERVES 6

⅓ cup sugar

2 tablespoons water

One 14-ounce can sweetened condensed milk

1 cup milk

4 large eggs

1 teaspoon pure vanilla extract

About 3 ounces shortbread cookies, broken into chunks (about 1¼ cups), plus (optional) cookies for serving

I LOVE ANY TYPE OF CUSTARD—FLAN, CRÈME caramel, crème brûlée. The Spaniards make flans with evaporated or sweetened condensed milk, which gives the custard a special texture that my wife adores. I make a version of that here, with the addition of shortbread, which provides a base for the custard. It can be made a day ahead.

I cook the caramel in a microwave oven. Since caramel is prone to burning, I cook the sugar for 3 minutes initially and then in 30-second increments until it is done.

||||||||||||||||||||||||||||||||||||||||||||||

Preheat the oven to 350 degrees.

Mix together the sugar and water in a 5- to 6-cup soufflé mold and place the mold in a microwave oven. Cook on high for 3 minutes, then check to see if the sugar has caramelized in the center. If it hasn't, cook for another 30 seconds and check again; repeat as necessary, cooking for 30 seconds at a time until the caramel is bubbling and has nice blond color.

Whisk together the condensed milk, milk, eggs, and vanilla in a bowl. Cover the caramel, which should be hard by now, with the shortbread chunks and pour on the egg mixture.

Put the soufflé mold in a large ovenproof saucepan or skillet and surround the mold with water to create a bain-marie, or water bath. Bake for about 50 minutes, or until the custard is light brown on top and set. To test, pierce the center with the tip of a paring knife; the knife should come out clean.

Cool, then cover and refrigerate the custard until chilled. At serving time, serve as is or with more shortbread cookies.

Mini Chocolate Truffles with Cognac

MAKES ABOUT 15 TRUFFLES

I ALWAYS MAKE CHOCOLATE TRUFFLES DURING the Christmas holiday season. You can replace the cognac in these with Grand Marnier or dark rum—or use no alcohol at all. The truffles can be coated with crushed nuts or confectioners' sugar instead of cocoa, or, if you prefer truffles with a hard exterior, dipped in melted chocolate to coat.

½ cup semisweet chocolate morsels (about 3 ounces)

3 tablespoons heavy cream

1 tablespoon cognac

1 tablespoon unsweetened cocoa powder

||||||||||||||||||||||||||||||||||||||||||||||||||||

In a microwave oven, heat the chocolate and cream in a microwavable bowl for about 45 seconds to melt the chocolate and heat the cream. Add the cognac and mix well with a rubber spatula until very smooth. Let cool, then refrigerate for about 1 hour, until the mixture is hard.

Using a small spoon, scoop out truffles the size of a medium olive and drop them onto a piece of plastic wrap. (You should have about 15.) Using your fingers, press each truffle into a rough, irregular ball so it resembles an actual truffle (the prized fleshy fungus eaten as a delicacy). Sprinkle on the cocoa powder and shake the plastic wrap to roll and coat the truffles all over with it.

Arrange the truffles in a single layer in a container with a lid, cover, and refrigerate until ready to serve.

Chocolate Pistachio Brittle

SERVES 4 TO 6

⅔ cup semisweet chocolate
   chunks

⅔ cup shelled pistachio nuts

1 cup sugar

¼ cup water

1 cup light corn syrup

⅛ teaspoon salt

1½ tablespoons unsalted
   butter

2 teaspoons baking powder

NO ONE I KNOW CAN STOP AFTER ONE BITE OF peanut brittle. I figured the classic candy would be that much more irresistible made with pistachios and chocolate. Using the microwave oven shortens the preparation time to a few minutes, but be sure to use a large microwavable bowl or other container (I use an 8-cup glass measuring cup) to make the caramel, because the mixture tends to rise up and foam. This brittle is equally good made with pecan or hazelnut pieces.

||||||||||||||||||||||||||||||||||||||||||||||||||

Line a baking sheet with aluminum foil. Sprinkle the chocolate chunks and pistachios on it and form them into a rough rectangle about 12 by 8 inches.

Combine the sugar, water, corn syrup, and salt in a large microwavable bowl or glass measuring cup and mix well. Cook in a microwave oven on high for 8 minutes. The mixture should be starting to caramelize in the center. You want to stop the cooking as soon as the caramel is pale blond, because it will continue to cook and darken after you remove it from the oven. If it isn't caramelizing in the center after 8 minutes, continue cooking it for 30 seconds at a time; it could take as long as 10 minutes total.

Remove the bowl from the microwave and, using a heat-proof spatula, mix in the butter and baking powder. The mixture will foam.

Pour the caramel on top of the chocolate pieces and nuts on the baking sheet and spread it out so it is about the same

thickness throughout. Let cool for at least 1 hour, refrigerated, until the brittle is hard.

Break into chunks to serve. Store leftovers in a plastic container for up to a few weeks.

||||||||||||||||||||||||||||||||||||||||||||||||||||||

NOTE: *The caramel can also be cooked on the stove in the conventional way.*

Chocolate Soufflés

SERVES 4

½ tablespoon unsalted butter, softened

¼ cup granulated sugar

¾ cup heavy cream

4 ounces bittersweet chocolate (at least 60% cacao), cut into ½-inch pieces

4 large egg whites (see Note)

ORANGE SAUCE
(OPTIONAL)

½ cup sour cream

1 teaspoon grated orange rind

1 tablespoon granulated sugar

1 teaspoon confectioners' sugar, for dusting the soufflés

4 Candied Rose Petals (page 388; optional)

A SOUFFLÉ IS ALWAYS AN IMPRESSIVE DESSERT. I like to prepare individual soufflés, which are easier to cook and serve than a single large one. Use good-quality bittersweet chocolate (containing at least 60% cacao) for the best results. The soufflés can be assembled a couple of hours before serving and kept in the refrigerator until ready to bake.

The orange sauce is optional, but it is a nice accompaniment.

||||||||||||||||||||||||||||||||||||||||||||||||||

Preheat the oven to 400 degrees. Butter four ¾-cup soufflé molds with the butter and coat with about 2 tablespoons of the granulated sugar.

Pour the cream into a microwavable bowl and heat it in a microwave oven for about 1½ minutes, until warm. Add the chocolate pieces and set aside for 1 to 2 minutes so the chocolate melts in the warm cream. Stir the cream with a whisk to incorporate the melted chocolate.

Beat the egg whites with a large balloon whisk in a large bowl until they hold a peak. Add the remaining granulated sugar and whisk for a few more seconds.

Combine the egg whites with the chocolate mixture, first using the whisk for a few seconds and then using a rubber spatula to finish folding in the whites. Divide the soufflé among the prepared molds. *(The soufflés can be prepared to this point and refrigerated for a couple hours before baking.)*

Place the soufflés on a baking sheet and bake for 15 minutes, or until puffy and set inside.

(continued on page 414)

MEANWHILE, FOR THE OPTIONAL SAUCE: Mix together all the ingredients in a small bowl.

Dust the tops of the warm soufflés with the confectioners' sugar and serve hot. If you like, garnish each plate with a candied rose petal, and accompany with the sauce, if desired, serving it on the side or pouring it over the soufflés.

Alternatively, let the soufflés cool to room temperature and unmold the soufflés onto dessert plates. (*Note:* The soufflés will deflate as they cool.) Serve.

||||||||||||||||||||||||||||||||||||||||||||||||||

NOTE: *You can reserve the egg yolks for another recipe, like the Sabayon with Madeira and Grapes on page 404.*

My Mistake

AFTER NEARLY SEVEN DECADES OF PROFESSIONAL COOK-
ing, I'm proud to say I have reached the level of proficiency where . . .
I still make mistakes. All the time. Any honest professional chef will
admit to the same thing. The difference between the pros and many
home cooks is that people who make their living cooking know that errors are part of the game and that you simply have to learn to roll with
the punches. Most of the time, mistakes can be fixed.

Some mistakes are small and easily remedied; others fall into an entirely different category. Once in Sacramento I joined several culinary
celebrities and prominent magazine editors for a cooking demonstration in front of an audience of four thousand in a huge auditorium. I decided to do a cheese soufflé, which presented a bit of a timing problem.
I could assemble the dish in a few minutes, but then it had to cook for
about 30 minutes. To get around this issue, I was to assemble the soufflé and pop it in the oven a half hour before the end of the presentation,
and then return triumphantly to pull out the beautiful, golden-domed
dish at the end of the presentation.

An appliance company had supplied a new state-of-the-art oven for
the demonstration. I set it at the correct temperature and tested it with
my hand to make sure it was warm before putting in the soufflé. Then I
had to leave the stage. My soufflé was at the mercy of the oven.

Through some mechanical malfunction, the oven spontaneously

went into the self-cleaning mode. The temperature inside soared to something like 750 degrees. When I returned for my voilà moment and opened the oven door, a puff of smoke emerged. My soufflé had not risen and the still-liquid interior was encased in a thick black crust.

Despite the disaster, mistakes rarely result in a dish that is unservable. Cooking is the art of compensation and recovery. Once while preparing what was to be a roulade of sponge cake wrapped around a buttercream filling, I overbaked the cake, and it cracked when I began to roll it. Disaster? Not at all. I cut the cake lengthwise into three slices and stacked them in layers with the buttercream in between, and no one was the wiser.

If a chicken comes out of the oven slightly overcooked, I simply extend the sauce and add a bit more garnish to give it more moisture. A slightly overdone piece of fish can be saved by a quick sauce of white wine, onion, and a bit of butter or olive oil spooned over the top.

Pastry can be trickier, because it is more formulaic than preparing meat and vegetables. If you forget to add vanilla to a cake batter, there's no going back later and adding it. But you can brush a simple syrup flavored with vanilla extract over the cake and it will soak inside. An overdone cake can get a similar syrup wash to add moisture.

By far the best way to avoid errors in the first place, though, is to taste as you go along. Add some salt if needed. Or sugar, if the dish is not sweet enough. Add a bit of milk or water to a batter or sauce that is too thick or too dry. If you constantly taste as you cook, mistakes can be discovered and corrected before it's too late.

But even irreparable kitchen disasters can sometimes have their own rewards. After I stood up with my smoldering soufflé in Sacramento, the audience rose to its feet and gave me one of the most thunderous ovations of my career.

Menus

CUISINE DE MA CHÉRIE
Herbed Omelet with Shrimp
Calamari Stew with Saffron and Cilantro Rice
Cucumber, Onion, and Mint Salad
Rice Pudding with Dried Cherries and Blueberry
  Sauce

VIVA MÉXICO
Hibiscus Flower Cocktail
Yucatán Ceviche
Fillet of Sole Riviera with Pico de Gallo
Beef Fillet Mini Steaks with Mushrooms and
  Shallots
Grapefruit Granité with Mango and Mojito
  Cocktail

LA COCINA OLÉ
Garlic and Pasilla Soup
Chicken with Chili Sauce and Achiote Rice
Banana Gratin

GLORIA'S FAVORITES
Pressed Caviar Canapés
Smoked Salmon on Corn Fritters
Hanoi Chicken Soup
Pork Kidneys with Mushroom and Vermouth
  Sauce
Fried Eggplant Fans

SWEET ENDINGS WITH SHOREY
Tartine of Confiture
Rhubarb-Honey Coupe with Creamy Yogurt
  Sauce
Chocolate Pistachio Biscotti
Peaches Marty
Croque Bébé
Mini Chocolate Truffles with Cognac

SHOREY'S PETIT APPETITE
Escargots in Baked Potatoes
Stuffed Tomatoes

Pain de Quatre Heures (Chocolate and Hazelnut
  "Sandwich")
Chocolate-Pistachio Brittle

JUST DUCKY!
Duck Liver Mousse with Apples
Sautéed Duck Breast with Arugula Salad and
  Cracklings
Lemon Mousseline

ALL IN THE FAMILY
Parisian Potage
Poulet à la Crème
Rice Soubise
Instant Orange Cake

TASTE BUD TEMPTATIONS
Tuna Tartare with Bagel Chips and Radishes
Tuna Mascarpone Cream
Spanish Tortilla
Caramelized Pear Custard
Strawberry Confiture

MENU MEMORIES
Salmon Scaloppine with Sorrel Sauce
Lamb Breast Navarin
Green Salad with Mustard Dressing
Coffee Panna Cotta

OCEAN HARVEST
Grilled Bacalao (Salt Cod) Steaks with Olive Sauce
Pasta and Shrimp with Pressed Caviar Shavings
Tuna à la Minute
Shrimp Burgers on Zucchini

COOKING FROM LE PÉLICAN
Egg and Swiss Chard Gratin
Kale, Sausage, Rib, and Lima Bean Stew
Stew of Radishes
Braised Veal Breast with Pearl Onions and
  Artichokes

AUTUMN LEAVES

Tomato Velvet
Red Cabbage, Pistachio, and Cranberry Salad with
    Blue Cheese
Sliced Tomato Gratin
Grilled Lamb Shashlik
Apple Galette

COOKING FOR THE PRESIDENT

Morel and Shrimp Eggs in Cocotte
Veal Chops Dijonnaise
Peas with Basil
Chocolate Soufflés

KITCHEN COMPANIONS

Octopus Stew with Onions, Paprika, and Wine
Venison in Sweet-and-Sour Sauce
Corn Soufflé
Prunes in Red Wine

COOKING CLEVER

Tomato and Potato Salad with Mustard Dressing
Mussels with Cream and Chives on Soft Polenta
Spaghetti à la Bolognese
Sautéed Radicchio

WONDERS OF THE SEA

Simple Seafood Salad
Spicy Shrimp with Cocktail Sauce
Blackfish Beignets with Spicy Sauce
Sautéed Tilapia

OFFAL GOOD

Chicken Livers in Mushroom Port Sauce
Tripe and Pigs' Feet Ragout
Beef Tongue with Ravigote Sauce
Tomato Tatin
Green Salad with Mustard Dressing

HEIRLOOM FAVORITES

Ricotta Quenelles
Flounder with Lemon Butter
Sauté of Rabbit with Mushrooms and Cream
Apples in Lemon Sauce

CUISINE ECONOMIQUE

Black Lentil Salad with Eggs
Pork Neck and Bean Stew
Spinach and Ricotta Lasagna
Carrots with Chives

CATCH O' THE DAY

Top Neck Clams with Vinegar and Scallion Sauce
Gloria's Linguine with Clam Sauce
Grilled Snapper with Olive Topping
Cod in Light Cream Sauce

TOAST TO JULIA

Sole Vin Blanc
Rack of Lamb with Spice Crust
Peas and Fennel with Lardons
Fried Potatoes
Wine-Sherbet Finale

JULIA REMEMBERED

Oyster Chowder with Potatoes, Spinach, and Corn
Hamburger Royale
Eggplant-Tomato Gratin
Cherry Crumble

FÊTE DE BOULES

Crab Chips with Salmon Caviar
Cannellini Bean Dip
Tabbouleh
Camembert with Pistachio Crust
Egg and Herb Treats
Smoked Ham Glazed with Maple Syrup

CHEF IN TRAINING

Fast Fougasse
Salmon Rillettes
Poussins (or Cornish Hens) à la Russe
Broiled Maple Sweet Potatoes

GLOBAL GASTRONOMY

Broiled Salmon with Miso Glaze
Chirashi Sushi
Grilled Chicken Tenders with Chimichurri
Sabayon with Madeira and Grapes

Producer's Acknowledgments

IT ALL BEGAN A LONG TIME AGO. FULL OF ideas and creativity and wanting to share his wealth of knowledge and talent, Jacques planted the acorn, and now, astonishingly, here we are, seemingly so soon—looking back at the mighty oak of Jacques's twenty-six-part television series for Public Television, *Jacques Pépin Heart & Soul*.

From the beginning, there was little doubt that the project would be firmly planted at KQED, the San Francisco station that has been Jacques's second home and that cultivated and maintained the relationship. With constant nurturing, we watched it grow, each step and each success built upon the last. But that does not happen in a vacuum. The frenzy must begin.

Planning, testing, tasting, building, writing, lighting, baking, painting, decorating, adjusting, propping, tweaking and retesting, blocking, shopping, practicing, and testing once again, and then there is the test that checks the original test! This is what we do. We built the set, installed the appliances, put the props in place, lighted the lights, primed the cameras, checked the mics, wrote the blockings to chart Jacques's every move, stocked the kitchen, unpacked equipment, stored the wine — in short, we set the stage. A remarkable group of talented, disparate individuals came together as a cohesive force to bring order to chaos as if in a structured, elaborate dance. And once we were in the studio, from the moment the director called "Action," the next weeks were a blur of activity, culminating in the fantastic series that will be Jacques's last.

For this complex and elaborate production, in all its glory and with all the twists and turns, I have so many people to thank. Toiling away by my side from beginning to end was the production team of June Mesina Ouellette, David Shalleck, and Christine Swett. I cannot thank them enough. Dana DeMercurio joined us this season, along with Jennifer Harrison to assist. Understanding the collective vision, director Paul Swensen artfully completed the team with great poise, patience, and sense of humor.

In the studio, stage managers Randy Brase and Cara Miller diligently hustled to ensure that every spatula and spoon was on set, while Alan Hereford, Greg Peterson, Mike Elwell, Greg Overton, and Jim McKee, backed by Tomas Tucker and Jennie Clark, caught Jacques's every move on camera. Rick Santangelo, Helen Silvani, and Eric Shackelford expertly completed the studio team. Kim McCalla and her aide, Simon Hui, supervised them all. Maintaining the buildings around us and setting up the back kitchen is no easy task, and Michael Welch, Robert Villegas, Dan Perez, and Wayne Henry organized everything, along with Anthony Spears.

Henry Rubin managed the technology and collected all the media in preparation for editor Byron Thompson, who brought everything together shot by shot to ensure that Jacques was seen as the amazing technician that he is. Byron doesn't miss an important moment or skip a relevant anecdote from Jacques's daughter, Claudine, or a peck on the cheek from his granddaughter, Shorey.

Furnishing and decorating the set to make it look like home, Andrea Pannes and Mimi Utley raided their own houses while also scouring local businesses to find that special something. Jenny Zielon adeptly powdered Jacques's nose and organized his wardrobe. Web producer Wendy Goodfriend not only built the website, but also took all the recipe close-ups, with the aid of David Shalleck and his assistant, Carrie Dove, who artistically styled the food for the web photographs. The graphic creations are those of Zaldy Serrano.

Laureen Chang took the marketing bull by the horns to make things happen, along with Janet Lim Young and David Shimada. Sandy Schonning stalwartly managed the project, keeping everything on track and on budget. DeLinda Mrowka headed up the Communications team of Evren Odcikin, Carly Severn, Sarah Hoffner, and Temi Adamolekun, while Lisa Landi and Katie Koskenmaki ensured complete distribution to national stations.

Our intrepid executive producer, Michael Isip, expertly took the lead from the very beginning to the very end. He championed the project from its inception and gave it its name of *Heart & Soul,* never underestimating Jacques or the commitment of the team.

So you see, it takes much more than a village; it takes a city full of individuals who speak the same language and have the same vision. Without each and every one, this series could not have been so very special. Thank you all.

And, finally, to our sponsors, without whom none of this would be possible—they gave us the means to produce our wonderful show:

La Posta Wines, Viña Casa Silva, Luca Wines

Supplying wonderful accommodations and great service while he was filming in San Francisco, Prescott Hotel, prescotthotel.com, continues to be Jacques' family's home away from home.

On the set, you'll see the best and latest equipment. We thank our suppliers:

Mauviel, mauvielusa.com
TriMark Economy Restaurant Fixtures,
    trimarkeconomy.com
Wüsthoff, wusthof.com
John Boos & Co., johnboos.com

A cooking show wouldn't get very far without food, and we thank Richard Ju and Kelly Gladstone, the two back-kitchen chefs who worked so closely with Jacques. Thanks especially to our volunteer extraordinaire, Mike Pleiss, who hasn't missed a single production in more than twenty-five years. Jean-Claude Szurdak, Jacques's best friend of more than sixty years, joined us once again and beavered away, supporting Jacques in so many ways in the kitchen, on the set, and in life. Others who provided support were Grace Sbrocco, Kim Kaechele, and Laura Pauli.

We thank the following organizations, who supplied us with some of the best-quality ingredients:

Greenleaf; greenleafsf.com
Straus Family Creamery; strausfamilycreamery.com
Gourmet and More
Kerrygold USA; kerrygoldusa.com
Modesto Food Distributors; modestofood.com
Monterey Fish Market; montereyfish.com
California Caviar Company, Inc.; californiacaviar.com
BiRite Foodservice Distributors; birite.com
Pacific Gourmet; pacgourmet.com
C. J. Olson Cherries; cjolsoncherries.com
Panorama Baking Company; panoramabaking.com
Equator Coffees & Teas; equatorcoffees.com
Nielsen-Massey Vanillas Inc.; nielsenmassey.com

Wine was provided by:

Barry + Tracy Schuler + Meteor Vineyard;
    meteorvineyard.com
Beni di Batasiolo; batasiolo.com
Burditch Marketing Communications
Cakebread Cellars; cakebread.com
Cairdean Estate; cairdeanestate.com
Casey Flat Ranch; caseyflatranch.com
Caymus Vineyards and the Wagner Family of Wine;
    wagnerfamilyofwine.com
Chappellet Vineyard; chappellet.com
DGB; dgb.co.za
GH Mumm; ghmumm.com
Giesen; giesen.co.nz
Grgich Hills Estate; grgich.com
Gruet Winery; gruetwinery.com
The Hess Collection Winery; hesscollection.com
Iron Horse Vineyards; ironhorsevineyards.com
Jamieson Ranch Vineyards;
    jamiesonranchvineyards.com
Jayson Woodbridge
Hundred Acre Wine Group; onetruevine.com
Jordan Vineyard & Winery; jordanwinery.com
Kermit Lynch Wine Merchant; kermitlynch.com
Les Voleurs Wines; lesvoleurswines.com
Liberty Imports, Inc.
Louis M. Martini Winery; louismartini.com
Luna Nuda; lunanudawines.com
Parallel Wines; parallelwines.com
Perrier-Jouët; perrier-jouet.com
Rob Murray Vineyards; rmvineyards.com
Robert Oatley; buywine.robertoatley.com.au
Robert Sinskey Vineyards; robertsinskey.com
Saffron Fields Vineyard; saffronfields.com
St. Amant Winery Lodi Native Project Marian's
    Vineyard; lodinative.com
St. Francis Winery & Vineyards; stfranciswinery.com
SakéOne; sakeone.com
Silver Trident Winery; silvertridentwinery.com
Stag's Leap Wine Cellars; cask23.com
Trefethen Family Vineyards; trefethen.com

Special thanks to

Antiques and Art Exchange;
    antiqueandartexchange.com
Floorcraft Carpet One; floorcrafthome.com
Ellington & French; ellingtonandfrench.com

Pottery Barn; potterybarn.com
Port & Manor; portandmanor.com
Soule Studio; soulestudio.com
Morgan and Company; morganandcompanysf.com
Isaac Mizrahi New York; isaacmizrahi.com
Ben Rupers
Let's Gel, Inc.; gelpro.com
Judith P. Diaz
Metropolitan Salon; metsalon.com

Thank you to everyone involved. I know that we all love to work with Jacques, that we all respect and treasure him and understand how lucky we are to be a part of this production. We all love to watch him cook and we learn from him as he moves through the kitchen with such skill, knife in hand, ready to transform simple ingredients into something extraordinary. We love the moments between segments when he'll chat with us and encourage us to taste a dish or share a sip of a new wine or rave about a piece of equipment. We love the end of the day when we are gathered in the back kitchen sipping wine from measuring cups and listening to his and Jean-Claude's stories. And knowing that this would be the last series made each moment with him more poignant and valuable; etching those moments into our collective memory became so important. We have enjoyed each and every minute of our time with him, and we walk away better for the experience.

I have worked with Jacques at KQED for more than twenty-five years, and knowing that this would be his last series added intense pressure and a desire to create an intimate portrait of the man as well as of the chef and teacher. I feel so honored to know him, to be a part of the team, and to be a part of *Jacques Pépin Heart & Soul.*

— TINA SALTER

Index

blueberry(ies): *continued*
  wine-sherbet finale, 392
blue cheese, red cabbage, pistachio,
    and cranberry salad with, 78
bluefish, 31
bok choy, in Hanoi chicken soup,
    60–62
Bolognese sauce, 286–87
Boston lettuce, in edamame
    ragout, 312
boules, 42–44
bread:
  baguette with pesto, 103
  black, and butter lattice, 32
  brioche, cherries with sweet
      wine and, 359
  cheese and anchovy toasts, 34
  country, 110
  croque bébé, 403
  croutons, 71
  crumb and mustard crust, 230
  crumbs, fried, 298–99
  crumpets, in tomato tartine, 25
  fougasse, fast, 108
  stuffed (*pain farci*), 111
  tartine of confiture, 384
brioche, cherries with sweet wine
    and, 359
brittle, chocolate pistachio,
    410–11
broccoli silk, 51
bulgur, in tabbouleh, 82
burgers:
  hamburger royale, 210–11
  shrimp, on zucchini, 181
butter:
  chive, 159
  fresh, 112–13
  garlic-herb, 138

C

cabbage:
  corned beef and, 213–14
  red, pistachio, and cranberry
      salad with blue cheese, 78

cakes:
  apple galette, 352
  orange, instant, 396
  pound, and prunes in red wine,
      374
  pound, and white peaches with
      Cointreau, 369
calamari (squid):
  sautéed, with tiny croutons and
      hot peppers, 182
  and shrimp patties, 45
  simple seafood salad, 140–41
  stew with saffron and cilantro
      rice, 184–85
calves' liver Lyonnaise style, 260
Camembert with pistachio crust,
    18
canapés:
  pressed caviar, 37
  see also hors d'oeuvres
candied rose petals and mint
    leaves, 388
cannellini bean(s):
  dip, 10
  fettuccine à la Playa, 278–79
  simple seafood salad, 140–41
caramel:
  bananas in, 357
  chocolate pistachio brittle,
      410–11
  custard with shortbread, 408
carpaccio of baby bellas, 24
carrots with chives, 302
cauliflower sauté à cru, 305
caviar:
  pressed, canapés, 37
  pressed, shavings, pasta and
      shrimp with, 290–91
  salmon, crab chips with, 38
  salmon or trout, in *chirashi
      sushi*, 175–76
celery gratin, 306
cellophane noodles (mung bean
    vermicelli), in Hanoi chicken
    soup, 60–62
ceviche, Yucatán, 125

cheddar cheese, in egg in pepper
    boats, 100
cheese, 20–21, 102–6
  to always have on hand, 276
  and anchovy toasts, 34
  blue, red cabbage, pistachio, and
      cranberry salad with, 78
  Camembert with pistachio
      crust, 18
  fondue with pesto, 102
  Fontainebleau, 19
  goat, tostadas, 13
  gougères with, 26–27
  mushroom and Gruyère pizza,
      106
  ricotta quenelles, 105
  and tomato towers, 17
  uses for leftover pieces of, 20,
      52–53
  see also Gruyère cheese;
      mozzarella
cherry(ies):
  crumble, 361
  dried, rice pudding with
      blueberry sauce and, 362
  with sweet wine and brioche,
      359
Chez Panisse, Berkeley, Calif., 98
chicken:
  with chili sauce and achiote rice,
      206
  jardinière, 202–3
  poulet à la crème, 199
  and rice with cumin and
      cilantro, 207
  soup, Hanoi, 60–62
  tenders, grilled, with
      chimichurri sauce, 200
chicken feet in hot sauce, 259
chicken liver(s):
  dirty rice for Gloria, 274
  mousse with apples, 47
  in mushroom port sauce, 258
chickpeas (garbanzos):
  spicy, 12
  and spinach, 308

Child, Julia, 250, 253–54
children:
    being part of cooking, 401–2
    introducing new foods to,
        400–401
chili sauce, chicken with, and
        achiote rice, 206
chimichurri sauce, 200
Chinese-inspired dishes:
    chicken feet in hot sauce, 259
    eggplant chinois, 320
    sautéed leg of lamb chinois, 236
chirashi sushi, 175–76
    Pépin's formulation of recipe
        for, 177–79
chive:
    butter, 159
    and cilantro pesto, 283
chocolate:
    croque bébé, 403
    and hazelnut "sandwich" (*pain
        de quatre heures*), 399
    mini truffles with cognac, 409
    pistachio biscotti, 398
    pistachio brittle, 410–11
    soufflés, 412–14
chowder, oyster, with potatoes,
        spinach, and corn, 58–59
chuck roast, small, with red onion
        sauce, 215
cilantro:
    chimichurri sauce, 200
    and chive pesto, 283
    freezing stems of, 184
    rice, 185
Claiborne, Craig, 132, 250, 254–55
clam(s):
    and mussel stew, 190
    packing in seaweed, 191
    sauce, linguine with, Gloria's,
        288
    steamers in hot broth, 192
    top neck, with vinegar and
        scallion sauce, 134–35
cocktails:
    hibiscus flower, 393

mojito, 364–65
cocktail sauce, 132
cod:
    grilled bacalao (salt cod) steaks
        with olive sauce, 166–67
    in light cream sauce, 165
coffee panna cotta, 406
cognac, mini chocolate truffles
        with, 409
Cointreau, white peaches with, 369
confiture:
    strawberry, 385
    tartine of, 384
corn:
    fritters, smoked salmon on, 119
    oyster chowder with potatoes,
        spinach and, 58–59
    and shallots with sun-dried
        tomatoes, 309
    soufflé, 310
corned beef and cabbage, 213–14
Cornish hens *à la Russe*, 196
cottage cheese and tarragon sauce,
        146
country bread, 110
crab:
    avocado, and tomato salad, 83
    chips with salmon caviar, 38
    cracklings, duck, 208–9
cranberry(ies) (dried):
    Camembert with pistachio
        crust, 18
    pears with honey and, 372
    red cabbage, and pistachio salad
        with blue cheese, 78
cream cheese–horseradish sauce,
        124
croque bébé, 403
croutons, 71
crumble, cherry, 361
crumpets, in tomato tartine, 25
crusts:
    mustard and bread crumbs,
        230
    rice coating, crispy, 218
    salt, for whole fish, 148–50

cucumber:
    onion, and mint salad, 73
    "vases," 23
custard:
    caramelized pear, 373
    with shortbread, 408

D

dandelion (pissenlit) salad,
        Lyonnaise, 69–71
desserts, 350–414
    chocolate pistachio biscotti,
        398
    chocolate pistachio brittle,
        410–11
    chocolate soufflés, 412–14
    coffee panna cotta, 406
    croque bébé, 403
    custard with shortbread, 408
    faux Savarins, 397
    mini chocolate truffles with
        cognac, 409
    orange cake, instant, 396
    pain de quatre heures (chocolate
        and hazelnut "sandwich"),
        399
    sabayon with Madeira and
        grapes, 404
    see also fruit desserts and
        preserves
dip, cannellini bean, 10
dirty rice for Gloria, 274
dressings:
    anchovy, 140
    mustard, 63, 76, 300
    mustard and cream, 301
    tapenade, 74
duck breast, sautéed, with arugula
        salad and cracklings, 208–9
duck liver mousse with apples, 47

E

edamame ragout, 312
egg(s), 84–100

mushroom(s):
    baby bellas, carpaccio of, 24
    beef fillet mini steaks with
        shallots and, 212
    and Gruyère pizza, 106
    marinated, in *pain farci* (stuffed
        bread), 111
    morel and shrimp eggs *en
        cocotte*, 92–93
    mussels with cream and chives
        on soft polenta, 188
    pasta and shrimp with pressed
        caviar shavings, 290–91
    port sauce, chicken livers in, 258
    sauté of rabbit with cream and,
        228–29
    stuffed tomatoes, 340–41
    veal chops Dijonnaise, 244
    and vermouth sauce, 268–69
    wild, foraging for, 64–68
mussel(s):
    and clam stew, 190
    with cream and chives on soft
        polenta, 188
mustard:
    and cream dressing, 301
    crust, baked rabbit with, 230
    dressing, 63, 300
    veal chops Dijonnaise, 244

N

noodles, cellophane (mung bean
    vermicelli), in Hanoi chicken
    soup, 60–62

O

octopus stew with onions, paprika,
    and wine, 187
oil(s):
    Asian, 277
    poaching fish in, 170
olive(s), 276
    black, asparagus with, and
        mustard dressing, 300

black, in prosciutto packages,
    46
black, in small potatoes in olive
    oil, 335
black, in tapenade dressing, 74
green, in fettuccine à la Playa,
    278–79
green, rice with cumin and, 273
sauce, grilled bacalao (salt cod)
    steaks with, 166–67
topping, grilled snapper with,
    160
omelets, 86–87
    herbed, with shrimp, 89
    Spanish tortilla, 91
onion(s):
    calves' liver Lyonnaise style, 260
    caramelized, 260
    cucumber, and mint salad, 73
    ravigote sauce, 262–63
    red, quick pickled radishes and,
        328
    red, sauce, 215
    steamed fish with Provençal
        vegetable stew, 151
orange:
    cake, instant, 396
    sauce, 412, 414
organ meats, 256–69
    Americans' appreciation of, 265
    beef tongue with ravigote sauce,
        262–63
    calves' liver Lyonnaise style, 260
    chicken feet in hot sauce, 259
    chicken livers in mushroom port
        sauce, 258
    duck liver mousse with apples,
        47
    pork kidneys with mushroom
        and vermouth sauce, 268–69
    pork neck and bean stew, 267
    tripe and pigs' feet ragout, 264
    veal tongue and lentil stew, 261
oyster(s):
    chowder with potatoes, spinach,
        and corn, 58–59

opening, 58
packing in seaweed, 191

P

pain de quatre heures (chocolate
    and hazelnut "sandwich"),
    399
pain farci (stuffed bread), 111
pancetta, in Lyonnaise pissenlit
    (dandelion) salad, 69–71
panna cotta, coffee, 406
pantry, ingredients to have on
    hand in, 275–77
Parisian potage, 50
Parmesan cheese, 20, 276
    eggplant with cheese crust, 313
pasilla and garlic soup, 56–57
pasta, 278–93
    fettuccine à la Playa, 278–79
    fusilli in spicy garlic tomato
        sauce, 280–81
    linguine with cilantro and chive
        pesto, 283
    linguine with clam sauce,
        Gloria's, 288
    and shrimp with pressed caviar
        shavings, 290–91
    spaghetti à la Bolognese, 286–87
    spaghetti with tomatoes and
        herbs, 284
    spinach and ricotta lasagna,
        292–93
pastries:
    gougères with cheese, 26–27
    shrimp gougères Provençal, 28
peaches:
    Marty, 370
    white, with Cointreau, 369
peanut butter, in *croque bébé*, 403
pear(s):
    caramelized, custard, 373
    with honey and cranberries,
        372
peas:
    artichoke hearts and, 296

Jacques and his longtime friend, neighbor,
fellow boules player, and photographer Tom Hopkins